WOMEN AND WORK CULTURE

Women and Work Culture
Britain c.1850–1950

Edited by

KRISTA COWMAN and LOUISE A. JACKSON
Leeds Metropolitan University, Leeds, UK

ASHGATE

Published by
Ashgate Publishing Limited
Gower House
Croft Road
Aldershot
Hants GU11 3HR
England

Ashgate Publishing Company
Suite 420
101 Cherry Street
Burlington, VT 05401-4405
USA

Ashgate website: http://www.ashgate.com

British Library Cataloguing in Publication Data
Women and work culture : Britain c.1850-1950.—(Studies in labour history)
    1.Women—employment—Great Britain—History 2.Sex role—Great Britain—
    History 3.Sexual division of labor—Great Britain—History 4.Work and family—Great
    Britain—History 5.Work—Social aspects—Great Britain—History
    I.Cowman, Krista, 1964- II.Jackson, Louise A. (Louise Ainsley), 1967-
    331.4'0941'09034

Library of Congress Cataloging-in-Publication Data
Women and work culture : Britain c.1850-1950 / edited by Krista Cowman And Louise A. Jackson.
    p. cm.— (Studies in labour history)
  ISBN 0-7546-5050-2 (alk. paper)
 1. Women—Employment—Great Britain—History. 2. Sex role—Great Britain—History.
3. Sexual division of labor—Great Britain—History. 4. Work and family—Great Britain—
History. 5. Work—Social aspects—Great Britain—History. I. Cowman, Krista, 1964- II.
Jackson, Louise A. (Louise Ainsley), 1967- III. Series: Studies in labour history (Ashgate (Firm))

HD6135.W566 2005
331.4'0941'09034—dc22
2005004121

ISBN-10: 0 7546 5050 2

Printed and bound in Great Britain by MPG Books Ltd, Bodmin, Cornwall

Contents

List of Figures and Table

Figures

Table

List of Contributors

Krista Cowman is a Principal Lecturer in the School of Cultural Studies, Leeds Metropolitan University. She has published *Mrs Brown is a Man and a Brother! Women in Merseyside's Political Organisations 1890–1920* (Liverpool, 2004) and is currently working on a study of paid organisers in the Women's Social and Political Union. She sits on the editorial boards of *Women's History Review* and *Labour History Review*.

Judy Giles is Reader in Gender and Cultural Criticism at York St John College and she has published extensively in the areas of women's studies and cultural history. Her latest book, *The Parlour and the Suburb: Domestic Identities, Class, Femininity and Modernity* (Oxford, 2004) explores women's relationship to domesticity in the first half of the twentieth century.

Sandra Stanley Holton is a Senior Research Fellow in the Institute for International Integration Studies, Trinity College, Dublin. She is completing a book on the women of the Bright circle, about whom she has also published a number of articles. Her previous books include *Feminism and Democracy* (Cambridge, 2002) and *Suffrage Days* (London, 1996).

Louise A. Jackson is a Senior Lecturer in the School of Cultural Studies, Leeds Metropolitan University. She is the author of *Child Sexual Abuse in Victorian England* (London, 2000) and has just completed a monograph on the history of women in the police service. She is a deputy editor of the journal *Women's History Review*.

Claire Jones is completing her doctorate 'Pure and Applied Women: Gender, Mathematics and Science around 1900' at the University of Liverpool. She has published in *Women's History Review* and was the joint winner of the Claire Evans Memorial Fund Prize Essay (1999).

Emma Liggins lectures in Victorian literature at Edge Hill College of Higher Education. She has published articles on sensation fiction and New Woman fiction in a range of journals. She is the author of *George Gissing, the Working Woman and Urban Culture* (Aldershot, 2005) and editor of *Feminist Readings of Popular Texts: Divergent Femininities* (Aldershot, 2001).

Kaarin Michaelsen is an Assistant Professor at the University of North Carolina, Greensboro. Her research interests include the intersection of gender, national, and medical politics in late nineteenth- and early twentieth-century Britain. She is revising her doctoral thesis 'Treating the Nation: British Medical Women and the Origins of the Welfare State' for publication.

Lucy Noakes is a Senior Lecturer in Social and Cultural Theory at the University of Portsmouth. Publications include *War and the British: Gender and National Identity* (London, 1998) and a forthcoming study of women and the British Army. She is on the editorial boards of *Women's History Review* and *National Identities*.

Joyce Senders Pedersen is Associate Professor of British Studies at the University of Southern Denmark at Odense. Her book *The Reform of Women's Secondary and Higher Education in 19th Century England: A Study of Elites and Educational Change* appeared in 1987. She is currently working on a study of men and women's friendships in nineteenth-century England.

Emma Robertson is currently a Research Associate at Loughborough University, studying the history of music in the workplace. She is completing a doctorate at the University of York, on women, gender and imperialism in the Rowntree chocolate industry. She is one of the editors of *The Feminist Seventies* (York, 2003).

David Sheridan is a doctoral student in modern British History at the University of Southern California and he is currently teaching at Eastern Kentucky University. His research explores issues of musical culture, gender and identity in modern Britain.

Angela K. Smith is a Senior Lecturer in English at the University of Plymouth. She has published two books on women's writing of the First World War (Manchester, 2000), edited a collection of essays on *Gender and Warfare in the Twentieth Century: Textual Representations* (Manchester, 2004) and just completed a book on the First World War and the Women's Suffrage Movement (Aldershot, forthcoming).

Stephanie Spencer is a Senior Lecturer in Education Studies at University College Winchester and co-editor of *History of Education Researcher*. She has published articles in *Women's History Review*, *History of Education* and

Paedagogica Historica. She is completing a book on gender and work in the 1950s.

Selina Todd was awarded her DPhil, entitled 'Young Women, Employment and the Family in Interwar England', from the University of Sussex and is now completing a book based on her thesis. She has recently completed an ESRC Postdoctoral Fellowship at the Institute of Historical Research, London, and is now a Research Fellow at Girton College, Cambridge.

Studies in Labour History
General Editor's Preface

Labour history has often been a fertile area of history. Since the Second World War its best practitioners – such as E.P. Thompson and E.J. Hobsbawm, both Presidents of the British Society for the Study of Labour History – have written works which have provoked fruitful and wide-ranging debates and further research, and which have influenced not only social history but history generally. These historians, and many others, have helped to widen labour history beyond the study of organised labour to labour generally, sometimes to industrial relations in particular, and most frequently to society and culture in national and comparative dimensions.

The assumptions and ideologies underpinning much of the older labour history have been challenged by feminist and later by postmodernist and anti-Marxist thinking. These challenges have often led to thoughtful reappraisals, perhaps intellectual equivalents of coming to terms with a new post-Cold War political landscape.

By the end of the twentieth century, labour history had emerged reinvigorated and positive from much introspection and external criticism. Very few would wish to confine its scope to the study of organised labour. Yet, equally, few would wish now to write the existence and influence of organised labour out of nations' histories, any more than they would wish to ignore working-class lives and focus only on the upper echelons.

This series of books provides reassessments of broad themes of labour history as well as some more detailed studies arising from recent research. Most books are single-authored but there are also volumes of essays centred on important themes or periods, some arising from major conferences organised by the Society for the Study of Labour History. The series also includes studies of labour organisations, including international ones, as many of these are much in need of a modern reassessment.

Chris Wrigley
British Society for the Study of Labour History
University of Nottingham

Acknowledgements

The editors would like to thank the School of Cultural Studies, Leeds Metropolitan University, and the British Academy for supporting the 2002 conference on 'Women and Work Culture c.1850–1950' from which this collection has grown. We would also like to thank all those who contributed papers and discussion at the conference. We are grateful, too, to Pat Cook and Elaine Newsome who were involved in its organisation and to Simon Gunn for sharing his wide knowledge of cultural history.

We wish to thank the following individuals and organisations who have given permission to reproduce copyright material: The Royal Society for the image of Hertha Ayrton (Chapter 9, Figure 9.1); Trustees of the Clark Archive, C. & J. Clark Limited, for quotations from the Millfield and Bancroft Papers (Chapter 2); Mrs J. Castle for quotations from her interviews with women workers in Coventry, MRC Archive, University of Warwick (Chapter 7); Judith Baines for quotations from Annie Purbrook's 'Notes 1914–18' (Chapter 10); Valerie Corden for quotations from Edith Airey's memoir (Chapter 10); David Wilby for quotations from the papers of George and Ethel Wilby (Chapter 10). We have been unable to trace the copyright holders for the manuscripts of Mrs G. Kaye, Mrs P.L. Stephens and Miss G.M. West (Chapter 10), which were deposited in the Imperial War Museum, Department of Documents, although every effort has been made to do so.

Introduction: Women's Work, a Cultural History

Krista Cowman and Louise A. Jackson

Women's work has fascinated historians since Alice Clark and Ivy Pinchbeck, writing in the early twentieth century, examined the effects of industrialisation on women's labour.[1] An earlier focus on the pay, conditions and occupational opportunities of predominantly blue-collar working-class women has been joined by an interest in other social and occupational groups (white-collar workers, clerical workers and professionals), in cultural representations of women's work and in the cultural practices of the work-place.[2] Initially the terrain of social and economic historians, the subject of work has attracted the interests of historians of popular culture and literary production, consumerism, art and design.[3] In 1987 Patrick Joyce introduced a collection entitled *The Historical Meanings of Work* by outlining his aim to map out 'a new history of work'. This project would recognise 'work as a cultural activity, rather than simply an economic one'.[4] Here we further demonstrate how sensitivity to the cultural practices and identities associated with work has impacted on the terrain of women's history over the last 20 years.

The search for continuity and change has been central to the historiography of women's work in the period c.1850–1950. Debates have focused on three questions: Was industrialisation beneficial or detrimental to women's social and economic position?[5] Did the construction of 'public' and 'private' spheres of activity result in the confinement of middle-class Victorian women?[6] Finally, did women's work during the First and Second World Wars contribute to their longer-term liberation?[7] Clear black and white answers have to a large extent been replaced with arguments about complexity, continuity and gradual change rather than seismic shift. An equation of the public sphere with a masculine world of work and the private with feminine domesticity has been overhauled by studies of, on the one hand, fatherhood, and, on the other, women's involvement in philanthropy.[8] Recent research has suggested that we need to move away from a characterisation of the early nineteenth century as a period of 'confinement' for middle-class women by highlighting their involvement (both formal and informal) in a range of economic activities.[9] Yet it is still important to consider the ways in which inequality was enshrined in the formal mechanisms of the law (such as the factory and mines legislation of the 1840s) as well as other regulatory institutions (for example, the professional associations and trades unions which developed exclusivity strategies that were gender-based).[10] Feminist campaigns led to access to higher education for women, as well as their admittance to the medical profession, in the last decades of the nineteenth century. Women's engagement in a wide variety of occupations in the First World War was finally rewarded with the vote through the Equal Franchise Act of 1928. The Sex Disqualification Removal Act of 1919 admitted women to all professions and enabled them to become magistrates and judges. These gains need to be offset against the continuation of both informal processes of discrimination as well as gender ideologies that stressed the centrality of marriage, maternity and domesticity. Whilst new occupations were opened up to women, their public role was invariably defined in terms of social maternalism (as they became associated with the caring professions), a result of assumptions about their maternal function. There was undoubtedly a continued 'gendering of "proper" spheres of activity for men and women', although these traversed public and private.[11] Furthermore, the proportion of all adult women engaged in paid work remained steady, at approximately a third, throughout the first half of the twentieth century. It was not until what Deirdre McCloskey has labelled the 'social earthquake' of the 1960s and 1970s that paid work became the norm across women's life-cycle.[12] Thus the relationship between structures, cultures and agency requires careful interrogation; the balancing of this relationship has shifted across time as a result of legislatory interventions.

Statistical profiles of women's relationship to work are notoriously problematic given that a great deal of women's work has, historically been hidden or 'free'. Working-class wives took in lodgers or laundry and engaged in casual labour or piecework as part of an economy of makeshift across the period. Middle-class women carried out important duties in the home supporting the work of their husbands and undertaking voluntary social work that involved considerable expertise and emotional labour.[13] The boundaries between home and the workplace were by no means clear-cut. Domestic service – work in the homes of others – continued to be the single largest employer of women until the Second World War and is now creeping back as a major form of employment.[14] Moreover, studies of work that distinguish between paid and unpaid simply perpetuate gendered ideologies that have valued work in business or industry over 'free' work in the home. Our contributors seek to unpack and problematise the concept of work itself, to analyse gendered discourses that delineated activities as masculine or feminine, and to examine the ways in which work and the workplace were negotiated, interpreted and experienced by women themselves across the modern period.

Each of the chapters in this book contributes to a cultural history of women's work by addressing the following set of questions: How have women created occupational and professional identities in the historical past? How have they negotiated cultural, legal and institutional practices that are masculine in derivation? How have women created feminine or feminist practices and environments? How has work been integrated with domestic responsibilities and identities? For which groups of women has the term career been meaningful? Finally, how has women's work been constructed and represented within wider cultural fields? Our collection focuses on five specific areas of investigation – i) the meanings attached to work; ii) factory labour; iii) youth; iv) medicine and science; and v) women and war – although debates that ensue cut across these areas. Before offering overviews of each of these specific areas, our introduction will explore some of the conceptual and methodological issues that are suggested by one further question: what is a cultural history of women's work?

Researching Culture

Culture is a difficult concept to define.[15] It is often used to refer to the production of both literary and material artefacts: novels, poetry, works of art or sculpture (as well as clothing and furnishings). It has also been equated with the aesthetics and politics of taste (a sense of 'the beautiful' and 'the cultured') as well as with ideas of civilisation and education (which have, historically, been constructed in opposition to 'nature' or 'savagery'). Anthropologists would suggest that 'culture' is the set of meanings, values and rituals that shape our understandings of everyday life. Furthermore, references to 'a culture' may invoke the idea of a community with a shared ethos. The term 'cultural history' is equally hard to pin down, since it can denote both a subject of study (that is, culture, however defined) and a set of methods and approaches (particularly when it is prefixed by the word 'new'). Hence it is possible to speak both of a 'social history of culture' (which uses methods derived from the social sciences to comment on cultural products and their audiences) and a 'cultural history of the social' (which views the 'social' itself as a cultural construct).[16] The turn towards cultural analysis within British historiography is often linked to the publication of E.P. Thompson's

The Making of the English Working Class in 1963. Thompson sought to analyse class consciousness by examining the way in which 'experiences are handled in cultural terms: embodied in traditions, value-systems, ideas and institutional forms'.[17] Gareth Stedman Jones's *Languages of Class* further separated class consciousness from what he saw as an overtly determinist economic framework, suggesting instead the significance of linguistic frameworks in the categorising and ordering of social life.[18] The idea of 'the new cultural history' was laid out most clearly in a collection of that title, edited by Lynn Hunt and published in 1989. Hunt identified a set of intellectual influences from other disciplinary areas – social and cultural theory, linguistics, anthropology and literary studies – which emphasised the centrality of language (and other forms of symbolic ordering) as a mediator or filter of all social encounters.[19] Language, it was argued, does not simply reflect social reality but represents it metaphorically. In terms of method, this meant a shift away from attempts to measure systems and structures towards forms of hermeneutic enquiry that aimed to deconstruct texts and to analyse the process of meaning-making; meanings were, moreover, viewed as fluid or unstable and, therefore, always under construction. Studies such as Judith Walkowitz's *City of Dreadful Delight* – which examined the gendered narratives of newspapers, novels, social commentaries and visual imagery that constructed *fin de siècle* London as a site of sexual danger – exemplified this approach within British historiography.[20] At the same time, feminist scholars researching British labour history pointed to the exclusion of both women (as a group) and gender (as a category of analysis) in the work of Thompson and Jones. Anna Clark and Sonya Rose examined the ways in which a language of gender was deployed within radical and Chartist rhetoric as plebeian women were increasingly defined in relation to a model of domesticity.[21] The turn to rhetoric and representation in history was paralleled, within literary criticism, by a focus on inter-textuality, which stressed the importance of comparing and contrasting fictional and non-fictional forms. Labelled 'new historicism' by its proponents, this approach invoked an inter-disciplinary connection with historical method.

The interest in representation and inter-textuality – including the analysis of fiction, poetry, popular magazines, advertising imagery, films and radio programmes – is apparent in this collection in essays by Judy Giles, Emma Liggins, Stephanie Spencer and Angela Smith. A focus purely on representation – on the text itself and, thus, on linguistic determinism – can be criticised for its inability to allow space for the agency of individuals and the processes of negotiation that are present in all forms of social interaction.

Mary Poovey has argued, however, that there is a need for a recognition of the 'interdependence of material conditions and representations'.[22] Each of our contributors seeks to depict the relationship between text and reader as a dynamic one. Although the creation of cultural stereotypes – in particular the stereotype of the rough, 'good-time', factory girl – is a central reference point across a number of chapters, our contributors also discuss the ways in which actual women positioned themselves in relation to it.

For those researching working-class women, oral history provides an important method for retrieving the 'experiences' of those who might otherwise be 'hidden from history'. Emma Robertson's study of shop-floor culture in Rowntree's chocolate factory in York is dependent on such a methodology. Oral testimonies, like written sources, are complex texts. Rather than providing clear windows onto an objective social reality, they are subject to processes of mediation; whilst charting personal 'experience', this term needs to be used with care. Joan Scott has argued that what we call 'experience' is in fact culturally constituted, involving the interpretation, ordering and labelling of events as part of the process of remembering.[23] Whilst Scott has been criticised for excluding the extra-textual, her approach does not necessarily mean that women's agency is once again obscured. As Kathleen Canning has argued, the task of the historian is 'to untangle the relationships between discourses and experiences by exploring the ways in which subjects mediated or transformed discourses in specific historical setting'.[24]

Understandings of culture as dynamic process have led oral historians to focus on the interplay between individual and collective memory and to view testimony as a dialogic process involving not merely a narrator but also a series of audiences. As testimonies have come to be viewed as fluid, so a stable notion of the self who is doing the telling has also been questioned. The notion that 'woman' is an essential and homogenous category has been replaced with a focus on 'identity': that is, a sense of being that is continually being re-made and is negotiated in relation to a series of 'others'.[25] The term 'identity' has not removed the key concepts of class, gender and 'race'/ethnicity (which linked history with social movements in the 1960s and 1970s). Rather it invites discussion of the complexity of ways in which individuals position themselves in the world; 'identity' involves the negotiation of these and a plethora of other markers (such as nation, region, occupation, sexuality, caste and religion) as well as the ways in which different identities can be prioritised at particular times. The significance of difference – in particular those between generations and social classes as well as between married women and single women – is highlighted across this collection.

These essays also reflect a range of further methods and research questions that have come to be associated with a cultural history approach. Anthropological interest in the ordering of space/place in terms of function and ritual is reflected in Liggins's analysis of the gendering of the city (and the work roles associated with it) as well as in Giles's discussion of the significance of cleanliness and dirt ('matter out of place') in housewifery. Spencer references the concepts of theatricality and performativity. 'Womanliness' is a 'mask' that is put on, a series of performances that are learnt through girls' magazines; appearance and demeanour were presented as central to 'womanly' duty and respectability in the first half of the twentieth century.[26] In a study of young women's work patterns, Selina Todd also draws attention to the connections between 'clothes, work and courtship'. Whilst young women's labour was to a large degree a necessity in terms of the family economy, any excess earnings might be invested in appearance/display, which was often associated with marital aspiration. In her discussion of the gendering of scientific work, Claire Jones demonstrates that the research laboratory was viewed as a site for manly display; as an arena that was associated with bravery and danger.

In promoting a cultural history of women's work we do not see it as replacing methods or approaches associated with social, economic or political history. Rather, we see it as a complementary addition, which raises questions about the relationship between economic, social, political and cultural spheres.

The Meaning of Work

What officially counts as 'work' has been subject to definition. Historians using census data to interrogate women's working lives must recognise that 'householders and enumerators varied the extent to which they regarded women's employment outside the home and paid work within it as an occupation'.[27] Furthermore, what, exactly, paid and unpaid labour has meant to individual women in Britain has been shaped by a whole set of variables, including religion, material circumstances and class culture as well as gender. These variables have affected the ways in which different forms of work have been viewed in terms of economic necessity, social aspiration (status), self-fulfilment, vocation, duty or service (or indeed any combination of these). The defining of work as skilled or professional has added to the status and value of certain forms of work. However, work that has been associated with women has tended to be devalued and seen as less skilled because of its gender association.[28] It is also clear that work that is viewed as 'clean' (such as shop work or office work) has often had more status for women workers than work that is viewed as 'dirty' (factory work), even though it might command a lower salary; arguably such a distinction has been crucial for women because of their cultural association with moral purity and the linking of women's respectability with sexual reputation.[29] The contested and variable meaning of 'work' is the focal point of the first three chapters in this collection, although other contributors return to the theme throughout.

Much of the literature on the relationship between working-class women and paid employment has centred on the workplace as a site of struggle, and the so-called double burden faced by women workers who worked out of economic necessity and also carried the majority of responsibility for their homes. Jeannie Mole, a prominent nineteenth-century socialist who took a special interest in promoting the rights of working-class women, offered this typical picture of the grim realities of life for women ropemakers in Liverpool: 'Many of [them] rise before five, tidy their little homes, prepare the day's food and pass the factory gate after a walk of two miles, before the steam whistle stops shrieking at 6.30'.[30] For middle-class women who moved into the field of paid employment throughout the nineteenth and twentieth centuries, it was accepted that work would hold a different meaning. Martha Vicinus has described the efforts of middle-class single women to enter into working environments in the nineteenth century as a 'revolt against redundancy' initiated by women who 'like their male counterparts ... believed passionately in the morally redeeming power of work; paid public work would give them dignity and independence'.[31] These women expected more than just a salary in exchange for their labour; work for them offered a sense of purpose and identity as they worked towards acceptance as professionals.

Although middle-class women sought a deeper meaning in work than one of financial remuneration, some realised that this search might not be restricted to women of one social class. Barbara Leigh Smith recognised that working-class women too might be seeking identity and fulfilment through their work. Women, she explained, wished to work, 'both for the health of their minds and bodies. They want it often because they must eat and because they have children and others dependent upon them – *for all the reasons that men want work*'.[32] Autobiographies suggest that many working-class women themselves took a different view of their work, and derived a sense of pride and identity from their occupation. This could be tied into the feeling of economic independence which paid work brought. Kathleen Dayus returned to work as an enameller in Birmingham's jewellery quarter when she was widowed in the

1930s; she also took time to 'get to know much more about the business side of the trade' which employed her.[33] She used this knowledge to establish her own business which both allowed her to reclaim her children from care but also offered her an unprecedented sense of freedom: 'I'd always been a jack of all trades but now I had my own business and I was independent for the first time in my life'.[34] For married women, the economic benefits of work were frequently connected to the desire to improve their children's status as Gwyneth, a South Wales miner's wife, explained to Jill Miller in 1986,

> … I don't think I ever wanted anything special … I just wanted the chance to live a comfortable life, with enough food on the table … Even when I was working and earning a wage as well as my husband … we only ever managed to make ends meet. I think everyone dreams of being able to give their children a bit more than they had …[35]

Although it is very recent, Gwyneth's view of her work echoes that of Lucy Luck, who worked as a straw-plaiter a century earlier: 'I always liked my work very much and although I had trouble with it when I first learned, it has been a little fortune to me. I have been at the work for forty-seven years, and have never missed one season, although I have a large family'.[36]

Joyce Senders Pedersen's essay explores the meaning that work held for early Victorian feminists and how ideas about work shaped their identities as women. Many of them drew on a broad tradition of dissenting and protestant beliefs and infused their discussions about work with religious overtones. In performing 'useful' work, women were drawing nearer to fulfilling the divine purpose for their lives although in order to fully achieve this, all work should be undertaken more for others than for self-advancement. Whilst this concept of work initially suggested a sense of solidarity between middle-class and working-class women, Pedersen demonstrates that this began to fracture as a more secularised view emerged which set those who worked primarily from economic need at odds with the more privileged middle-class woman who could develop a sense of professionalism.

Much of the feminist historical writing of the 1970s reflected the increasing secularisation of western society and ignored religious motivation in the lives of historical subjects. Although the religious affiliation of women in the past was often mentioned it was rarely analysed as a key component of their lives, partly, as Jane Haggis has suggested, because interpreting religious writing and thought became so difficult from 'a secular feminist location' in the late twentieth century.[37] Recent writing has begun to challenge this trend and attempt to return religion to the central place that it played in the lives of historical subjects.[38] Sandra Holton's essay here builds on her discussion of the importance of religion in the life of Alice Clark to examine how a common Quaker faith underpinned the understandings of work developed by three generations of the Bright-Priestman-Clark circle.[39] She suggests that for each of these women, 'work' involved 'family and community service' and thus became imbued with spiritual value.

Holton's essay also uses the approach of prosopography or collective biography, which has proved invaluable in attempts to chart what work has meant for groups of women in practical terms. The utility of this approach is threefold. Firstly, given the paucity of sources that are available to research any marginal or subaltern group, the piecing together of small fragments pertaining to the lives of a sizeable group may help to reconstruct the experience that eludes us if we only focus on the individual. Secondly, prosopography offers particular strengths when studying the work of any 'group of like-minded individuals'.[40] The subtleties of individual perspectives, which can make the subjects of individual biographies appear anomalous, can be seen as combining towards a single strand of thought or way of proceeding. Finally, prosopography enables us to study the precise operation of family, kin and friendship ties, which were often key informal support mechanisms for women. Family and friendship networks often promoted extensive correspondence, which offers a wealth of insight into women's public and private lives.[41] As well as being useful for women's historians, collective biography has much to offer the political historian as its broader focus can unravel many of 'the deeper interests ... behind the rhetoric of politics ... [including] the workings of a political machine'.[42] Sandra Holton has used collective biography for her research into the British women's suffrage movement. In *Suffrage Days*, she follows the lives of seven individuals previously on the margins of historical narratives, finding that although individually each subject remained a shadowy figure, collectively their experiences combined to produce a very different narrative in which 'the object of the historical gaze' was reconfigured.[43] Here she engages with four women whose collective lifespan stretched from the late eighteenth century to the 1930s to study experiences of work.

As discussed above, increasing secularisation in the West has been one reason why religion has slipped from historical analyses of women's lives. Historians of the more contemporary past have also noted that material rather than spiritual aspirations have shaped women's lives in the twentieth century. Judy Giles's essay suggests that soft furnishings and white goods offered housewives a particular niche in emerging consumer culture. Centring on the housewife, Giles also tackles the tension that many historians have suggested laid between paid and domestic work. In locating the home as a key site of identity formation in the modern era, she offers a re-evaluation of housework which challenges many current conceptualisations of the differences between public and private locations of work.

Factory Work

Whilst most feminist historians would acknowledge that women participated in many forms of work, there has been a tendency when studying the post-industrial era to follow the definition advanced by Louise Tilly and Joan Scott who used work in this era to 'denote ... only market-oriented, or wage-earning jobs'.[44] Consequently the majority of historical investigations into women and work are centred around the figure of the working-class woman in paid employment. The starting-point for much of this research remains Ivy Pinchbeck's *Women Workers and the Industrial Revolution*, first published in 1930. Pinchbeck's main focus was the woman worker employed in the large factories and mills that typified the landscape of industrialised Britain. Although she herself recognised in the 1968 preface to the reprinted edition of her work that there was still great 'historical neglect ... [of] many new occupations' which opened up to women in the later nineteenth century, the woman factory worker still remains central to narratives of women and work.[45]

Part of the reason for the continued fascination of the female factory worker comes from the power she held over the Victorian imagination. As Meg Gomersall noted in her study of young women workers in Lancashire, 'concern about the factory employment of women was widespread across all social ranks'.[46] The factory girl was a very visible presence on the streets of many industrial towns. Her freedom of movement suggested lack of parental authority which was exacerbated by her obvious economic power represented by a penchant for cheap, showy clothes. Concern over the figure of the woman factory worker spread through newspapers and literature into parliamentary debates. Deborah Valenze's study has found this to be so pervasive that 'factory workers influenced all working women' through the way that public opinion perceived them.[47] Reactions to this concern took many forms but increasingly concentrated on the power of the factory to shape the lives of its employees both within and beyond the workplace. Barbara Harrison and Melanie Nolan have demonstrated that one of the effects of this was to add impetus to the campaign for women factory inspectors who could not only monitor the progress of the Factory Acts but simultaneously police the moral welfare of workers.[48] The Factory Acts had been contentious for the feminist movement as many opposed what was seen as an attempt by the state to curb women's economic freedom, solving the perceived problem of the woman factory worker by effectively preventing her from working. The paradox of the state expanding one layer of opportunities for women's work by restricting another has made woman factory inspectors difficult figures for historians. Harrison has suggested that their 'contribution … has been neglected … as if it were not possible to countenance such middle-class state officials in this light'.[49]

Whilst Harrison and Nolan have reminded us of the complexity of the category of 'woman worker' within the factory, little attention has been paid to the role of women from different classes in shaping public concern around the figure of the female factory worker. Emma Liggins's essay attempts to open up this debate by considering the work of female (and feminist) social investigators such as Clara Collet and Clementina Black. Liggins examines such categories as Collet's pleasure-seeking work-girl who refused to avail herself of the leisure advantages through which middle-class philanthropists aimed to mould her into a 'respectable' factory girl. Liggins traces the influence of female social investigators on the novels of realist writers such as George Gissing, which fed popular concerns surrounding the perceived immorality of working-class girls. Considering their work from this perspective reminds us of the many ways in which the category of 'woman' can be cleaved by other categories, in this case class. Thus the experience of work did not unite women inspectors with the working-class women whose occupations they charted; rather, the work which was done became a divisive factor between them.

Emma Robertson's chapter also concentrates on factory women, but considers their work from their own perspective rather than from that of external investigators or commentators. Looking at the Rowntree factory in York in the twentieth century, Robertson uses oral history to allow women factory workers to shape their own narratives and frame their own experiences of work so that the reader encounters the factory through their eyes rather than through those of an investigator from a different social class. Difference also features in Robertson's work, with marital status and age emerging as potentially divisive factors within an all-female workforce, although in most instances her interviewees felt that friendships forged at work could ultimately overcome these. Despite a time gap of 50 to 100 years, Robertson's factory women recognised the 'rough' stereotype which Clara Collett had helped to establish, but were quick to disarm her, suggesting that much of the impropriety associated with factory workers was verbal rather than physical in nature.

Youth

Along with gender and class, the category of age – in particular, the ways in which specific stages within a lifecycle have been demarcated, labelled and interpreted – is increasingly recognised as an important tool for historical analysis. Clearly the passing of time is always embodied in a physical and physiological sense; yet the meanings attached to these processes is historically and culturally specific. What it meant to be a 14-year-old working-class girl in 1850 was very different from 1950 and these meanings were constituted through law and medicine as well as a range of other cultural fields.[50] She had, for example, been reconstituted in terms of sexual status (as a result of the raising of the age of consent from 13 to 16 in 1885); she had also been transformed from worker into scholar as a result of the raising of the compulsory school-leaving age (to 14 in 1918 and to 15 in 1944). The late nineteenth century also saw the medical identification of adolescence as a period of development which separated childhood from adulthood. Within a wider popular culture, as Sally Mitchell has demonstrated, this had been paralleled with a delineation of girlhood as a specific state for those aged 8–18.[51]

Carol Dyhouse has depicted the Victorian and Edwardian concept of girlhood as a largely conservative construction and she argued that the idealisation of 'service' and 'self-sacrifice' as 'womanly behaviour' were the dominant ideological messages that shaped girls' socialisation into adulthood. These ideals were inculcated through family life (in which rigid sexual division of labour was entrenched), through schooling and through youth organisations such as the Girls' Friendly Society, the Girls' Club Movement and the Girl Guides.[52] Sally Mitchell, on the other hand, has depicted what she sees as the emergence of a 'girls' own culture' in the period 1880–1915 as a celebration of 'free space'.[53] The culture of the 'new girl' (which was related to the discourse of the 'new woman') was promoted through a proliferation of publications, including magazines, advice literature, careers novels, and popular fiction. Aimed at a lower-middle-class-audience, the *Girls' Own Paper* (which promoted careers in the professions) replaced the older idea of service 'with a newer ethic of self-sufficiency', whilst *Girls' Best Friend*, targeted at working-class girls, presented a glamourised ideal of office work to feed aspirations.[54]

The contrasting findings of Dyhouse and Mitchell result, in part, because they examine different sites of acculturation. Given the diversity of experience and the number of variables in terms of family background, class, occupational and regional identities, it is difficult to draw resounding conclusions. Yet the contrasts are also a function of a central dilemma that occurs in historical research on children and young people. Primary sources such as popular literature enable us to examine adult constructions of youth, whilst oral history and autobiography gives access to recollection and memory of youthful experience. It is extremely difficult, however, to evaluate the ways in which representations of youth were read or consumed by their target audience at time of publication. Similarly, first-hand accounts of family life, written by children and young people, have rarely survived. Whilst unable to solve this central problematic, the chapters by Selena Todd and Stephanie Spencer nevertheless seek to advance debates about the 'work' experiences of girls in their teens as they move beyond the timeframe of Dyhouse and Mitchell to later decades of the twentieth century.

Todd explores the involvement of young women aged 14–24 in paid work in inter-war England, demonstrating the importance of their salaries to family economies. Whilst a great deal of emphasis has been placed on domesticity as a feminine ideal, she reminds us that the majority of young women were, in fact, in employment. She uses working-class autobiography to consider the limited choices made by girls on entering employment, arguing that working-class girls were often sceptical of social and occupational mobility; family contacts and financial considerations often outweighed aspirations of acquiring status or respectability, particularly during the industrial contraction and poverty of the 1920s. By the 1930s, material aspirations, including the desire for a home of their own (also highlighted in Judy Giles's chapter), might be more readily invoked. However, a sense of family responsibility and service or duty, were still dominant, echoing Dyhouse's study. Spencer's study focuses on the 1950s and the ways in which the process of 'becoming a woman' was constituted as work in the magazine *Girl*. Preparation for adulthood involved the embodiment of femininity through deportment, dress and correct exercise. It also involved the acquisition of knowledge about the world of work through glamourised representations of the nurse and the air hostess, once again depicted in terms of care and duty. Spencer uses girls' letters to the magazine to begin to unpack the relationship between the adult producers of popular culture and its youthful consumers, highlighting points of tension and resistance in their negotiation of femininity.

Science and Medicine

The construction of 'woman' as an object of scientific knowledge and of the masculine medical gaze has been detailed in recent cultural histories of science. Rather than viewing the scientific paradigm of the Enlightenment as an objective uncovering of 'truth', scholars such as Ludmilla Jordanova and Ornella Moscucci have shown that the findings of medicine and physiology were profoundly shaped by gendered ideologies, into which they also fed.[55] Gender difference was gradually located in every part of the body (skeletons and individual cells as well as the reproductive organs) during the course of the nineteenth century.[56] 'Woman', equated with 'nature', was to be unveiled or revealed by the medical man, whose masculinity was associated with culture and rationality. Thus the body itself was culturally constructed or interpreted through medical science. Moreover, the less rational woman became characterised in terms of her reproductive function; this equation was used to frame socio-biological and Darwinian arguments (presented as 'truths') about women's limited capacity for intellectual and physical work. As Moscucci has argued 'ideologically charged beliefs about the biological foundations of femininity ensured that medical men became chief protagonists in debates over women's social duties and responsibilities'.[57] This is not to suggest that such thinking went unchallenged; rather medical 'knowledge' was continually debated and contested. In 1874 Elizabeth Garrett Anderson poured scorn on the suggestions of Darwinian psychiatrist Dr Henry Maudsley that women were essentially pathological as a result of menstruation:

> It is a great exaggeration to imply that women of average health are periodically incapacitated from serious work by the facts of their organization. Among poor women, where all the available strength is spent upon manual labour, the daily work goes on without intermission ...[58]

Whilst the nineteenth-century 'battle' for the acceptance of women doctors has been charted in detail, it was not necessarily 'won' by the end of the First World War.[59] Although there were 2100 women on the medical register in 1921, the inter-war period also saw a 'Sex War' in medicine: in London, four out of seven co-educational training colleges decided to revert to all-male entry.[60] Kaarin Michaelsen's essay is concerned with the gendered politics of professionalism in this period, as women doctors developed strategies to advance both their own interests and those they considered to be in the interests of the nation. Her work can be usefully set alongside studies of the networks and resources that were created or utilised by women working in teaching, law, social work and other occupations that aspired towards professional status. It is clear, however, that the legacies of the biological construction of womanhood in terms of reproduction shaped women's professional experiences and tactics well into the twentieth century. Indeed, the concept of social maternalism – the assumption that women, by virtue of their sex, were naturally carers and nurturers – was used by both conservatives and feminists to justify an expanded welfare role for middle-class women. In relation to medicine, social work and, indeed, women's venture into policing, it was frequently suggested that women professionals were required to work with children and with their own sex. As Michaelsen demonstrates here, concepts of 'equality' and gender 'difference' were not necessarily antithetical; indeed the valuing of the feminine has been an important strand within radical feminisms of the last hundred years. Michaelsen examines the politics of difference versus equality and of separatism versus assimilation in her study of the multifunctional Medical Women's Federation.

Michaelsen follows the work of Hilary Sommerlad and Ian Sandersen (who have studied the gender politics of the legal profession) in using the differing concepts of 'capital' (as outlined by Pierre Bourdieu) to explore the relationship between women and professionalism. Bourdieu has distinguished between 'economic capital' (property) and forms of 'cultural capital' and 'social capital', which may be converted into economic assets 'on certain conditions'.[61] Of particular significance here is the concept of 'cultural capital', which may be 'embodied' through appearance, gesture or pronunciation; it involves the ability to 'look the part', which may, as a result, facilitate advancement. 'Cultural capital' is also located in material goods, which one has to know how to appreciate in order to display taste. Furthermore, 'cultural capital' may be institutionalised through formal educational qualifications; it is less what you know that counts, more that your knowledge has been sanctioned by the state. The term 'social capital' is used by Bourdieu to refer to one's position within a network of social relationships. However, the effectiveness of the network is dependent on the extent to which each of its members possesses both 'economic capital' and 'cultural capital'. Thus the 'success' of 'the old boys' network' lies in its basic purchasing power as well as in the status accorded to middle-class masculinity; the network serves to enhance the effects of those other forms of capital.

Middle-class women seeking to enter the professions in the nineteenth century found their entry blocked by their lack of both 'institutionalised' cultural capital (their inability to possess educational qualifications) and 'embodied' cultural capital (on account of their femininity). In winning the right to train and to qualify they lacked the necessary social capital to secure advancement. A different strategy was required. More significantly, women faced the choice of adopting partially separatist strategies – the creation of structures and networks of women – or seeking absorption into existing networks in which masculinity was intrisically valued. Differing routes were tried and tested within different occupational fields. The separatist model was influential within Nightingale nursing and, as Michaelsen demonstrates, represented an important paradigm within medicine.[62] Within law, however, women preferred absorption. In policing, aspects of both were combined as women sought admission to police forces in the interwar period but remained segregated within each institution, with separate structures of pay and promotion. [63] The adoption of a separatist strategy was to many a double edged sword; it led to initial success in the forging of a distinctly feminine professional identity and role, but, within a wider occupational culture, ultimately failed to acquire sufficient 'cultural capital' for further advancement. As Michaelsen implies, the tactics and strategies adopted by the MWF were influenced by and, in some cases, learnt from, women's previous experience of political campaigning and lobbying.

Whilst Michaelsen's essay uses medicine as an example to discuss women's experience of professionalisation and, indeed, the politicisation of 'work', Claire Jones's essay is centrally concerned with women's involvement in scientific practice. Jones's analysis of the culture of physical science research laboratories at the turn of the century reveals them to be places of manly display as well as sites of the production of knowledge. Experimental laboratories were represented as masculine spaces where heroic qualities – such as physical and psychological bravery, stoicism and patriotism – could be tested, developed and exhibited. Focusing on the career of physicist and electrical engineer Hertha Ayrton, Jones demonstrates that women's presence in the laboratory could be viewed as trangressive. Ayrton had difficulty in achieving credibility for her work, despite becoming a media favourite. Because of her gender, Hertha was unable to take any visible post in an institutional laboratory but equipped a laboratory in her drawing room. Nevertheless, she refused to be stereotyped as a *woman* in science and argued that her work should be 'studied from the scientific, not the sex, point of view'.

Women and War

Our final section considers women's work in wartime. The concept of 'total war' has been used by twentieth-century women's historians when investigating the contribution that women made to national efforts during the First and Second World Wars. The related concept of a 'Home Front' which brought war to the domestic population in an unprecedented fashion underpins much of the historiography. For participants and historians alike, total war was no longer a conflict entirely experienced on the battlefield. Understandably, women's war work has again been central. As Sheila Meintjes has noted, 'one common element of wartime in virtually all twentieth century examples is that war provides women with employment and, sometimes, educational opportunities'.[64] In Britain investigations of women in the workplace have provided some of the most enduring images of female participation. Gail Braybon and Penny Summerfield have examined the scope and extent of work opportunities offered for women in both conflicts whilst Angela Woollacott has interrogated the experience of women munitions workers, arguably the archetype of women war workers during the First World War.[65]

Whilst commentators such as Arthur Marwick have suggested that the novelty of women's war work resulted in political, economic and social gains, feminist historians have been more open to acknowledging continuities between the figure of the working woman before, during and after war.[66] Irene Andrews, the contemporary observer who assessed the economic effects of the war on women and children for the Carnegie Foundation, was aware as early as 1918 that the visibility of women workers during the First World War did not equate to an enormous rise in the numbers of women coming into the workforce.[67] Rather, it was the *nature* of work done by women that altered. Working-class women initially faced unemployment as trades such as dressmaking and domestic service closed down under a drive for national economy and self-sacrifice. It was these women, already used to the world of work, who moved into the new wartime industries. The experience of war thus brought them opportunities for different, and often better-paid jobs rather than the chance to participate in paid work for the first time. It also allowed married women greater freedom to re-enter the labour market, Sarah Boston's study suggesting that they may have accounted for the rise in the total figure of employed women noted by Andrews.[68] In both wars the expansion of women's work to encompass previously masculine occupations was for the 'duration' only and was seen as auxiliary in nature, particularly in the case of married women when restrictions sometimes extended to allowing them into certain trades to temporarily take over from their husbands.

War itself is a 'gendering activity' and women's work tended to be cast in terms of a feminine duty to the nation.[69] Furthermore, as Susan Kingsley Kent and Sonya Rose have shown, the rhetoric of gender difference re-occurred in post-war policy and commentary, as national reconstruction was articulated in terms of maternity/maternalism.[70] Nevertheless, women's experiences of wartime work fed into feminist campaigning and undoubtedly contributed to shifts in the terms of debate. The relationship between war work and the shifting of gendered ideologies continues to be a subject of intense discussion.[71] Studies that measured the gendering of labour participation have been joined by cultural histories of wartime and its legacies, which have examined a range of artefacts including cinema, advertisements and women's magazines to explore the construction of wartime identities.[72] Arguments that wartime is an accelerator of social change have been challenged by others that seek to understand the ways in which ideas about gender difference are continually reconstructed and renegotiated through a wide variety of discourses and interventions.

The relationship between representations of wartime, memory and personal experience is discussed in Angela Smith's essay in this volume, which revisits the familiar First World War workplace of the munitions factory. Smith's main focus is on the cultural constructs of fictional figures such as Irene Rathbone's Pamela Butler, the embittered and bereaved heroine of the 1932 novel *We That Were Young*. This cultural perspective shifts the focus from the experiences of actual war workers to the broader meanings that war work came to hold for many participants and observers. Smith demonstrates how the literary imagination of writers like Rathbone reshaped the experience of munitions workers in post-war representations to argue for a parity of service between the Home and the Western Fronts.

Whilst better-paid jobs were clearly available for working-class women, research has also shown that wartime conditions blurred the very boundaries between paid and voluntary employment as the 'meaning' of women's work was articulated through the rhetoric of citizenship and duty (rather than economic necessity). Many middle- and upper-class women who had not necessarily been in paid employment in the years leading up to war, continued to be active in voluntary work.[73] The new conceptualisation of this as 'war *work*' with equal value to more obvious forms of paid employment such as munitions work, came almost immediately, and coloured official attitudes towards what constituted work on the 'Home Front'. The Imperial War

Museum, established in 1917 to commemorate the Great War, immediately inaugurated a Women's Work Sub-Committee. Its leaders Lady Norman and Agnes Conway invited women workers to deposit records of their activities to form part of the official collective picture of the war. The ensuing collection ranges from nursing to knitting and from munitions work to housing Belgian refugees. Its contents also demonstrate the extent to which voluntary workers were able to draw on pre-war feminist [and philanthropic] networks to enhance and sustain their efforts.[74]

'Volunteering' for the war effort was a politically loaded activity and its meaning was controversial. Often those who had been active in pre-war suffrage campaigns took diametrically opposed positions. Some, including Emmeline Pethick Lawrence, followed the trajectory identified by Ann Wiltsher and campaigned for an end to hostilities.[75] Others followed the lead of Emmeline and Christabel Pankhurst and devoted their campaigning skills and energies towards recruiting women as war-workers and men as army volunteers. The jingoistic tone of much of the Pankhurst's wartime campaigning was distasteful to many of their former allies in the Women's Social and Political Union and has also not sat comfortably within many feminist analyses of the suffrage campaign. However, more recent accounts of women's work during the First World War have drawn on approaches of gender history to analyse women's patriotism. Whilst Nicoletta Gullace has studied the motivations of those women who attempted to goad men into fighting, Krisztina Robert and Janet Watson have looked specifically at women who moved beyond the rhetoric of equality at this stage to claim a place for themselves in the uniformed auxiliary branches of the British armed services.[76] Here, Lucy Noakes' essay continues this trend, considering the gendered meaning of the work done by women within the British military between 1915 and 1918. Noakes shows how the exceptional circumstances of the First World War enabled women to gain a foothold in the military workplace, an area which had previously been exclusively male. She argues that women in charge of auxiliary forces, particularly in the Women's Army Auxiliary Corps, recognised the contentious nature of their status, and were at pains to emphasise the distinctiveness of their work, taking on jobs such as tending war graves which would present them as carers and nurturers rather than combatants. In this way, gendered divisions of labour were ultimately preserved in a conservative fashion, despite the outwardly revolutionary spectacle of women in uniform.

David Sheridan's essay also engages with women's wartime work by considering their part in shaping national identity during the Second World War.

Sheridan investigates the cultural work done by women as Music Travellers, who toured wartime Britain organising a series of concerts aimed both at spreading access to the culture of classical music and also boosting public morale. Sheridan reminds us that for women musicians these performances were war work and allowed them to challenge the predominantly male world of arts performance and administration whilst he simultaneously investigates the role of such work in devising and promoting a common British identity.

The woman as Music Traveller, traversing the British landscape in her Morris motorcar to bring 'culture' to the regions, is a very fitting image for the end of the book. This woman worker has come along way from Florence Nightingale's mid-nineteenth-century thoughts on work. She has choice, freedom and responsibility. Liberated and unchaperoned, she does not give rise to the social concern occasioned by the factory girl, although she is still functioning within a masculine world of work. She unites the desire for leisure and entertainment with the national project of winning a war. Her work gives her fulfilment and duty. Yet, ultimately it is performed through economic necessity, for a wage, making her more similar to the nineteenth-century working-class woman than she may realise.

Notes

1   Alice Clark, *Working Life of Women in the Seventeenth Century* (London, 1919); Ivy Pinchbeck, *Women Workers and the Industrial Revolution 1750–1850* (London, 1930).

2   For example, Meta Zimmeck, 'Strategies and Stratagems for the Employment of Women in the British Civil Service, 1919–1939', *Historical Journal*, 27, 4 (1984); Karen Sayer, *Women of the Field: Representations of Rural Women in the Nineteenth Century* (Manchester, 1995); Anne Clendinning, '"Deft Fingers" and "Persuasive Eloquence": The "Lady Demons" of the English Gas Industry 1888–1918', *Women's History Review*, 9, 3 (2000).

3   For example Erica Diane Rappaport, *Shopping for Pleasure. Women in the Making of London's West End* (Princeton and Oxford, 2000); Judy Attfield and Pat Kirkham (eds), *A View from the Interior: Feminism, Women and Design* (London, 1989).

4   Patrick Joyce (ed.), *The Historical Meanings of Work* (Cambridge, 1987).

5   See Katrina Honeyman, *Women, Gender and Industrialisation in England 1700–1870* (Basingstoke, 2000).

6   Leonora Davidoff and Catherine Hall, *Family Fortunes* (London, 1987); Amanda Vickery, 'Golden Age to Separate Spheres? A Review of the Categories and Chronologies of English Women's History', *Historical Journal*, 36 (1993). Whilst these first two debates focus on the period 1780–1830, they inform the ways in which women's history of the later nineteenth century is presented.

7   See Adrian Bingham, 'An Era of Domesticity? Histories of Women and Gender in Inter-War Britain', *Cultural and Social History*, 1, 2 (2004).

8   John Tosh, *A Man's Place: Masculinity and the Middle-class Home in Victorian England* (New Haven, 1999); Frank Prochaska, *Women and Philanthropy in Nineteenth-Century England* (Oxford, 1980).

9   Eleanor Gordon and Gwyneth Nairn, *Public Lives: Women, Family and Society in Victorian Britain* (New Haven, 2003).

10 Anne Witz, *Professions and Patriarchy* (London, 1992); Jane Humphries, 'Protective Legislation, the Capitalist State, and Working-Class Men: the Case of the 1842 Mines Regulation Act', *Feminist Review*, 7 (1981); Sonya O. Rose, 'Gender Antagonism and Class Conflict: Exclusionary Strategies of Male Trade Unionists in Nineteenth-century Britain', *Social History*, 11 (1988).

11 Gordon and Nairn, *Public Lives*, p. 235.

12 Deirdre Mcloskey, 'Paid Work', in Ina Zweiniger-Bargielowska (ed.), *Women in Twentieth-Century Britain* (Harlow, 2001), p. 169. See also Angela John (ed.), *Unequal Opportunities: Women's Employment in England 1800–1918* (Oxford, 1986).

13 Davidoff and Hall, *Family Fortunes*; Gordon and Nair, *Public Lives*.

14 Judy Giles, 'Help for Housewives: Domestic Service and the Reconstruction of Domesticity 1940–50', *Women's History Review*, 10, 20 (2001).

15 Raymond Williams, *Keywords*, pp. 87–93; William H. Sewell, 'The Concept(s) of Culture', in Victoria E. Bonnell and Lynn Hunt (eds), *Beyond the Cultural Turn* (Berkeley, 1999).

16 For an example of the social history of cultural forms, see Robert W. Malcolmson, *Popular Recreations in English Society, 1700–1850* (Cambridge, 1973). For an example of the cultural history of the social, see Mary Poovey, *Making a Social Body: British Cultural Formation 1830–64* (Chicago, 1995).

17 E.P. Thompson, *The Making of the English Working Class* (Harmondsworth, 1963), p. 10.

18 Gareth Stedman Jones, *Languages of Class: Studies in English Working-Class History 1832–1982* (Cambridge, 1983).

19 Lynn Hunt (ed.), *The New Cultural History* (Berkeley, 1989). Hunt cited the work of Clifford Geertz, Michel Foucault, Jacques Derrida, Roland Barthes and Hayden White. For a later critique and discussion of the 'new cultural history', see Bonnell and Hunt (eds), *Beyond the Cultural Turn*.

20 Judith Walkowitz, *City of Dreadful Delight: Narratives of Sexual Danger in Late-Victorian London* (London, 1992).

21 Sonya O. Rose, *Limited Livelihoods: Gender and Class in Nineteenth-century England* (Berkeley, 1992); Anna Clark, *The Struggle for the Breeches: Gender and the Making of the British Working Class* (Berkeley, 1995).

22 Mary Poovey, *Uneven Developments: The Ideological Work of Gender in Mid-Victorian England* (London, 1988), p. 17.

23 Joan Scott, 'The Evidence of Experience', *Critical Enquiry*, 17 (1991).

24 Kathleen Canning, 'Feminist History after the Linguistic Turn: Historicizing Discourse and Experience', *Signs: Journal of Women in Culture and Society*, 19, 2 (1994), pp. 373–4, quoted in Penny Summerfield, *Reconstructing Women's Wartime Lives* (Manchester, 1998), p. 12.

25 Denise Riley, *'Am I that Name?' Feminism and the Category of 'Women' in History* (London, 1988).

26 Joan Riviere, 'Womanliness as Masquerade', *International Journal of Psychoanalysis*, 10 (1929); Judith Butler, *Gender Trouble: Feminism and the Subversion of Identity* (London, 1990).

27   Edward Higgs, 'Women, Occupations and Work in the Nineteenth Century Censuses', *History Workshop Journal*, 23 (1987).

28   Witz, *Patriarchy and the Professions*; Cynthia Cockburn, *Brothers: Male Dominance and Technological Change* (Cambridge, 1983).

29   Elizabeth Roberts, *A Woman's Place: an Oral History of Working-class Women, 1890–1940* (Oxford, 1984).

30   *The Liverpool Labour Chronicle*, October 1895, cited in Krista Cowman, *Mrs Brown is a Man and a Brother! Women in Merseyside's Political Organisations, 1890–1920* (Liverpool, 2004), p. 35.

31   Martha Vicinus, *Independent Women: Work and Community for Single Women 1850–1920* (London, 1985), p. 6.

32   Barbara Leigh Smith, 'Women and Work', quoted by Jane Rendall, 'Friendship and Politics', in Susan Mendus and Jane Rendall (eds), *Sexuality and Subordination* (London, 1989), p. 161.

33   Kathleen Dayus, *Where There's Life* (London, 1985), p. 215.

34   Ibid., p. 219.

35   'Gwynneth', in Jill Miller, *You Can't Kill the Spirit: Women in a Welsh Mining Valley* (London, 1986), p. 104.

36   'Lucy Luck, Straw-plait Maker (1848–1922)', in John Burnett (ed.), *Useful Toil: Autobiographies of Working People from the 1820s to the 1920s* (London, 1974), p. 77.

37   Jane Haggis, 'A Heart that has Felt the Love of God and Longs for Others to Know it: Conventions of Gender, Tensions of Self and Constructions of Difference in Offering to be a Lady Missionary', *Women's History Review* 7, 1 (1998).

38   For example Sandra Stanley Holton, Alison Mackinnon and Margaret Allen, 'Introduction', in 'Between Rationality and Revelation: Women, Faith and Public Roles in the Nineteenth and Twentieth Centuries', *Women's History Review* special edition, 7, 1 (1998).

39   Sandra Stanley Holton, 'Feminism, History and Movements of the Soul: Christian Science in the Life of Alice Clark (1874–1934)', *Australian Feminist Studies*, 13 (1998).

40   Ludmilla Jordanova, *History in Practice* (London, 2000), p. 179.

41   For example, Tierl Thompson (ed.), *Dear Girl: The Diaries and Letters of Two Working Women 1897–1917* (London, 1987).

42   Lawrence Stone, *The Past and the Present Revisited* (London, 1987), p. 45.

43   Sandra Holton, *Suffrage Days: Stories from the Women's Suffrage Movement* (London, 1996), p. 1.

44   Louise Tilly and Joan Scott, *Women, Work and the Family* (London, 1978), p. 3.

45   Pinchbeck, *Women Workers and the Industrial Revolution*, p. v.

46   Meg Gomersall, *Working-class Girls in Nineteenth-century England: Life, Work and Schooling* (London, 1997), p. 28.

47   Deborah Valenze, *The First Industrial Woman* (Oxford, 1995), p. 98.

48   Barbara Harrison and Melanie Nolan, 'Reflections in Colonial Glass? Women Factory Inspectors in Britain and New Zealand 1893–1921', *Women's History Review*, 13, 2 (2004).

49   Barbara Harrison, *Not Only the Dangerous Trades: Women's Work and Health in Britain 1880–1914* (London, 1996), p. 196.

50   Anna Davin, 'What is a Child?', in A. Fletcher and S. Hussey (eds), *Childhood in Question: Children, Parents and the State* (Manchester, 1999).

51   Sally Mitchell, *The New Girl: Girls' Culture in England, 1880–1915* (New York, 1995).

52   Carol Dyhouse, *Girls Growing Up in Late Victorian and Edwardian England* (London, 1981).

53   Mitchell, *The New Girl*, p. 173.

54   Ibid., p. 29.

55   Ludmilla Jordanova, *Nature Displayed: Gender, Science and Medicine* (London, 1999); Ornella Moscucci, *The Science of Woman: Gynaecology and Gender in England 1800–1929* (Cambridge, 1990).

56   Catherine Gallagher and Thomas Laqueur (eds), *Sexuality and the Social Body in the Nineteenth Century* (Berkeley, 1986).

57   Moscucci, *Science of Woman*, pp. 40–41.

58   Elizabeth Garrett Anderson, 'Sex in Mind and Education: A Reply', *Fortnightly Review*, 21 (1874), quoted in Anne Digby, 'Women's Biological Straitjacket', in Mendus and Rendall (eds), *Sexuality and Subordination*. Anderson was responding to Maudsley's article in *Fortnightly Review*, XXI (1874).

59   Witz, *Professions and Patriarchy*; E. Moberly Bell, *Storming the Citadel: the Rise of the Woman Doctor* (London, 1953); Catriona Blake, *The Charge of the Parasols: Women's Entry to the Medical Profession in Britain* (London, 1990).

60   Carol Dyhouse, 'Driving Ambitions: Women in Pursuit of a Medical Education, 1890– 1939', *Women's History Review*, 7, 3 (1998), p. 321; Carol Dyhouse, 'Women Students and the London Medical Schools, 1914–39: the Anatomy of a Masculine Culture', *Gender and History*, 10, 1 (1998).

61   Pierre Bourdieu, 'The Forms of Capital', in A.H. Halsey, Hugh Lauder, Philip Brown and Amy S. Wells (eds), *Education: Culture, Economy, and Society* (Oxford, 1997), p. 47.

62   Anne Summers, 'Public Functions, Private Premises: Female Professional Identity and the Domestic-Service Paradigm in Britain c.1850–1930', in Billie Melman (ed.), *Borderlines: Gender and Identities in War and Peace, 1870–1930* (London, 1998).

63   Hilary Sommerlad and Peter Sanderson, *Gender, Choice and Commitment: Women Solicitors in England and Wales and the Struggle for Equal Status* (Aldershot, 1998).

64   Sheila Meintjes, 'War and Post-war Shifts in Gender Relations', p. 65 in Sheila Meintjes, Anu Pillay and Meredeth Turshem, *The Aftermath: Women in Post-Conflict Transformation* (London, 2001), pp. 63–77.

65   See for example Gail Braybon and Penny Summerfield, *Out of the Cage: Women's Experiences in Two World Wars* (London, 1987); Angela Woollacott, *On Her Their Lives Depend: Munitions Workers in the Great War* (Berkeley, 1994).

66   Arthur Marwick, *Women at War 1914–1918* (London, 1977), p. 157.

67   Irene O. Andrews, *The Economic Effects of the War upon Women and Children in Great Britain* (Oxford, 1918).

68   Sarah Boston, *Women Workers and the First World War* (London, 1989), p. 49.

69   Margaret R. Higgonet, Jane Jenson, Sonya Michel and Margaret C. Weitz (eds), *Behind the Lines: Gender and the Two World Wars*, 'Introduction', p. 4.

70   Susan Kingsley Kent, *Making Peace: The Reconstruction of Gender in Interwar Britain* (Princeton, 1993); Sonya O. Rose, *Which People's War? National Identity and Citizenship in Wartime Britain, 1939–1945* (Oxford, 2003).

71   Summerfield, *Reconstructing Women's Wartime Lives*; Bingham, 'An Era of Domesticity'.

72   Christine Gledhill and Gillian Swanson (eds), *Nationalising Femininity: Culture, Sexuality and British Cinema in the Second World War* (Manchester, 1996).

73   On the Women's Voluntary Service, see James Hinton, *Women, Social Leadership and the Second World War: Continuities of Class* (Oxford, 2002).

74 See Lucy Bland, 'In the Name of Protection: the Policing of Women in the First World War', in Julia Brophy and Carol Smart (eds), *Women in Law: Explorations in Law, Family and Sexuality* (London, 1985).

75 Ann Wiltsher, *Most Dangerous Women: Feminist Peace Campaigners of the Great War* (London, 1995).

76 Nicoletta Gullace, 'White Feathers and Wounded Men: Female Patriotism and the Great War', *Journal of British Studies*, 36 (1987); Krisztina Robert, 'Gender, Class, and Patriotism: Women's Paramilitary Units in First World War Britain', *International History Review*, 19, 1 (1997); Janet S.K. Watson, 'Khaki Girls, VADs, and Tommy's Sisters: Gender and Class in First World War Britain', *International History Review*, 19 (1997).

PART I

WHAT DO WE MEAN BY WORK?

Chapter 1

Victorian Liberal Feminism and the 'Idea' of Work

Joyce Senders Pedersen

The demand for expanded opportunities for work was a key concern of the women's movement in Victorian England.[1] Barbara Leigh Smith's *Women and Work*, which appeared in 1857, was one of many mid-Victorian tracts to address the problem. Like many period pieces, the essay is a somewhat disconcerting collage of religious pronouncements and highly practical material concerns. In one breath, readers are admonished to 'think seriously over my words: and if they have truth in them, it is a matter between God and your own souls that you act on them'. In the next, new employment opportunities for women are mooted and advice is given about suitable clothing for working women; cork-lined boots, waterproof cloaks, and skirts between the ankle and the knee are recommended.[2]

Smith's essay is prefaced by two quotes. The first, from St Paul, summons a Christian vision of a community bound by a common faith that transcends all differences, including those of sex.[3] The second, from Elizabeth Barrett Browning's *Aurora Leigh*, associates work with the value of self-dependence. Asserting that *all* honest work promotes God's purposes in the world, it proclaims that without work women are doomed to serfdom.[4] Subsequently, Smith informs her readers that God's purposes for the world encompass individual self-development: 'Think of the noble capacities of a human being. Look at your daughters, your sisters, and ask if they are what they might be if their faculties had been drawn forth, if they had liberty ... to become what God means them to be'.[5]

This complex of associations, identifying work with religious aspirations as well as practical material concerns and with hopes for communal integration as well as individual freedom and self-development, was characteristic of women and men who were active in women's rights causes in the mid-Victorian years. However, the linkage between these various dimensions of work – between the metaphysical and the material and the communal and the self-promotional – is not obvious. The following discussion seeks to understand this 'idea' of work, its logic and its attractions for Victorian feminists.

Far from viewing work as a regrettable necessity, feminists of this generation saw work as a desideratum for all individuals regardless of sex and invested work with existential hopes that were both religious and secular in character. They recognised that for many women work was a matter of urgent material need. They wanted women who engaged in waged work to be adequately remunerated and wished a greater range of paid employments to be opened to women. However, their 'idea' of work – particularly for individuals like themselves – was not that of a relationship dictated by economic imperatives. Rather, it was rooted in a non-materialist worldview that aligned Protestant religious convictions with a contemporary strand of liberal thought. The former associated work with a sense of moral/spiritual agency, transcendent purpose, and an understanding of community as a community of believers united by faith in a common cause. The latter assumed that self-interested individual striving would ultimately promote the common good but identified the higher self-interest with altruistic orientations. Blurring the distinction between waged and unwaged work and domestic and public employments, this 'idea' of work, while not *necessarily* gendered, included elements that were compatible with conventional ideals of middle-class womanhood and thus *could* carry gendered overtones.

In practice this 'existential' view of work had class implications, assuming a freedom of choice that was largely limited to the privileged few. More particularly, it was closely attuned to emergent professional ideals, which assumed a measure of independence from immediate market constraints and were oriented to an ethic of public service rather than a direct pursuit of private gain. However, its early proponents did not understand this 'idea' of work as being class-specific. On the contrary, they assumed it to be potentially accessible to all and as promoting bonding across lines of class and sex. By the late nineteenth and early twentieth century, when class-related issues (including working-class conditions of employment) were acquiring greater salience, this vision of work as a secular calling was becoming increasingly class-specific, feeding into the formation of professional identities and the concept of a career.

* * *

For most mid-Victorian feminists the 'idea' of work remained heavily freighted with religious associations: with a quest for transcendental meaning, a hope (however faint) of immortality, a view of life as a pilgrim's progress towards spiritual/moral enlightenment, and a search for spiritual fellowship. Work was often projected as a religious imperative incumbent on all human beings. In Barbara Leigh Smith's words:

> God sent all human beings into the world for the purpose of forwarding ... the progress of the world. We must each leave the world a little better than we found it ... To do God's work in the world is the duty of all, rich and poor, of all nations, of both sexes.[6]

Her views were echoed by Josephine Butler, who also believed that it was against God's will that any be 'cumberers of the ground'.[7] This religious vision of work dovetailed with a strain of contemporary liberal thought, associated especially with the later works of John Stuart Mill, that envisaged a meritocratic society in which individuals were rewarded for their works but at the same time recognised their responsibilities for promoting the larger, public good. As Mill related, he and his wife Harriet Taylor Mill:

> ... looked forward to a time when society will no longer be divided into the idle and the industrious; when the rule that they who do not work shall not eat will be applied ... impartially to all ... and when it will no longer either be, or be thought to be, impossible for human beings to exert themselves strenuously in procuring benefits which are not to be exclusively their own, but to be shared with the society they belong to.[8]

The 'idea' of worldly work as a Godly calling of course had roots reaching far back in the Protestant tradition. While work retained religious associations for many individuals of this generation, it was but loosely attached to any particular doctrinal or denominational moorings. Although their religious sensibilities differed, Barbara Leigh Smith, a Deist from a radical Unitarian family, and Josephine Butler, an Evangelical, vested similar hopes in the 'idea' of work,[9] and their hopes were broadly shared by many earnest doubters, including Mill. Eliding moral and spiritual values, Mill considered that individuals might find something at least akin to religious satisfactions in labouring to realise the new moral order that he believed destined to prevail:

> A battle is constantly going on, in which the humblest human creature is not incapable of taking some part, between the powers of good and those of evil ... even the smallest help on the right side has its value in promoting the very slow ... progress by which good is gradually gaining ground from evil, yet

gaining it so visibly at considerable intervals as to promise the very distant but not uncertain final victory of Good. To do something during life ... towards bringing this consummation ever so little nearer, is the most ... invigorating thought which can inspire a human creature; and that it is destined, with or without supernatural sanctions, to be the religion of the Future I cannot entertain a doubt.[10]

In working for the good of humankind, Mill noted, noble-minded individuals might hope to achieve a form of immortality in being honoured forever in the memory of their fellow human beings.

For many thoughtful individuals of this generation who struggled with religious doubts, however they resolved them, the quest for work assumed a special urgency. Whether or not they were believers they were determined to find a sense of transcendent purpose in this life and some way of leaving their footprints in the sand. Jane Rendall has provided a moving account of the young Barbara Leigh Smith's and her good friend Bessie Rayner Parkes's quest for work that would provide a sense of purpose in their lives. Writing to her friend about '*work & life*' and urging the necessity of 'fixing early on a train of action', Barbara reflected 'what is so sad so utterly black as a wasted life .... I believe there are thousands & tens of thousands who like you & I ... *intend working* but live & die, only intending'.[11] Also familiar is Florence Nightingale's heartfelt cry for work, and her outrage at what seemed to her the appalling waste of life that conformity to the small rituals of private social concourse entailed. '[I]s it a wonder', she demanded, 'that all individual life is extinguished [in this context]'?[12] Millicent Fawcett, a perfunctory Anglican, devoted much of her later life to working for the cause of women's suffrage. As her sister wrote to her: 'I felt ... that the cause is to you what religion was to dear mother'.[13]

These feminists' 'idea' of work was comprehensive. It included both waged and unwaged labour and might include women's domestic responsibilities as well. Bessie Parkes, who edited the *English Woman's Journal* from 1858–63, intended it to be a 'Working Woman's Journal'. She included in the ranks of 'working woman':

> [A]ll women who are actively engaged in any labours of brain or hand, whether they be the wives and daughters of landed proprietors, devoted to the well-being of their tenantry, or ... other labourers in the broad field of philanthropy ... teachers ... professional artists; or are engaged in any of those manual occupations by which multitudes ... gain their daily bread.[14]

Insisting on the equivalency of women's domestic work and other forms of work, Barbara Leigh Smith explained:

> Women who act as housekeepers, nurses, and instructors of their children, often do as much for the support of the household as their husbands; and it is very unfair for men to speak of supporting a wife and children when such is the case. When a woman gives up a profitable employment to be a governess to her own family, she earns her right to live. We war against idleness, whether of man or woman, and every one is idle who is not making the best use of the faculties nature has given them.[15]

For Smith, then, it was the nature of the work, not the setting or its remuneration, that were of crucial interest.

However comprehensive their definition of work, these individuals did not consider all forms of labour equally valuable. Consistent with their Protestant origins, they insisted on the importance of inner motivation in determining the ethical value of work. In their view, ideally work was undertaken in a disinterested, altruistic spirit, whether or not the work was waged and whatever the benefits that accrued incidentally to the individual worker. 'The ideal life', Florence Nightingale explained, 'is passed in noble schemes of good consecutively followed up, of devotion to a great object, of sympathy given and received for high ideas and generous feelings'.[16] Frances Power Cobbe took a similar view: '[A]ll faithful work – be it in the fields of art or science, or disinterested labour of any kind – is as truly work for God as the toil of the most devoted philanthropists'.[17]

These individuals' claims for work for women were tailored to a worldview in which claims to esteem and power were based on individuals' moral and mental merit (they were inclined to elide the two). As Alice Rossi observed in connection with the American women's movement, identification with worthy moral causes played a compensatory role for individuals whose status was insecure.[18] '[T]o enlarge the working sphere of woman', Anna Jameson noted, '… to give her a more practical and authorised share in all social arrangements which have for their object the amelioration of evil and suffering, is to elevate her in the social scale'.[19] Emphasising the 'duty of mental and spiritual cultivation for both men and women', Emily Davies considered that claims to authority should rest on a moral and spiritual rather than on a physical and legal basis.[20] The 'best' women, she explained, cared for little but serving others:

> I believe the best women think more of duties and responsibilities than of rights and wrongs, and care comparatively little for any 'right' but that of

giving their best in the service of God and humanity, by the development of whatever capacities of usefulness they possess.[21]

To Barbara Leigh Smith it seemed that salvation was best found by concentrating on the ills of this world rather than indulging in selfish hopes about one's fate in the next:

> By working for the salvation of the world, we may chance to achieve our own in another, but never by any other means. To set to work to save our own souls is as foolish as for a man on horseback to try and pull up his fallen horse.[22]

Frances Power Cobbe took a similar line. Criticising Anglican Sisterhoods for encouraging a spirit of blind obedience, she asserted that: 'They must bear in mind that their object is not *to earn salvation for themselves* by penitential practices and meritorious 'works', but *to do good for others*'.[23] Work, then, in its most admirable guise might incidentally promote individual self-interest, but it was not undertaken primarily with an eye to self-advancement.

Mid-Victorian feminists were not indifferent to women's material needs.[24] On the contrary, armed with census data, they were at pains to publicise the fact that many women (including middle as well as working-class and married as well as single and widowed women) in fact engaged in waged work and urgently needed an expanded range of employment opportunities in order to support themselves and their dependents.[25] Josephine Butler was of the opinion that 'A much greater number of women must support themselves now than has been the case at any other time. The agitation for the enlargement of woman's sphere of work has a real and pressing cause'.[26] Bessie Parkes agreed:

> [E]xcept for the material need which exerted a constant pressure over a large and educated class, the 'woman's movement' could never have become in England a subject of popular comment, and to a certain extent of popular sympathy.[27]

These individuals devoted time, effort, and sometimes money to extending women's employment opportunities and supported educational schemes intended to qualify women for a wider range of occupations. However, their 'idea' of work was embedded in a non-materialist worldview. Protestant and liberal commitments alike directed their attention to the crucial importance of the inner life in deciding individual destiny. All human progress, including material success, appeared to turn on individual moral and mental development. As Maria Grey, a leading figure in the movement for women's educational reform, explained: 'for the higher purposes of life, beyond the simple preservation of the species, it is moral purpose and intellect … that is decisive'.[28]

Given such assumptions, it was natural that these individuals fixed their attention above all on the relationship between work and character. In her *Hints on Self-Help; A Book for Young Women* Jessie Boucherett (1825–1905), the founder of the Society for Promoting the Employment of Women, showed her readers that success in work was predicated on a well-ordered character. Acknowledging her debt to Samuel Smiles's 'book for young men', Boucherett, like Smiles, aimed to encourage a spirit of self-dependence by presenting case histories of exemplary individuals whose lives demonstrate the character traits associated with success.[29] Whereas women figure in Smiles's book only as assisting self-helping males, Boucherett's female exemplars go about their own work.

A comparison of the two tracts suggests that self-help was distinctly more problematic for women than for men. The subtext of Smiles's book, with its myriad examples of men successful in many walks of life, is that a wealth of opportunities exist for men prepared to seize them. By contrast, Boucherett directs attention to women's limited employment opportunities, and unlike Smiles's tales, some of her stories have unhappy endings (including cases of women who, moved by a false sense of family obligation, are victimised by unscrupulous relations). Moreover, whereas Boucherett indicates that a woman may have to choose between family obligations and going 'out into the world to push her fortunes', Smiles's heroes face no such choices.[30] In effect, household responsibilities continued to be construed as women's work.

This said, the two tracts share many common assumptions. Both assume that qualities of character are crucial to success in life and that the same character traits make for success in women and men. Thus, for example, Boucherett laments that all too often 'a silly girl, whose reason is obscured by idleness' believes that women by virtue of their sex are excused from acquiring habits of 'order, punctuality, and method'. 'Such an idea', readers are informed, 'is a complete bar to success in life'.[31] Smiles cites Caroline Chisholm's advice to Harriet Beecher Stowe ('"that if we want anything *done*, we must go to work and do: it is of no use merely to talk"') as universally applicable (without identifying either woman's achievements) and fulsomely acknowledges the importance of maternal example in promoting male success, tacitly suggesting that similar character traits make for success in the public and domestic domains.[32] Both authors regard paid and unpaid work as equally

meritorious, and both associate idleness with moral delinquency and view
work as potentially morally improving.

Feminists anticipated a variety of moral gains from expanding women's
opportunities for work. On a practical level, they urged that improved prospects
for paid employment offered a solution to the material want that tempted all
too many women to evil ways, driving some to prostitution and others to
marry simply to obtain a maintenance (which most feminists regarded as but
a form of prostitution).[33] Convinced that marriage should be entered upon in a
disinterested spirit, Josephine Butler, for example, urged that marriage should
not be 'degraded to the level of a feminine profession'.[34] On a more abstract
level, work was associated with the elevation and realisation of individuals'
moral nature. Undertaken in the proper spirit, work was associated with an
expansion of individuals' mental and moral horizons, encouraging them to
look beyond narrowly personal or familial concerns. Explaining that not only
'humble' women but also women of the 'better classes' required work, Butler
suggested that: '[T]he very condition of their moral existence is, that efforts
made by them should answer to some part of the needs of the community'.
She predicted that: '[E]ducation, earnest work in trades and professions,
and a share in grave national interests will correct the foolish sentimental
tendencies' too common amongst women.[35] Emily Davies took a similar
line. Idleness, she asserted, was morally injurious: '[T]he absence of any
definite settled occupation … is … calculated to encourage a trifling habit
of mind, injurious not only to the women who indulge in it, but to everyone
with whom they have to do'.[36] Whereas a man 'may find in his daily work
the mental and moral discipline he needs', women, Davies considered, were
all too often indifferent to any but family interests. They tended to discourage
their husband from interesting himself in anything other than '[m]aking money
and getting on in the world by means of it'.[37] It was a common complaint.
Lydia Becker (1827–90), a leading figure in the early suffrage movement,
expressed similar concerns:

> The inert mass of deadness to public interest … is the bane of national and
> personal nobleness. This is fostered by inculcating the duty of indifference
> in women – and they drag down the men to their own enforced level of
> indifference.[38]

Seen in this light, rather than being narrowly self-serving, work appeared an
antidote to family selfishness and to promote the altruistic orientations that
these feminists prized.

Leonore Davidoff and Catherine Hall have shown the centrality of religious commitments in buttressing middle-class attachment to a work ethic and in underwriting middle-class claims to status and power in the period 1780–1850.[39] Most mid-Victorian feminists were middle class in origin, and in one of its aspects their advocacy of a work ethic can be seen as advancing a middle-class ideal, distancing them both from the idle rich and the destitute poor. Barbara Leigh Smith, for example, distinguished both between 'work' and mindless toil ('WORK – not drudgery, but WORK is the great beautifier') and between 'work' and merely self-gratifying activity: [a]ccomplishments, [music, drawing, etc.] which are amusements only,' she indicated, are 'killing to the soul'. However, she continued:

> Do not misunderstand: all 'accomplishments' may be works, serious studies; and may, by helping others to bear life better, and giving pleasure to those who have none, be made worthy work for women; but for this end they must be studied faithfully, and with self-devotion.[40]

Isabella M.S. Tod took a somewhat similar tack. Applauding the middle classes as the 'substance and sinew of the country' and the chief source of its prosperity, she regarded them as free both from the 'mingled suffering and recklessness which poverty creates, and ... luxurious idleness and self-worship which surrounds great wealth, their very condition compels the exercise of many of the higher faculties of heart and mind'.[41]

It was the assumed association of work with the 'higher' qualities of heart and mind that these individuals especially valued, not the material rewards that work might entail. A distaste for strictly profit-oriented behaviour pervades their works. Bessie Parkes considered that the 'operations of commerce, while tending to the greatest happiness of the greatest number, devour any small obstacles in the way'. How, she wondered, could the principle of benevolence be brought to counteract men's selfishness? She acknowledged that interfering with the 'laws of political economy' would create less wealth, but concluded that 'luxuries' must be sacrificed to considerations of human well-being.[42] Frances Cobbe distinguished between 'mere money-getting' and other pursuits. The latter, she thought, could be classified in three great orders, as pursuing the True (science, literature, philosophy), the Beautiful (art, including 'poetic literature'), or the Good (politics and philanthropy). 'The philosopher ... the artist ... the statesman or philanthropist', she suggested, '... all these in their several ways are God's seers'.[43] Consistent with this view, although Barbara Leigh Smith was prepared to attack the prejudice against ladies taking money for their work, she was *not* prepared to defend the profit motive *per se*. Instead, she suggested that payment be viewed as proof that work was actually serving the wants of others.[44]

These individuals were writing at a time when the professions were slowly becoming disentangled from the old status hierarchy and a new version of professionalism, emphasising intellectual expertise, an ethos of public service, and formal certification, was in the process of being defined. Many of them belonged themselves to the professional middle classes, and they can be seen as voicing the ideals of what Harold Perkin has termed 'the forgotten middle class' – professional, as opposed to entrepreneurial – who functioned at a certain remove from the market.[45] Like other contemporary proponents of the professional ideal, they sought to distance themselves at once from a life of opulent idleness and 'mere money-getting'.

Feminists construed women's philanthropic work and domestic occupations as ideally involving similar skills and orientations to those associated with paid professional work. '[W]hy', queried Anna Jameson, 'should not charity be a profession in our sex, just ... as religion is a profession in yours [male clerics]?'[46] Emily Davies advised that unpaid public service when seriously undertaken was virtually equivalent to 'definitely professional work'. Considering the relation between 'professional' and 'domestic life', she argued that the same education equipped upper- and middle-class women equally for both, noting that household management, like many public pursuits, required skills of 'government' and 'administration'.[47] In a similar spirit, Maria Grey advised young women to train as kindergarten teachers as a preparation for motherhood.[48]

Projecting themselves (however problematically) as existing above the fray of the market place, liberal feminists identified with an ethos of public service that pointed towards social integration rather than an ethic of competitive individualism.[49] Thus, while it is true that they often employ the language of class in discussing women's work, class assumes a somewhat spectral appearance in their writing, being associated as much with qualities of mind and character as with differences in material circumstances. Often they spoke in terms of differences of 'education' or 'intelligence' rather than differences of wealth or market position. Calling attention to the plight of 'educated women' who were prey to the vicissitudes of middle-class life but not trained to provide for themselves, Bessie Parkes, for example, urged that such women be schooled in the virtues of self-help and strenuous exertion: 'the women of the middle classes', she admonished, '... should heartily accept the life of those classes, instead of aping the life of the aristocracy'.[50] However, an ethic of self-dependence and strenuous exertion had appeal to women of quite varied social origins, and, as noted above, Parkes's 'idea' of work accorded precedence to this shared ethos, rather than focusing on waged versus unwaged labour or differences in market position.[51]

Parkes and other activists took it for granted that women were destined for different types of waged employments depending on their socioeconomic circumstances, and that their domestic responsibilities, too, would differ. However, for feminists of this mid-Victorian generation, the salience of social formations based on shared material interests, whether of social class or sex, was always qualified by the importance they accorded the individual inner life and their preference for a social economy based on moral and mental merit and geared to an ethic of altruism. Jessie Boucherett, for example, thus cast her discussion of class in terms of differences of intellect:

> There are the labouring classes, who want instruction in household and domestic matters, to enable them to become good servants and useful wives for working men ... and there are the middle classes, such as the daughters of tradesmen, clerks, &c., who require another kind of teaching of a more intellectual nature to enable them to become saleswomen or bookkeepers, and engage in other situations requiring intelligence ... Each [class] from want of instruction and discipline, are apt to fall into great distress ... but all attempts at aid must be kept quite separate.[52]

Boucherett also considered that women's disadvantaged position in the world of work provided them with common interests. However, her emphasis was on the incentives this provided for 'sisterly love' and fostering bonds of union amongst women, rather than its potential for generating conflicts with men:

> When we reflect how many interests in common women have, it is sad to see how little union there is among them ... Like sticks in the fable, they are easily broken one by one, instead of being bound together by the ties of sisterly love and mutual sympathy. Great and good men are trying to raise the position of women, but these efforts will be unavailing unless zealously seconded by the women themselves. Every woman who has her own livelihood to earn ... has suffered ... either from a deficient education, or from ill-judged restrictions excluding her from well-remunerated employments ... [T]his common suffering ought to form a strong bond of union among all who work for their bread, whether they belong to the higher or lower sections of society.[53]

Urging the need for mutual assistance, she suggested that 'benefit clubs and co-operation societies' be established for women with an eye to fostering 'public spirit'.[54]

Millicent Fawcett's sketches of *Some Eminent Women of Our Times* offers another case in point. Her volume was intended to encourage 'working women' and young people by showing 'how much good work had been done in various ways by women'. Included are individuals of very various social provenance (ranging from Queen Victoria to Sarah Martin, a poor dressmaker) whose claim to eminence is shown to rest on their earnest, disinterested striving in their chosen fields of endeavour. Martin is applauded for having taken up 'good work' as a prison visitor, despite poverty, and for her determination to leave the world a better and happier place than she found it. The Queen is commended for her active devotion to duty. 'Simplicity of daily life and daily hard work', we learn, 'are the antidotes which she has constantly applied to counteract the unwholesome influences associated with royalty'. In effect, Queen Victoria and Sarah Martin are regarded by Millicent Fawcett primarily in the light of fellow workers, not as representatives of royalty or the working class.[55] In this way, a particular 'idea' of work as oriented to the general good tended to blunt awareness of differences based on socioeconomic class.

This association of work with an ethic of altruism accorded quite readily with conventional ideals of self-sacrificing womanhood, and in some cases it carried gendered overtones. Although most of these activists believed women should be free to choose their employments, most envisaged that women would be inclined to make different occupational choices from men. Barbara Leigh Smith predicted that women would be drawn particularly to those 'professions' which 'have in them something congenial to their moral nature'. She thought it unlikely that large numbers of women would enter conflict-oriented occupations, such as the military, politics, or the bar:

> Perhaps we may say that women will only enter those professions which are destined to be perpetual, being consistent with the highest moral development of humanity, which war is not. The arts, the sciences, commerce, and the education of the young in all its branches – these will most strongly attract them.[56]

Rather than being hardened by work outside the home, as conservative critics feared, women would be inclined to enter occupations that would enable them to continue to occupy the moral high ground.

Maria Grey thought that women should be left unfettered in their choice of employments but considered it unlikely that many women would succeed in work generally done by men. Her understanding of women's 'natural' work drew on conventional gender stereotypes but encompassed a broad swathe of non-domestic employments:

> The woman in virtue of her motherhood, is the natural educator of the race, the natural helper and comforter of the helpless and comfortless, and therefore the natural guardian of the poor and minister of charity. She is the natural physician of her own sex and nurse of both; the natural counsellor of the combatants in the actual struggles of life, which ... she can survey with the calmer, clearer vision of a looker-on. She is above all, the natural ally of law and order ... of the ideal, as against the material; of moral, as against physical force; the natural priestess of all the pieties and sanctities of life, and therefore of religion.[57]

In effect, she staked women's special claim to the 'caring' professions. However, Grey also noted that 'a vast quantity of the best work of the world is of no sex. It is the work of preserving and enlarging the general inheritance of mankind ... moral progress, knowledge in all its branches, art in all its forms, literature, culture'.[58]

If there was sometimes a gendered inflection to these feminists' 'idea' of work, it was part of a general 'culture of altruism' which, as Stephan Collini has shown, flourished amongst male 'public moralists' in Victorian England (including Mill), who saw an ethic of altruism as desirable for all – not just for women.[59] Consistent with this orientation, Mill's view of women's employment emphasised the opportunities for public service that a free labour market entailed:

> [B]y leaving them [women] the free choice of their employments ... [the result] would be that of doubling the mass of mental faculties available for the higher service of humanity. Where there is now one person qualified to benefit mankind and promote the general improvement, as a public teacher, or an administrator of some branch of public or social affairs, there would then be a chance of two.[60]

Rather than stressing the competitive implications of women's entry into the labour market, Mill primarily emphasised the long-term benefits that would accrue to all society. By focusing attention on future gains rather than present costs and always assuming the right motivation, *all* work that answered to human wants might be seen as partaking of the nature of 'good works' aimed at benefiting humanity. Rejecting the idea that 'ladies should not take the bread out of the mouths of the poor working-man or woman by selling in their market', Barbara Leigh Smith reminded her readers that:

> The riches and material well-being of the country consist in the quantity of stuff in the country to eat and to wear, houses to live in, books to read ... etc.

Anyone who puts more … of these things into the country adds to its riches
and happiness. The more of these things, the easier is it [sic] for all to get.
Do not think of money until you see this fact. This is why we bless steam-
engines; this is why we would bless women. Steam-engines did at first take
the bread out of a few mouths, but how many thousands have they fed for one
they have starved![61]

In effect, by stretching things a bit and eliding enlightened self-interest and
altruistic intent, an ideal of disinterested service rooted in religious values
might peacefully co-exist with liberal economic paradigms.

Davidoff and Hall have suggested that for men and women of the middle
classes who came to maturity in the years 1780–1850 an ideology of separate,
gendered spheres was a core constituent of middle-class cultural identity.[62]
Feminists of the mid-Victorian generation rejected this notion, and their 'idea'
of work was crucial to this rejection, serving to blur the distinction between
the private and the public spheres.

As we have seen, mid-Victorian activists were inclined to reject
the conventional distinction between 'work' and women's domestic
responsibilities, emphasising instead that similar skills and ethical orientations
were required for both. 'You are all … preparing … for *service*', Maria Grey
informed public school girls.[63] Centred on disinterested motivations, her idea
of 'service' included domestic responsibilities and philanthropic work as well
as paid employment. Emily Davies, too, wished both public and private life to
be informed by an altruistic ethic. Through a moral trickle-down effect, she
envisaged that gradually the whole moral tone of society would be raised 'by
the insensible influence of the employing class, whose ideas, unconsciously
communicated to their subordinates, gradually leaven all the classes below
them'. This, Davies thought, would prove an antidote to the 'want of hearty
sympathy' between different social classes that she regarded as 'one of the
most serious impediments to social progress'.[64] Josephine Butler took a similar
view. Deploring a pattern of family life that was selfish and exclusive, she
wished to bridge the separation between home and society. Home life, she
thought, should be characterised by larger, more generous public concerns;
public life would benefit from the 'giving forth of the influences of Home …
for the common good'.[65] Urging that there was 'work on every side waiting
to be done by women', who were 'waiting to be prepared for service', Butler
thought that women could 'bridge over … many a gulf between class and class
which now presents a grave obstacle to social and political progress'.[66]

There was disagreement as to whether waged work for married women was
generally desirable. As Jane Rendall has shown, although as a young woman

Bessie Parkes made no very clear distinction between work and marriage, by the 1860s her views had become more conservative.[67] Although she continued to approve the 'principle of vocations to religious and also to intellectual and practical life apart from marriage' for a minority of women, she stated that she 'never wished or contemplated the mass of women becoming breadwinners'.[68] Barbara Leigh Smith took a contrary view. 'Adult women', she thought, 'must not be supported by men, if they are to stand as dignified, rational beings before God'. Associating work with an expansion of individuals' moral and mental horizons, she considered that extra-familial commitments promoted nobility of character and ultimately improved the quality of family life: 'Work will enable women to free themselves from petty characteristics and therefore ennoble marriage'. 'Let women take their places as citizens in the Commonwealth', she concluded, 'we shall find they will fulfil all their home duties the better'.[69] John Stuart Mill's view was probably more common. He left the door open for exceptions but assumed that: 'Like a man when he chooses a profession, so, when a woman marries, it may in general be understood that she makes the choice of the management of a household, and the bringing up of a family, as the first call on her exertions'.[70] Positing equivalencies between household and professional commitments in terms of their potential moral claims and worth, Mill was not troubled by the prospect that this would condemn the majority of wives to a life of *de facto* economic dependency. For this generation of feminists, whether or not they approved of paid work for married women, it was the implications of work for the individual's inner life that were of paramount interest.

In effect, these individuals' mental landscape approximated a Marxist world turned upside down. Instead of being the site at which conflicts of interest were apt to be most nakedly revealed, their 'idea' of work emphasised its integrative potential, promoting social harmony across lines of class and sex. As Diane Worzala has argued, rather than highlighting the possibility of gender wars, feminists of this generation sought 'the union of the now divided sexes … at every stage and in all phases of life'.[71] Consistent with this view, Barbara Leigh Smith considered that shared work constituted the best fundament for a happy marriage: 'The happiest married life we can recall ever to have seen is the life of two workers, a man and a woman equal in intellectual gifts and loving hearts; the union between them being founded in their mutual work'.[72] Although what M. Jeanne Peterson has termed a 'shared career' between husband and wife seems hardly to have been the norm amongst the Victorian upper middle classes, a number of prominent feminists (including John Stuart and Harriet Taylor Mill and Millicent and Henry Fawcett) did enjoy partnerships in which shared work constituted an important bond,[73] and many of their friendships were geared to a shared commitment to some form of work, especially disinterested work in public causes.

Writing of her campaign to eliminate state regulated prostitution, Josephine Butler recalled 'sweet friendships taking their rise in a common aim'.[74] Although work for a common cause did not necessarily erase consciousness of class or sex differences, it might point up mental and moral affinities that at least suggested the possibility of cross-class and cross-sex friendships. Writing of a working man's wife – 'a grand, clever woman' – Butler remarked: 'What a difference there is between the intellect of such working women and some Society ladies whom I have met! I could make a companion of this woman at any time'.[75] Similarly, the suffrage activist Helen Blackburn (1842–1903) considered that work for the cause resulted in 'new ties of friendship and common interest for the common good, between men and women as well as between women themselves'.[76]

Barbara Leigh Smith, who in addition to her philanthropic interests was a professional artist, entertained a vision of an 'Outer and Inner Sisterhood' united by their commitments to their work:

> The Inner, to consist of the Art-sisters bound together by their one object ... the Outer Sisterhood to consist of women, all workers, and all striving after a pure moral life, but belonging to any profession, any pursuit. All should be bound to help each other in such ways as were most accordant with their natures and characters.[77]

In a similar spirit, the reforming headmistress Dorothea Beale hoped to establish a sisterhood of women teachers.[78] Although these visions failed to materialise, they reflected an 'idea' of work that combined social bonding and self-realisation, as these figures understood it.

Addressing her 'dear Friends and Fellow-workers', Josephine Butler assured them that 'We are of those ... who represent the imperishableness of principles, one of the many assurances of immortality'.[79] Emphasising the importance of shared principles rather than ties of material interest (whether based on birth or class) in social bonding, these feminists' 'idea' of work was compatible with a Christian vision of community as a community of believers, defined by their commitment to a common faith. This Christian vision was closely aligned with a strand of liberal thinking that posited linkages between individual self-development and an ethic of altruism. It was above all the 'idea' of work as the expression of a blessed inner life that enabled this generation of feminists to square the circle, reconciling the ideals of social integration and self-advancement. Although projected as a free-floating ideal accessible to all, this 'idea' of work was most compatible with a middle-class perspective that associated moral worth with individual achievement and entertained hopes that through individual striving a better future might be in the making. It had particular appeal to the professional middle classes whose claim to authority rested on an ethic of disinterested public service as well as their expertise.

* * *

The 'idea' of work advanced by mid-Victorian liberal feminists was embedded in a culture – a sustaining complex of ideas and feelings – in which Christian and materialist paradigms were quite readily aligned. Although many educated Victorians of the period confronted doubts about the truths of revealed religion, most continued to entertain high hopes for the future for humanity, finding comfort in the belief that 'There is … an essence of immortality in the life of man, even in this world … No man's acts die utterly; and though his body may resolve into dust and air, his good or his bad deeds will still be … influencing generations for all time to come'.[80] If mid-Victorians such as Barbara Leigh Smith could move without embarrassment between the material world of work and that of the spirit, directing attention now to God's purposes for the world, now to working women's need for sensible shoes, it was because they believed in the moral/spiritual equivalence of these realms, anticipating if not a heavenly future then at least a future in which humankind was advancing toward moral/spiritual perfection. Theirs was a world that was but semi-disenchanted.

In the late nineteenth and early twentieth century, more materialist outlooks gained ground. Writing in 1889, Maria Grey lamented that increasingly 'work, meaning paid work, and independence, [meaning a] life apart from the home life' were seen by public schoolgirls as 'essential to honourable womanhood'.[81] Similar concerns were voiced by Alice Zimmern at the turn of the century. Fearful that the few desirable paid employments open to educated women were becoming hopelessly overcrowded, she urged teachers 'to check the untrue notion in girls' mind that no work is worthy of the name unless it is paid'. 'Unpaid service', she observed, 'is the pride of Englishmen; why not of English women'? Still, she acknowledged, there *was* a problem: '[F]or most service money is the fitting reward, and some measure of independence belongs by right to every adult, whether man or woman'. Perhaps, she mused, wealthy parents could pay daughters a fair salary for services rendered at home 'to make life at home a worthy substitute for a professional career'.[82] In a more materialist, less optimistic age, the 'idea' of 'worthy' work was increasingly coming to be associated with paid employment. However, elements of the Victorian liberal feminists' 'idea' of work lived on to influence middle-class women's construction of a 'professional career'.

Notes

1   Olive Banks, *Becoming a Feminist: The Social Origins of 'First Wave' Feminism* (Brighton, 1986), p. 66.
2   Barbara Leigh Smith, 'Women and Work', in Candida Ann Lacey (ed.), *Barbara Leigh Smith Bodichon and the Langham Place Group* (New York and London, 1987), quote p. 37, clothes p. 63. Originally published in London, 1857, the tract is reprinted in full, together with a selection of other related contemporary pieces, in the Lacey collection. References here are to the Lacey edition. Barbara Leigh Smith, later Mme. Bodichon, was a leading figure in a number of early campaigns, including those aimed at securing women's property rights, educational reforms, and the vote. See Pam Hirsch, *Barbara Leigh Smith Bodichon 1827–1891: Feminist, Artist and Rebel* (London, 1998).
3   'For we are all the child of God by faith in Christ Jesus; for there is neither Jew nor Greek, there is neither bond nor free, there is neither male nor female, for ye are all one in Christ Jesus.' Smith, 'Women and Work', p. 36.
4   'Be sure, no earnest work / Of any honest creature, howbeit weak / Imperfect, ill adapted, fails so much / It is not gathered as a grain of sand / For carrying out God's end. No creature works / So ill, observe, that he's cashiered. / The honest, earnest man must work; / The woman also; otherwise she drops / At once below the / dignity of man, / Accepting serfdom.' Ibid., p. 36.
5   Ibid., p. 42.
6   Ibid., p. 37.
7   Josephine E. Butler (ed.), *Woman's Work and Woman's Culture* (London, 1869), p. xiii. Best remembered for her leading role in the campaign against state regulated prostitution, Butler, 1828–1906, was also active in efforts to extend women's educational opportunities. See Nancy Boyd, *Josephine Butler, Octavia Hill, Florence Nightingale: Three Victorian Women Who Changed Their World* (London and Basingstoke, 1982) and Barbara Caine, *Victorian Feminists* (Oxford, 1992), chapter 5.
8   John Stuart Mill, *Autobiography of John Stuart Mill* (New York, 1964), p. 168.
9   On the radical Unitarians see Kathryn Gleadle, *The Early Feminists: Radical Unitarians and the Emergence of the Women's Rights Movement, 1831–51* (New York, 1995) and Ruth Watts, *Gender, Power and the Unitarians in England 1760–1860* (London and New York, 1988). On Evangelicalism and the origins of modern feminism see Jane Rendall, *The Origins of Modern Feminism: Women in Britain, France and the United States, 1780–1870* (Basingstoke and London, 1985), chapter 3 and Olive Banks, *Faces of Feminism. A Study of Feminism as a Social Movement* (Oxford, 1981).
10 John Stuart Mill, 'Theism', in J.M. Robson (ed.), *Collected Works of John Stuart Mill*, X (Toronto and London, 1969), pp. 488–9.

11 Quoted in Jane Rendall, 'Friendship and Politics: Barbara Leigh Smith Bodichon (1827–91) and Bessie Rayner Parkes (1829–1925)', in Susan Mendus and Jane Rendall (eds), *Sexuality and Subordination: Interdisciplinary Studies of Gender in the Nineteenth Century* (London and New York, 1989), p. 149.

12 Florence Nightingale, 'Cassandra', in Ray Strachey, *The Cause: A Short History of the Women's Movement in Great Britain* (London, 1978), p. 405.

13 Quoted in Ray Strachey, *Millicent Garrett Fawcett* (London, 1931), p. 230. On Millicent Fawcett (1847–1929) see David Rubinstein, *A Different World for Women: The Life of Millicent Garrett Fawcett* (London, 1991).

14 Quoted in Jane Rendall, '"A Moral Engine"? Feminism, Liberalism and the English Woman's Journal', in Jane Rendall (ed.), *Equal or Different. Women's Politics 1800–1914* (Oxford, 1987), p. 115.

15 Smith, 'Women and Work', p. 41.

16 Nightingale, 'Cassandra', pp. 414–15.

17 Frances Power Cobbe, 'Female Charity, Lay and Monastic', in *Essays on the Pursuits of Women* (London, 1863) p. 141. Cobbe (1822–1904) was active in a variety of women's causes, including the suffrage movement and campaigns to secure women's property rights. See Caine, *Victorian Feminists*, chapter 4.

18 Alice S. Rossi (ed.), *The Feminist Papers: From Adams to de Beauvoir* (New York and London, 1973), pp. 269–72.

19 Mrs [Anna Brownell] Jameson, *The Communion of Labour: A Second Lecture on the Social Employments of Women* (London, 1856), p. 24. Like her friend Harriet Martineau (1802–76), Anna Jameson (1794–1860) belonged to an older generation of professional women writers who championed an expansion of women's opportunities for work in the mid-Victorian years. On Jameson see Clara Thomas, *Love and Work Enough: The Life of Anna Jameson* (Toronto, 1978).

20 Emily Davies, *Home and the Higher Education* (London, 1878), p. 18; Emily Davies, *The Higher Education of Women* (London and New York, 1866), p. 184. Davies is best remembered for her work for women's education, but she was also active in the movement to extend women's employment opportunities and the suffrage cause. On Davies see Caine, *Victorian Feminists*, chapter 3 and Daphne Bennett, *Emily Davies and the Liberation of Women 1830–1921* (London, 1990).

21 Emily Davies, 'Letters addressed to a Daily Paper at Newcastle-upon-Tyne, 1860', in E. Davies, *Thoughts on Some Questions Relating to Women 1860–1908* (Cambridge, 1910), p. 5.

22 Smith, 'Women and Work', p. 38.

23 Frances Power Cobbe, 'Female Charity: Lay and Monastic', in *Essays on the Pursuits of Women* (London, 1863), p. 141.

24 On feminists' early engagement in women's work issues see Diane Mary Chase Worzala, 'The Langham Place Circle: The Beginnings of the Organized Women's Movement in England 1854–1870' (University of Wisconsin, Madison, unpublished PhD, 1982) and Lee Holcombe, *Victorian Ladies at Work: Middle Class Working Women in England and Wales 1850–1914* (Newton Abbott, 1973), chapter 1.

25 Jessie Boucherett, 'On the Obstacles to the Employment of Women', in Lacey (ed.), *Barbara Leigh Smith Bodichon*; H. Martineau, 'Female Industry', *The Edinburgh Review*, CCXXII (April, 1859). Josephine E. Butler, *The Education and Employment of Women* (London, 1868).

26 Butler, *Woman's Work*, p. xv.

27   Bessie Rayner Parkes, 'The Changes of Eighty Years', in *Essays on Women's Work* (London, 1865), p. 55.

28   Mrs William Grey, 'Men and Women', *The Fortnightly Review*, 155, 26, New Series, (1 November 1879), p. 675. Maria Grey (1816–1906) née Shirreff, is primarily remembered for her work for women's education but also championed women's suffrage. See Edward W. Ellsworth, *Liberators of the Female Mind: The Shirreff Sisters, Educational Reform, and the Women's Movement* (Westport, CN, 1979).

29   Jessie Boucherett, *Hints on Self-Help: A Book for Young Women* (London, 1863), p. viii. On the Society for Promoting the Employment of Women see Worzala, 'The Langham Place Circle', pp. 185–215. Originally published in 1859, Samuel Smiles's *Self-Help* grew out of talks given to young male artisans.

30   Ibid., p. 50.

31   Ibid., p. 19.

32   Samuel Smiles, *Self-Help* (Harmondsworth, 1986), pp. 221, 219. Caroline Chisholm promoted reforms in the conditions of emigrants to Australia; the American novelist Harriet Beecher Stowe achieved fame as the author of *Uncle Tom's Cabin*.

33   Boucherett, *Hints on Self-Help*, p. 50.

34   Butler, *Woman's Work*, p. xxxi.

35   Ibid., pp. xxiii, xxxiii.

36   Davies, 'Letters addressed to a Daily Paper at Newcastle-upon-Tyne, 1860', p. 6.

37   Emily Davies, 'On Secondary Instruction as Relating to Girls', in *Thoughts*, pp. 80, 75–6.

38   Quoted in Helen Blackburn, *Women's Suffrage: A Record of the Women's Suffrage Movement in the British Isles with Biographical Sketches of Miss Becker* (New York, 1971), p. 42. John Stuart Mill, 'On the Subjection of Women', in Alice S. Rossi (ed.), *John Stuart Mill and Harriet Taylor Mill. Essays on Sex Equality* (Chicago and London, 1970), pp. 225–6.

39   Leonore Davidoff and Catherine Hall, *Family Fortunes. Men and Women of the English Middle Class 1780–1850* (London, 1987), Part I.

40   Smith, 'Women and Work', pp. 44, 39.

41   Isabella M.S. Tod, *On the Education of Girls of the Middle Classes* (London, 1874), p. 3. Tod was active in the movement to promote reforms in girls' secondary education in Belfast.

42   Bessie Rayner Parkes, 'Social Economy', in *Essays on Woman's Work* (London, 1865), pp. 226–7, 239–40.

43   Frances Power Cobbe, 'Old Maids', in Lacey (ed.), *Barbara Leigh Smith Bodichon and the Langham Place Group*, p. 364.

44   Smith, 'Women and Work', p. 64.

45   Harold Perkin, *The Origins of Modern English Society 1780–1880* (London and Toronto, 1969), pp. 252–70.

46   Jameson, *Communion of Labour*, p. 122.

47   Davies, *The Higher Education of Women*, pp. 110–11, 100.

48   Maria G. Grey, *Last Words to Girls* (London, 1889), p. 253.

49   Harold Perkin, *The Rise of Industrial Society in England since 1880* (London and New York, 1989), pp. 116 and 123.

50   B.R. P.[arkes], 'What Can Educated Women Do? Part II', *The English Woman's Journal*, IV (1 January 1860), p. 595.

51   Ibid., pp. 4–5.

52   Boucherett, *Hints on Self-Help*, p. 136.
53   Ibid., p. 146.
54   Ibid., p. 145.
55   Mrs Henry Fawcett, *Some Eminent Women of Our Times: Short Biographical Sketches* (London and New York, 1889), pp. v, 49, 52 (quote).
56   Smith, 'Women and Work', p. 64.
57   Maria G. Grey, 'Men and Women. A Sequel', *Fortnightly Review*, 1 June 1881, p. 791.
58   Ibid., p. 788.
59   Stefan Collini, *Public Moralists: Political Thought and Intellectual Life in Britain 1850–1930* (Oxford, 1991), chapters 2 and 4.
60   Mill, 'On the Subjection of Women', pp. 220–21.
61   Smith, 'Women and Work', pp. 62–3.
62   Davidoff and Hall, *Family Fortunes*, chapter 3.
63   Grey, *Last Words to Girls*, p. 5.
64   Davies, 'On Secondary Instruction as relating to girls', pp. 77–8.
65   Butler, 'Woman's Work', pp. xxxix, xxvii–xxviii.
66   Josephine E. Butler, *The Education and Employment of Women* (London, 1868), p. 22.
67   Rendall, 'Friendship and Politics', p. 161.
68   Parkes, 'Social Economy', p. 226; Bessie R. Parkes, 'The Balance of Opinion in Regard to Woman's Work', *The English Woman's Journal*, IX, 53 (1 July 1862), p. 342.
69   Smith, 'Women and Work', pp. 41, 43.
70   Mill, 'On the Subjection of Women', p. 179.
71   Quoted from 'Passing Events', *The English Woman's Journal* (1858) in Worzala, *The Langham Place Circle*, p. 365.
72   Smith, 'Women and Work', p. 41.
73   M. Jeanne Peterson, *Family, Love, and Work in the Lives of Victorian Gentlewomen* (Bloomington and Indianapolis, 1989).
74   Josephine E. Butler, *Personal Reminiscences of a Great Crusade* (Westport, CN, 1976), p. 243.
75   Ibid., pp. 24–5.
76   Blackburn, *Women's Suffrage*, p. 102.
77   Quoted in Hirsch, *Barbara Bodichon*, p. 54.
78   Elizabeth Raikes, *Dorothea Beale of Cheltenham* (London, 1910), p. 249.
79   Butler, *Personal Reminiscences*, p. 243.
80   Smiles, *Self-Help*, p. 220.
81   Grey, *Last Words to Girls*, pp. 239–40.
82   Alice Zimmern, *The Renaissance of Girls' Education in England: A Record of Fifty Years' Progress* (London, 1898), pp. 247–8. Zimmern (1855–1935), an educator, promoted reforms in women's education and women's suffrage.

Chapter 2

Religion and the Meanings of Work: Four Cases from among the Bright Circle of Women Quakers[1]

Sandra Stanley Holton

Studies of the changing position of women among middle-class families in the nineteenth century have demonstrated the importance of cultural as well as structural factors to that process. The role of evangelical religion especially, and the domestic cultures to which it gave rise, has been explored in terms of the relation between notions of gender difference and the formation of middle-class consciousness.[2] This article focuses on four women Quakers from the middle class, members of a church, the Religious Society of Friends, that saw a continuing struggle in the nineteenth century between its longstanding quietism and the newer forces of evangelicalism and rational religion. More specifically, it takes four cases from among succeeding generations of the women of the Bright circle.[3] These families sympathised with the evangelical emphasis on good works and on the value of the scriptures. But they continued to give primacy to the Quaker doctrine of 'the Light within', the belief that every individual holds within themselves the capacity for knowledge of the will of god.[4]

More particularly, all four women sympathised to a varying extent with reform politics. And all but one went further, and engaged actively in middle-class radical politics and in the campaigns for women's rights. In so doing, they challenged a longstanding commitment of their church to quietism and the avoidance of 'creaturely' activities. They also resisted conventional understandings of gender roles. This chapter asks how religious beliefs informed the meanings that these four women attached to the various and varying kinds of work in which they engaged. It suggests that they drew on an alternative current to evangelicalism within the Society of Friends, a current I have elsewhere identified as 'oppositionism'.[5] My discussion uses an expansive definition of work that includes family and community service, so as to explore the role of religious values in the meanings attaching to work, especially in terms of changing class and gender consciousness.[6] The four cases are:

a) Margaret Wood (1783–1859), was aunt to one of the first Quaker MPs, John Bright. She became, through her own efforts, a classic example of the *petite bourgeoise*, a woman able to live on income from the investment of a small capital sum, accumulated over a 'working life' that ended, by such a limited definition of work, in her early 40s. She provides a starting point of comparison for the three further case studies from succeeding generations of women among her kinship circle;

b) Margaret Tanner (1817–1905), (previously Priestman, and then Wheeler: her second married name will be used throughout the main body of the paper for simplicity, and as the name by which she is now best remembered). She was sister-in-law to John Bright, and became a close friend to him and his sisters, especially Priscilla Bright, after the early death of her own sister, Elizabeth Bright. She came to know and respect Margaret Wood through these lifelong friendships among the Bright and Priestman families;

c) Helen Priestman Bright (1840–1927, subsequently Clark), was the daughter of Elizabeth and John Bright, niece and sometime charge of Margaret Tanner, and great niece and sometime companion to Margaret Wood;

d) Alice Clark (1874–1934), the daughter of Helen Priestman Bright Clark, was an industrialist and early historian of women's work.

Margaret Wood

Margaret Wood's parents had a shoemaking business in Bolton, a business her father had begun as a clogger, after leaving the family farm in the lake district. The family was never prosperous, and lived in the same premises as its shop. When John Wood died in 1809 his widow appears to have kept the business going for some years more – shopkeeping was the largest single occupation among middle-class women in this period.[7] Margaret Wood was the only one of her siblings, comprising one brother and three sisters, to remain single. Family memory records her as a pastry cook and in later life she used her cookery skills to run a confectionary shop of her own.[8] The first record of her in trade directories appears in 1814 and shows that at some time prior to that date she had moved to Rochdale, where she was a partner in a confectioner's shop of which she became sole owner the following year. Her own recollections suggest that her widowed mother assisted her in the early years of this business, while her letters show also that the two women kept house together in Rochdale.[9] Here they were also near neighbours of another of the Wood sisters, Martha Bright, and her husband, Jacob, a former handloom weaver turned cotton manufacturer, who were the parents of John Bright.

Her work as a confectioner was the means by which Margaret Wood earned a living as a spinster from a family of small means. But it was, of course, also much more than that, as her letters, diaries and apocryphal sayings reveal. It formed her sense of herself as a member of 'the industrious classes', an identity that embodied both her social-economic and religious values, values that in turn shaped her political views. Firstly, it made clear the separation she celebrated between herself (and her kin) and 'the idle classes', a landed aristocracy headed by a monarch, and living parasitically and uxoriously on the wealth produced by the labour of such as herself. So when, as a small child, her niece, Priscilla Bright, rushed to her aunt's window to watch the procession of civic loyalty that attended the coronation of George IV, she commanded: 'Come away lass, he's na' but a pauper and I have to keep him'.[10] This notion of 'the industrious classes' allowed, of course, a conceptual merging of the owners of small enterprises with those they might employ in shop and factory, a merger that similarly shaped the radical rhetoric of her nephew, John Bright, in his rise as the 'Tribune of the People'.

Among the industrious classes, she recognised also a sub-grouping, 'the poor', with whom her sympathies were unwavering but with whom her sense of identity was more equivocal. By the poor, she meant those who had not sufficient resources to tide them over in bad times, whether these were times of high food prices or poor trade and low employment, war, famine or pestilence. On the one hand, she had earlier in her life felt the space between herself and the poor to be worryingly small, a period when she had clearly held fears of falling into that pitiable state. Numbers of her immediate kin had struggled to maintain their families as farmers or tradesman in Britain, and had emigrated to the United States. They included her only brother, John Wood, and his departure around 1819 had almost certainly entailed the division of her family's small capital, and the exporting of a substantial part of it. Her mother maintained herself subsequently on the rent of a few cottages, presumably purchased from her share when the family shoe business in Bolton was wound up. As a young man, Margaret Wood recalled, her brother had frequently bemoaned having four sisters to support.[11] Ironically, he did not prosper in the United States, produced a large family, some of whom he failed to establish in skilled trades or businesses, and in old age became dependent on Margaret Wood for a small annuity to supplement his own meagre income. Her letters are full of fond but exasperated references to him and his successive business failures, and anxiety concerning her nieces and nephews in the United States. Their plight might well have been hers.[12]

But she worked herself free from such danger, and in her later years had a clear sense also, therefore, of her distance from 'the poor'. She had escaped their condition, she believed, through divine providence, but her route to that providence had been hard work, humble ambitions and a deep if unostentatious piety. By middle age she had secured herself from any danger of falling among 'the poor'. She had come to enjoy what she sometimes referred to as a 'snug' independence, firmly established as a *petite bourgeoise* able to live comfortably on a modest income deriving from bank dividends, small rents, and a little interest on loans she was able to make to some of her kin in the United States.[13] Her sense of herself as an independent woman of modest means among the industrious classes shaped also her political sympathies, which were Whig rather than Radical. Her religious affiliation informed the oppositionism that most characterised her political values, especially in her hostility to the established church. This together with her lack of respect for the landed classes ensured that the Tories would never have her sympathies. But such oppositionism did not extend, as it did with her nephew, to an adherence to Radical politics.[14] She felt distaste for parliamentary politics and feared the social instability that might follow from a Radical programme that included, at this time, annual parliamentary elections.[15]

If fear of poverty had been a spur to her own enterprise, her religious values shaped her attitude to wealth. This attitude in turn informed her anxieties for her numerous nieces and nephews, especially the Brights, but also the Woods, and the family of Elizabeth Bancroft, another of her sisters, who had also emigrated with her husband and children to the United States in the early 1820s. In the case of the Brights, her concern arose from the prosperity of their father, Jacob Bright, and his pursuit of still more wealth through the continuing expansion of his mills. That expansion continued when John Bright and his brothers added the production of carpets to their business. Margaret Wood remained a fond aunt, but her accounts of John Bright took on an increasingly critical tone. She reported, for example, how, when planning to marry, he began to build himself a house of some grandeur, one that cost in all £1,200 to build, and another £1,000 to furnish. Describing it for their kin in the United States, Margaret Wood commented: 'so you see they are beginning high enough … I don't like to see them begin in so large a way, but I hope they will sometime see the folly of it'. John Bright remained in her eyes 'a very aspiring man', and she meant this not as a compliment.[16]

So Margaret Wood continued to advise her younger kin that shopkeeping was a particularly desirable occupation for Friends. It needed far less capital to start a shop than a mill, and tied up far less capital in equipment and stock. In consequence, it was less risky financially, a consideration that she felt ought to be a serious one for any member of the Society of Friends – bankruptcy was one of the grounds for disownment by the church. She was delighted, then, when two of her unmarried Bancroft nieces followed her example. They set themselves up with a small drapers shop in association with their eldest brother's tallow-chandlery business – and soon provided evidence to support her claims for shopkeeping: their enterprise succeeded to such an extent that that were shortly able to offer employment to her namesake and niece, another Margaret Wood, one of the vulnerable children of her hapless brother.[17] But she remained uneasy when contemplating the establishment of mills by Bancrofts and Woods, fearing that financial ruin might result. Not only was such large-scale manufacturing financially hazardous, it was also, in the view of Margaret Wood, spiritually dangerous, motivated by the pursuit of wealth far beyond a modest independence.[18] She herself had retired from business in her early forties, once she had achieved the means to her snug independence, thereby protecting herself from the spiritual danger that she associated with wealth. The correspondence of others within this kinship network similarly expresses an attitude to business enterprises as a temporary resort, to be given up in good time to prepare spiritually for death.

If Margaret Wood's was a down-to-earth religiosity, she valued her retirement none the less for allowing her more time now to read the journals of Quaker founders like George Fox and contemporaneous ministers like Job Scott, to follow the affairs of her church in the pages its *Annual Monitor*, and also to travel to major events in the church calendar, such as the Yearly Meeting of the Society of Friends in London. She expressed a mix of confidence and humility with regard to her religious beliefs: a confidence borne of the conviction that the pursuit of right living might ensure salvation after death; a humility that sprang from her adherence to a key belief among Friends, the indwelling of God within every individual. She saw her main spiritual task as a constant search for guidance from this 'Light within'. But with that conviction necessarily went a tolerance of the views of her co-religionists whom she recognised as similarly committed to that task. Spiritual arrogance, dogmatism and intolerance were, from such a perspective, to be firmly resisted. She feared that worldly advancement only encouraged such pride: 'Oh it is a good safe thing to be low in our minds keep from being too much exalted it is then we shall be taught "His Way" which are indeed pleasantness and all his paths are Peace'.[19] On this count, she was especially concerned for the spiritual wellbeing of her American kin, and continued to offer religious counsel as part of a kinship obligation as sister and aunt.

For the Bancroft family was prominent among a schismatic group within the Philadelphia Yearly Meeting, followers of the minister, Elias Hicks, who had opposed a shift to evangelical beliefs among American Friends.[20] Only her sister, Elizabeth Bancroft, continued to attend the religious meetings of the 'orthodox' Yearly Meeting there, while a number of her nephews and their wives had ceased to attend any meeting because they were themselves divided on the issue, and preferred not to make public such domestic disharmony. Initially, Margaret Wood chided her Bancroft nieces and nephews about their involvement in this breakaway group, and suggested the need for greater spiritual humility. But she herself was worried by the growing strength of evangelicals within London Yearly Meeting. She noted a decreasing readiness of women ministers opposed to this influence to speak there. She also recorded the mockery that met one such woman minister when she attempted to conciliate between London Yearly Meeting, and an English schism, the Beaconites, who had sought to strengthen the place of evangelical doctrine within the church discipline of the Society. A visit to the United States confirmed her in her sympathy with the Hicksites, and thereafter she saw it as her religious duty to defend them among English Friends critical of that schism, even as she urged her Hicksite kin to seek reconciliation.[21]

Her retirement from shopkeeping meant that Margaret Wood was able to assist members of her family, and of her community, in a variety of practical ways: nursing, childcare, financial advice, letter writing. So in her retirement, Margaret Wood was praised by one of her nephews for remaining a 'useful old maid'. The phrase indicated the continuing reliance of many families on the unpaid labour of unmarried women kin.[22] She cared for her mother and two of her sisters through their last illnesses between 1829 and 1831. Jacob Bright built a new house for her after her mother's death, near to his own.[23] So on Martha Bright's death, she was at hand to help him and his oldest daughter, Sophia Bright, in the care of the younger Bright children. She also saw it as her duty to help maintain and strengthen bonds of kinship, bonds that had been stretched thin by the migration of her brother and sister. It was important to her that the younger generation of her American kin knew who were their closest relations in England, as well as something about their forebears, no doubt in large part because of the mutuality that was encouraged among Quaker families. Such mutuality could be of great assistance in times of financial insecurity. As part of this work of kin she also began, following the death of her mother and two sisters, to keep a chronicle of family events. Maintaining such bonds between geographically separated kin necessarily involved her also in extensive letter writing, a task for which, she constantly complained, she was not well fitted.[24]

Even after Margaret Wood retired from shopkeeping, she remained a woman of affairs. In such a capacity this useful old maid was able also to serve her neighbours in ways that extended the more commonplace community work habitual to middle-class women. She might act as postal service for her less literate neighbours, passing on messages between them and relatives in the United States, or investigating labour markets and wage rates there for those contemplating emigration from, or return to, Britain. Nor did she restrict her moral surveillance to her own family. She maintained a watchful eye over elderly parents left behind by those who emigrated, or women and children left behind by deserting husbands, providing for the needy even as she chased after those she believed ought properly to carry that responsibility.[25] In sum, Margaret Wood understood her working life and her life in retirement equally in terms of a combination of ethical precepts deriving from her Quaker beliefs, the kinship duties that might fall to an unmarried woman, and the social obligations that attached to her modest education and means. She sought to enact her religious values through both her work as a confectioner and as a useful old maid. Such work was the basis of the quiet satisfaction she was able to take in her place as an independent woman among the 'industrious classes', and the challenge those classes might offer the established order of society.

Margaret Tanner

As in the case of Margaret Wood, much of the work of kin that filled the life of Margaret Tanner derived from the relationship of sister and aunt. When her sister died after less than two years of marriage, she stepped in for a while to help Priscilla Bright in the care of their infant niece, and in the management of John Bright's household. Subsequently, she married twice. She was also widowed twice, first after only two years of marriage, during a large part of which she nursed Daniel Wheeler through his last illness. Her second husband, Arthur Tanner, died while she was still in early middle age, so that she lived as a single woman once more for almost another four decades.

Unlike Margaret Wood, however, Margaret Tanner never had to go outside her family to earn a living. Her first husband was of independent means, having earlier in his life established a successful milling company in Finland, sold up and retired to England where he invested largely in the rapidly expanding railways. Her second husband ran a struggling paper mill in the Mendips, an offshoot of his family's timber business in Bristol. She enjoyed something approaching a genteel style of life, with considerably higher expectations of consumption on houses, furniture, and servants than Margaret Wood.[26] Yet she worked for a large part of her life, and often arduously: as a young woman she had assisted her mother in the management and maintenance of a large household; shared in her family's involvement in humanitarian and moral reform activities, including the anti-slavery and temperance movements; nursed the sick among her numerous extended family, including the two of her sisters who died of tuberculosis in young adulthood; helped care for her motherless infant niece. Unlike Margaret Wood she shared the political radicalism of John Bright, and as a single woman she campaigned energetically on behalf of the Anti-Corn Law League.

During both marriages she was an active housewife, busy in storeroom, kitchen, garden and field, visiting the poor and sick of her neighbourhood, and helping to teach in local schools for the children of the poor. During her second marriage she also kept the complex accounts that arose from the mixing of personal, household and business finances (for her first marriage had left her a woman of independent, if modest, means).[27] During her first widowhood she became an occasional governess to her niece, Helen Priestman Bright, in whose care as a baby she had helped.[28] At other times she served as nurse/companion to elderly aunts and uncles. During her second widowhood, her skills were once more turned to a political end, as honorary treasurer of the Ladies National Association for the Repeal of the Contagious Diseases Acts, and as office holder in a range of other women's rights and reform and political associations.

Margaret Tanner's modest wealth derived from industrial manufacturing and from investments made from the profits of such enterprises. In many respects, her life and that of Margaret Wood appear to be quite different, not simply in terms of marriage status, but in patterns of consumption, and in their relation to radical politics. But there remains one significant similarity, and that is a readiness to engage with a market through work (rather than solely as a consumer). Margaret Tanner was never an entrepreneur in the sense of establishing her own business. But she demonstrated a similar capacity for, and enjoyment in, enterprising activity, especially as a fund-raiser for the political causes that she supported. This was particularly evident in her work while still single for the Anti-Corn Law League – her tea parties, soirees, and bazaar stalls on its behalf were managed by her in a thoroughly businesslike manner, and with a keen eye for profit, even though that profit went into other coffers than her own.[29] After marriage and widowhood she became more staid, even stately, in manner. But throughout her life, she continued to give garden parties, and to organise other fund-raising events for the political and reform associations to which she belonged. As a housewife, and especially in the straightened circumstances of her first widowhood, she sought various ways to make her housekeeping pay – through cutting the costs of maintaining her home by allowing close kin and a friend to share her house, and by selling her garden produce to a local woman shopkeeper.[30]

Familial service also provided Margaret Tanner with the further means for managing economic necessity when she found herself with a rapidly declining income during the banking and railway crises of the late 1840s. She managed this time of stringency by returning to her parents' home for six months of the year, where she acted as governess to her niece, Helen Priestman Bright (also reliant on Priestman hospitality at this time as a way of managing her unhappy relationship with her stepmother). In the other half of the year, she took her niece home with her to Bristol, continuing her education there. At other times, Margaret Tanner nursed kin such as her aunts, or her sister-in-law, Priscilla Bright McLaren, in her confinements.[31] Such work was formally unpaid, but it paid none the less. For by such means she further saved on her own housekeeping expenses. Such help might also be reciprocated in the form of holidays and hospitality, and in legacies that at least in part recognised her nursing care. At some points, then, her work of kin merged into work that paid, albeit in payment that was largely hidden.

Works of benevolence and moral reform were equally central to her sense of identity as a middle-class Quaker woman. She had been raised in a family committed to community service, a commitment that reflected to some degree the influence of evangelical religion on their faith. Some of her mother's kin were among the evangelical Beaconite schism, and the religion in which she had been raised was an anxious one, constantly fearful of personal unreadiness for salvation. But the Priestmans were opposed to schism, just as Margaret Wood was. Margaret Tanner's grandmother had spent the years of her retirement from the family shop studying the bible for guidance on the question of baptism, for example (such sacraments had been rejected by the founders of the Society of Friends, but many evangelical Quakers wished their return). She left memoranda containing her reflections, and the grounds on which she came to uphold Quaker teaching against such sacraments. The Priestmans were careful not to leave their children too much in company of kin whose evangelical leanings they felt to be too extreme. They also accepted with considerable regret the resignation of a much-valued governess, a member of their household for many years, when she decided her evangelical beliefs led her to sympathise with the Beaconites.[32] The religious culture of Margaret Tanner's family of birth emphasised, then, the importance of good works to personal salvation but also held to the founding tenets of Quakerism. Such values encouraged an engagement with the world, and especially with projects of social and moral reform. So, much of Margaret Tanner's youth was given over to such work: poor visiting, adult schools, temperance and anti-slavery bazaars.

But her greatest enthusiasm was for her altogether unconventional work, as a woman, on behalf of the Anti-Corn Law League, work that was classed by the Tory press of the time as political prostitution, and that led eventually to her involvement in the movement for women's rights.[33] In many respects this looks like an abrupt break with the previous generation of Quaker women like Margaret Wood, suspicious of too close an engagement with the wider world. But it also reflected a fresh response by the next generation to a shared religious legacy in the foundation of their church among the Levellers of the English Civil War. In early adulthood Margaret Tanner responded more actively to the enfranchisement in 1832 of the class from which both women came, and took a lively interest in parliamentary elections.[34] Though the Reform Act did not extend the vote to any women (indeed for the first time this legislation expressly excluded them from the franchise by virtue of their sex), it did serve to place Quakers of this class in a new relation to the established order.

For men like John Bright such change now made it a Quaker's duty to participate in parliamentary politics. Margaret Wood might declare of the debates in Rochdale that preceded the election of 1832, 'I take no interest in the choice'. But by 1840 she was referring to local repealers as 'our people', and declaring the oppressiveness of the bread tax to her kin in the United States. She regarded John Bright's election to parliament in 1843 as a personal misfortune that had to be borne. By contrast, Margaret Tanner had watched his efforts to win a seat with growing enthusiasm, and offered him her moral support in the controversy to which this course had given rise among their kin, and co-religionists more generally.[35] Her own campaigning on behalf of the League required her appearance in public places, not least in seeking male custom for the goods she and other women made for sale at League bazaars. Shop work had been part of the everyday life of her grandmother, as of Margaret Wood. Now it required Margaret Tanner's transgression of the conventional bounds of behaviour for a woman of her social standing. Margaret Wood wryly observed, as her Bright nieces took up similar work in Manchester, that these young women were likely to be 'kept shopkeeping for a considerable time'.[36]

Bread had become for this generation of middle-class radicals both a political as well as a domestic fact of life. Such a conjunction made nonsense of the separation of the spheres of men and women, elaborated in the rhetoric of a domestic ideology that informed conventional notions of gender difference among the middle classes at this time. Feeding the poor and needy was a religious responsibility that fell to Quaker women such as these in the ordinary, everyday division of labour within their families. Margaret Tanner might, in consequence argue equally with John Bright that her obligations to the less fortunate among the industrious classes required her to join the campaign to secure 'the people's bread'. In sum, through her work for the Anti-Corn Law League, Margaret Tanner gave expression to religious values, to an opposition to the established order, and to a sense of class struggle that she shared with Margaret Wood, even though her generation enacted those values differently.

Helen Bright

Helen Bright learned the meaning of work within the domestic cultures of the Bright and Priestman families.[37] Margaret Wood and Margaret Tanner were important figures in her early life, and from them she learned the importance of personal autonomy, independence of mind, courage to act according to her values, and the obligation to serve family and community. These she combined with an enthusiasm for political life learned from her father, with whom she also shared a forceful self-assurance. Her Priestman grandparents and her aunt, Margaret Tanner had provided her with alternative homes when her tempestuous and unbending nature caused relations with her stepmother to become strained and full of conflict. She was indebted to Margaret Tanner for an education that was advanced for a girl at this time, one she completed at a school in Brighton with a similarly advanced curriculum.

At the end of her schooling, Helen Bright returned at last to a permanent home in her father's household. But she was reluctant to assist her stepmother in the care and education of the seven younger children of the family, close though she was to her stepbrothers and sisters. She much preferred to act as an amanuensis to her father when he was at home, helping him sort his papers, and organise his library. This became her sanctuary where she sought escape from some of the duties that fell to an oldest daughter, and where she also continued her own education, for she shared the intellectual curiosity of Brights and Priestmans. She saw this love of reading, however, as a kind of self-indulgence, and a rejection of one sort of women's work in the domestic routines of the Bright household.[38]

She soon succeeded in establishing a more autonomous role by involving herself in an adult school for the employees in the Bright factories, and taking on the secretaryship of the local book society. Whenever the circumstances allowed, too, she decamped to the far more modest home of her great aunt, a household containing only Margaret Wood, her servant-companion, Eliza Oldham, and sometimes another of her nieces, Jane Crosland. Helen Bright's pretexts for such extended absences from her own home might include the wish to make more room for guests at her father's house, to learn some cooking skills, to provide companionship when Eliza Oldham and Jane Crosland were absent, or to care for her great aunt as her health began to deteriorate in the years immediately before her death in 1859. Whenever she could, she pursued the family service expected of young women in the care of her great aunt, and in assisting her Priestman aunts with their family responsibilities.[39] She and Jane Crosland together eased the deathbed of Margaret Wood, and Helen Bright long mourned this energetic, humorous and capable old maid, 'a host in herself'. Margaret Wood's memory as a model of independent womanhood was preserved and passed on to succeeding generations of women kin.

Her Priestman and Bright aunts also inspired Helen Bright, and most especially with their aspirations for greater freedoms for her sex. Her engagement to William Clark, a Somerset shoe manufacturer, followed only after many months of confused and anxious deliberation on her part (she had already rejected a previous proposal of marriage to a man of whom she remained fond all her life). Marriage meant turning her back on the models of independence provided her by her great aunt and a number of her aunts. But she also wished for a home and family of her own, something she felt she had lacked since her father's remarriage. So part of her courtship correspondence was aimed at making very clear her desire to maintain her independence and autonomy within marriage. The couple were similar in their social background, and Helen Bright was happy in the prospect of marrying a manufacturer, seeing honour and respectability in work that produced such necessities of life as shoes, though she acknowledged she would have felt less happy about marrying a shopkeeper (presumably because retailing was not in itself productive of anything but profit). Her future husband invested in his role as capitalist a heavy social and moral responsibility, for his family firm became the largest employer in the area. Helen Clark imbued her position as his wife with a similar burden, especially in terms of promoting activities aimed at self-improvement among their employees.[40]

Such unity of purpose was not weakened by the religious differences between Helen Clark and her husband, differences that were never fully resolved. William Clark shared his family's sympathies with the evangelical current among Friends – though not with the schismatics within it. She leaned towards Unitarianism, and shared her father's suspicion of religious enthusiasm and of evangelical attempts to introduce formal doctrine into the discipline of the Society of Friends. The Clark and Bright families were united, however, in their commitment to radical causes, including anti-slavery, franchise reform and the emerging Liberal party. Helen Bright was also able shortly to turn William Clark into an enthusiast for women's rights, a commitment already evident in his mother and some at least of his sisters.[41] So through her new domestic role as wife, Helen Clark was able to express the values of neighbourliness and social service that were part of her religious outlook, and part of her legacy from her mother's and her father's families.

Her marriage into another family of political reformers also allowed her to continue her immersion in radical politics. She spent much of the last few months of her single life with her father in London, mixing with his parliamentary colleagues, visiting luminaries from revolutionary and nationalist movements in Europe, fugitive slaves and leading abolitionists, black and white, and proponents of women's rights. Some of her Priestman and Bright aunts were founding members of the early suffrage societies, and she herself helped in collecting petitions for women's enfranchisement. She canvassed for signatures even as she prepared for her wedding, and afterwards joined her husband's mother and sisters in the collection of signatures for a further petition in her new hometown.[42]

Prior to marriage, Helen Bright had also made clear the kinds of community service she preferred to undertake. In Rochdale she had started a Sunday school, but had found she had no 'vocation' for it. Nor did she favour 'systematic' visiting among the poor. She preferred personal philanthropy, built upon neighbourliness and friendship, and carried on this preferred pattern of sick and poor visiting after her marriage. Changes in local government franchises in the 1890s meant that women might vote and stand for local boards of poor law guardians and she joined the Wells board at this time. Her work there became her most absorbing interest in the last decades of her life, joining with a number of other women guardians in attempts to alter the culture of poor law provision, especially as it related to the care of pauper children. She also took a far greater interest in the provision of schools in Street once this question was politicised with the establishment of elected school boards under the 1870 Education Act.[43] In all these activities she was giving expression to her religious values, to a sense of class identity and of class contestation, and to the political values embodied in that identity.

She understood her lifelong involvement in Liberal politics in similar terms, as the best way available to someone of her social standing to reform an unjust society. Helen Clark's most active period in politics was also the period when she was raising her family of six children. The Clarks and their Morland in-laws were among those who helped establish the Liberal party in Somerset, not an easy task in a county comprising a number of rural constituencies mainly controlled by Tory gentry and agricultural, brewing and cider-making interests. Brights, Priestmans and Clarks had all been early advocates of temperance, and of teetotalism. It was a subject in which Helen Clark had taken only a limited interest as a single woman. But after her marriage she became as dedicated to teetotalism as her husband's family, in part, at least, because of the links she saw between the advance of liberalism and women's rights, and control of the drink industry. To this end also she helped establish local branches of the Order of Good Templars, and a temperance hotel and coffee house opposite the factory gates, supplanting an old cider house.[44] The formation of the Women's Liberal Federation in the late 1880s provided Helen Clark with an organisation through which she increasingly pursued not only her radical politics, but also her commitment to women's rights. Its creation had been inspired in part by the efforts of her Priestman aunts to establish local Women's Liberal Associations in the early 1880s, as they fell out of sympathy with the national leadership of the suffrage movement.[45]

Helen Clark was descended from a line of women ministers on the Priestman side, but her own spirituality was more akin to her father's and was similarly expressed through this-worldly concerns. She shared, however, the commitment of Priestman and Clark women to reforming the position of women within the Religious Society of Friends. She and her husband served on the governing body of a nearby Friends' school at Sidcot, and pursued improvements to the educational provision for girls there. They were also both active members of the Education Committee of the Society of Friends that had a more general oversight of Quaker schools.[46] With her Priestman aunts and some of her Clark women kin, Helen Clark also set about reforming more fundamentally the position of women within the government of the Society.

Quaker women might be recognised as ministers, elders and overseers, and had won the right to hold their own monthly, quarterly and yearly meetings after a prolonged struggle at the end of the eighteenth century. But these separate women's meetings had no standing within the government of their church. Through their local Bristol Quarterly meeting, the women of the Priestman and Clark families, together with kin among the Sturge family, began to challenge this exclusion from 1873. It proved a long process, but led eventually to women gaining access to all the governing bodies of the Society of Friends by the early twentieth century.[47]

Her working life came to an end in the years following the First World War. An attack of shingles in 1917 left her with a weakened heart, and her memory also began badly to fail. The diary she had kept from childhood provides saddening evidence of the steady decline of her mental powers.[48] She retired from the public work that had previously been so central to her sense of who she was, an independently minded woman of some means, an authoritative figure in her church and community, a political activist on behalf of social reform, and a campaigner on behalf of sexual equality.

Alice Clark

Family memory records that Helen and William Clark had always hoped that one of their four daughters might enter the family firm alongside their two sons. In 1893 they confronted a family crisis. Their eldest son, John Bright Clark was diagnosed with tuberculosis, and his case was considered serious. After extensive medical consultation they settled on treatment at a sanatorium in the Black Forest. Even if he survived, such treatment would necessitate a long absence from home for John Bright Clark, leaving his father short of managerial support at the factory. Alice Clark was at this time about to leave school, having taken her Cambridge entrance examinations. Now, to the surprise of her headmistress, Alice Clark agreed to leave academic ambitions behind, and enter the factory in preparation for following in her brother's footsteps.[49]

In the years that followed she completed an informal apprenticeship in the various departments of the family firm, including the processes undertaken in the men's shops. She also worked for a time in a superior shoe shop in Edinburgh so as to gain some experience of the retail trade. At this time she lived in an attic apartment that she shared with two other working women, enjoying the novelty of life in a 'hen-household' free of the accustomed restraints of life as the daughter of the house. In time she took on responsibility for running the women's workrooms at C. & J. Clark, and occasionally had the supervision of the entire factory. She became one of the company's five directors, an appointment for life. Alongside her factory responsibilities, Alice Clark ran an adult school for the women of the factory, participated in the associational life of Street, notably its temperance societies, took part in electioneering on behalf of the Liberal party, helped build a branch of the Women's Liberal Federation in Street, and campaigned actively for women's suffrage.[50]

All this activity came to a stop, however, when she, too (and for the second time), became a victim of tuberculosis in 1909. Her recovery was slow and the treatments she underwent weakened her. She was evidently not strong enough to return to the factory in a full-time managerial capacity, though she remained a director, and took on special responsibility for the development of a welfare department in the firm from 1913. Paradoxically, her illness left her freer to choose a different way of life. She had long had an interest in history, and while convalescing had read Olive Schreiner's *Woman and Labour*.[51] Now she determined to examine the position of women historically, and in 1912 begun private research in the records kept at Friends' House Library. At the same time, she returned to an active part in the suffrage movement, by becoming honorary Assistant Parliamentary Secretary to the National Union of Suffrage Societies.[52] This new work required her being in London most of the time, so once again she lived in shared accommodation with communities of like-minded women. Helen Clark missed the support of a daughter at home, and was uncertain about this new life: 'A flat does not sound very comfortable'. But she kept up a lighthearted banter on the subject: 'Surely Chenies St [Chambers] is a sort of rabbit warren of worthy women?'[53]

Her historical research led to Alice Clark's appointment, late in 1913, to the Shaw Fellowship at the London School of Economics, a fellowship established to promote research by women on women's work. Here her industrial experience and the research on which she was already embarked made her a preferred candidate over another applicant who held a university degree. Her work for the National Union also brought her into closer contact with labour and socialist women, as this wing of the suffrage movement sought a working alliance with the Labour Party from 1912. The First World War interrupted this dual career, however. She became involved in a range of activities aimed at relieving distress occasioned by the war, activities that brought an end to her fellowship at the LSE.[54] In 1915 she began training as a midwife, intending to help her sister, Dr Hilda Clark, in her work among refugee women and children fleeing the war zone. This training brought her face to face with the 'simply appalling' conditions of life for the working-class women of Battersea, and gave her 'furiously to think'. Her experience here led her to conclude that the demand for the vote was too limited a route to women's emancipation, and she began from this time to think in terms of the need for a 'feminist' (her term) campaign to secure the economic independence of married women.[55] She also put aside her longstanding Liberal party affiliations and lent her support to the Independent Labour Party. After the war she finished and published her *Working Life of Women in the Seventeenth Century*, whilst engaged in the Quaker relief of the famine in Europe that followed the war.[56]

The war also saw a new direction in her religious life, with her growing involvement from 1917 with the Church of Christ Scientist. The radical idealism of this church, its promise of victory over disease, and over evil, all appealed to her mystical religious sensibilities.[57] She eventually resigned from the Society of Friends in the late 1920s, after having served as clerk of her monthly meeting. Her new religious orientation seems also to have displaced entirely her interest in history, and she never wrote a second book as she had planned. Instead, she returned to her post as daughter of the house, as Helen Clark had so long hoped she might do. She also returned to her work at the factory, where she oversaw the development of a modern personnel office from the firm's welfare department. In this period she gradually extended also the scheme for day-release study for young school-leavers to half-time study, and the necessary development of the Continuation School that C. & J. Clark had helped establish in 1913. Here, and in her concern for the interest of the women employees at the factory, she had sometimes to contend with the resistance of her fellow directors. She saw the company's centenary pension scheme, established in 1925, as a commemoration of her father, and the business ethics for which he had stood. Tuberculosis finally took her life in 1934. In a final service to her community, she requested that money be set aside from her estate to build a swimming pool for the women and children of Street. That pool was opened for use (by both sexes) in 1937, and still stands today, opposite the house in which she was born, and the old factory site of C. & J. Clark.[58]

* * *

For the four women examined here, work, whether gainful or otherwise, was an activity informed by the ethical and religious values of their church. Those same values also shaped their attitude to wealth. The obligations that they attached to personal prosperity ensured none would choose a leisured existence. They shared a religious outlook deriving from the egalitarian, oppositional foundations of their church, and resistant to the full influence of evangelical religion. Indeed, their religious values legitimated their altogether unconventional public intervention on issues such as the Corn Laws. Through such work these women Friends also found a new means of expressing their sense of class identity and of class contestation. This class consciousness led all but Margaret Wood into an active involvement in political activism – and even her interest in politics increased later in life, following the enfranchisement in 1832 of men of her class, and the representation of towns like Rochdale.

Notions of gender difference undoubtedly shaped the work chosen by these four women in market, family, church and community. But such notions did not restrict them to a secluded, sequestered domesticity. Rather, their homes were outward looking centres of service to church and community. Family bonds might impose obligations on single as much as on married women that might circumscribe freedom of action. But, equally, the strength and complexity of their kinship ties provided them with a valuable asset in building a social movement around the question of women's rights. Their stories help identify a liberal current within Quakerism, distinct from evangelical Quakerism and drawing on an 'oppositional' perspective, that provided such women with the impetus to active, independent lives, and to the pursuit of social betterment, and greater freedoms for their sex.

Notes

1   I use the term 'Bright circle' for convenience, as a term that crops up in recent studies in women's history. For the purposes here, I include in that circle members of the Wood, Bancroft, Crosland, Bragg, Priestman, Tanner and Clark families.

2   L. Davidoff and C. Hall, *Family Fortunes: Men and Women of the English Middle Class, 1780–1850* (London, 1992 edn); see also, C. Hall, 'The Early Formation of Victorian Domestic Ideology', in her *White, Male and Middle-class: Explorations in Feminism and History* (Cambridge, 1992), pp. 75–93. The research presented here provides a point of comparison with these two studies, as it concerns families from similar sections of the middle class, but ones that resisted aspects of evangelical religion within the Society of Friends. On this issue, see also n. 20. On the domestic culture of this kinship circle, and Quaker families more generally, see n. 36.

3   The papers of these women are held in several locations: the main body forms part of the Millfield Papers (henceforth MP), in the Archives of C. & J. Clark, Street, Somerset (henceforth, CA); most of the correspondence of Margaret Wood cited here is among the Sarah Bancroft Clark papers (henceforth, SBCP), CA, and is also held on microfilm at the Somerset Record Office (henceforth, SRO); some of the genealogical information

presented here draws on the research on family history in the W. Bancroft Clark Papers (henceforth, WBCP), CA. My thanks to the trustees of the Clark Archive for permission to work in this archive and present some of the findings here.

4   On these doctrinal divisions, see T.D. Hamm, '"A Protest against Protestantism": Hicksite Friends and the Bible in the Nineteenth Century', *Quaker Studies*, 6 (2002), pp. 175–94; T.C. Kennedy, *British Quakerism 1860–1920: The Transformation of a Religious Community* (Oxford, 2001), esp. pp. 86–119; E. Isichei, *Victorian Quakers* (London, 1970), esp. chapter 2.

5   Davidoff and Hall, *Family Fortunes*, p. 21, makes reference to an 'oppositional culture' among the provincial middle classes, but my usage of 'oppositionism' here is more specific, and relates to the radical political stance of a particular current within Quakerism. For a more extended discussion, see S.S. Holton, 'John Bright, Radical Politics and the Ethos of Quakerism', *Albion*, 34 (2002), pp. 584–605.

6   R. Williams, *Keywords: A Vocabulary of Culture and Society* (London, 1976), pp. 280–82, examines the multiple meanings of 'work', and related vocabulary. Though concerned with a different class, A. Vickery, *The Gentleman's Daughter: Women's Lives in Georgian England* (New Haven, 1998) provides a further point of comparison, especially in its discussion of the complex relation of women of 'polite society' to public worlds. In particular I take up here her notion of women's 'work of kin'.

7   J.T. Mills, *John Bright and the Quakers* (London, 1935, 2 vols), vol. 1, p. 171 and W. Robertson, *The Life and Times of the Right Honorable John Bright ...* (Rochdale, 1883), pp. 34–5, provide some background on the Wood family. On women and shopkeeping see, Davidoff and Hall, *Family Fortunes*, esp. pp. 301–4; Hall, *White, Male and Middle-class*, pp. 98–101, 109–23.

8   S.B. Clark, 'Aunt Wood', BC249/1, WBCP, CA.

9   This account of Margaret Wood and her mother (also Margaret Wood) derives from Index and Returns for Bolton, 1811 Census; *The Commercial Directory for Rochdale*, 1814–15, and 1816–17 (Manchester, 1814 and 1816); *Pigot and Dean's New Directory of Manchester, Salford, Etc* (Manchester, 1820); 2 rolls of recipes, MIL 17/06, MIL 28/01(g), MP, CA; M. Wood to M. Bancroft, 6 May 1827, BAN 1/13, SBCP, SRO.

10   Reported in Clark, 'Aunt Wood'.

11   Reported in Clark, 'Aunt Wood'.

12   See, e.g. M. Wood to M. Bancroft, 6 May 1827, BAN 1/13; M. Wood to J. Bancroft, 9 December 1839, BAN 1/81, SBCP, both SRO.

13   M. Wood frequently discussed her financial affairs in letters to her American nephew, Joseph Bancroft, and increasingly so as she prepared for death, e.g. 21 February 1851, 10 July 1852, 16 June 1854, and see also M. Wood to John and Susannah Bancroft, 9 June 1843, all BAN 2/3, SBCP, CA.

14   Compare, Holton, 'John Bright'. S. Wright, *Friends in York: The Dynamics of Quaker Revival 1780–1860* (Keele, 1996), pp. 85–107, discusses Quaker involvement with town and city politics in York from the late eighteenth century, and the retreat this involved from the earlier quietism of Quaker religious culture.

15   M. Wood to R. Bancroft, 2 November 1832, BAN 1/13; M. Wood to J. and S. Bancroft, 5 August 1839, 1/81, SBCP, SRO.

16   M. Wood to R. Bancroft, 7 December 1839, BAN 1/13; M. Wood to J. Bancroft, 9 December 1839, BAN 1/81, both SBCP, SRO. Davidoff and Hall, *Family Fortunes*, p. 24 provides a helpful analysis of the internal differentiation among the middle class at this time, and an analysis of the differing characteristics of its lower and higher ranks that would place

Margaret Wood clearly among the lower ranks, and the three other cases discussed here among the higher ranks.

17　M. Wood to J. Bancroft, 14 April 1829, BAN 1/81; M. Wood to R. Bancroft, 2 November 1832, BAN 1/13; M. Wood to R. and M. Bancroft, 5 April 1838, BAN 1/13, all SBCP, SRO.

18　M. Wood to R. Bancroft, 2 November 1832; M. Wood to M. Bancroft, 7 December 1836, both BAN 1/13; M. Wood to J. Bancroft, 9 December 1839 BAN 1/81, all SBCP, SRO. Her father was recorded as a cotton spinner at the time of his death (not as a clogger or shop owner, though that business appears to have continued for some years after that date). A few years on, her brother was also identified as a cotton spinner and accountant, but subsequently as simply an accountant, suggesting that an earlier Wood spinning concern may have failed.

19　M. Wood to J. Bancroft, 14 April 1829, BAN 1/81, SBCP, SRO.

20　H.L. Ingle, *Quakers in Conflict: the Hicksite Reformation* (Knoxville, 1986).

21　M. Wood, Journal of her visit to the United States, 1831–32, MIL 17/8, MP, CA. Margaret Wood's sense of a challenge to the spiritual leadership of women within the Yearly Meeting further supports the findings in H. Plant, 'Gender and the Aristocracy of Dissent: a Comparative Study of the Beliefs, Status and Role of Women in Quaker and Unitarian Communities, 1770–1830, with Particular Reference to Yorkshire' (University of York, unpublished DPhil, 2000), esp. pp. 57, 74–7, but compare with the discussion in Wright, *Friends in York*, esp. pp. 30, 31–50, 67. Wright finds that evangelical women ministers dominated the York Monthly Meeting, and helped spread the influence of evangelicalism more widely within the Society. She also suggests that the relatively strong position of women within Quaker domestic culture allowed them to take only what was found to be empowering within the domestic ideology. Yet it is noteworthy that evangelical women Friends were not evident in the beginnings of the women's suffrage movement. Some found other routes to greater freedom through a form of religious sensibility that emphasised women's 'mission' to reform church and society. For a further perspective on this question see also, E.A. O'Donnell, '"On behalf of all young women trying to better than they are": Feminism and Quakerism in the Nineteeth-century: The Case of Anna Deborah Richardson', *Quaker Studies*, 6 (2001), pp. 37–58.

22　T. Bright to M. and R. Bancroft, 17 February 1839, BAN 1/84, SBCP, SRO.

23　M. Wood to J. Bancroft, 14 April 1829, BAN 1/81, SBCP, SRO.

24　M. Wood to M. Bancroft, 6 May 1827; M. Wood to E. Bancroft, 10 March 1833,10 March 1833, all BAN 1/13; M. Wood to J. and S. Bancroft, 6 April 1838, BAN 1/81, all SBCP, SRO; M. Wood, 'Chronicle of Family and Other Events, 1808–58', MIL 17/2, MP, CA.

25　M. Wood to J. Bancroft, 20 July 1832, BAN 1/81; M. Wood to R. Bancroft, 2 November 1832; M. Wood to E. Bancroft, 10 March 1833; M. Wood to M. Bancroft, 7 December 1836; M. Wood to Rebecca and M. Bancroft, 5 April 1838, all BAN 1/13, all SBCP, SRO.

26　M. Wheeler [Tanner] to M. Priestman, 19 November 1847, 27 January 1848, MIL 31/1 (2), CA provides her sister with a description of her first marriage home, 'Ashley Grange', Cotham, then on the outskirts of Bristol. She employed a cook, housemaid, gardener/handyman, and sometimes a boy to assist him. She and her first husband had not the means, however, to keep a carriage and horses.

27　For accounts of her housekeeping activities in her new home, Oakridge, in Sidcot, see M. Tanner to S. Tanner, 25 June, 23 October 1855, 20 October 1858, MIL 32/1 (1), MP, CA.

28　For reports on her teaching of her niece, see M. Wheeler [Tanner] to M. Priestman, 13 March 1850, 10 February 51; to M. and A.M. Priestman, 11 December 52, all MIL 32/1 (2), MP, CA.

29   E.g., M. Priestman [Tanner] to P. Bright, 18 January 1842, 7 October 1842, 25 February 1843, 20 July 1843, 14 July 1844, 15 October 1844 (postmark), MIL 31/1(4), all MP, CA.

30   M. Wheeler [Tanner] to S. Tanner, 8 and 10 September 1849, 29 October 1849, 7 December 1850 MIL 32/1(1), MP, CA.

31   See, for example, M. Wheeler [Tanner] to P. Bright, 7 December 1851, MIL 31/1(4); and to J. and M.E. Bright, n. d. [1850], 19 December 1850, MIL 31/1(2); M. Wheeler [Tanner] to S. Tanner, 1 November 1851, MIL 32/1(1), all MP, CA.

32   M. Bragg, notes on 'Dogma and Discipline', MIL 11/4; E. Stickney to R. Priestman, n. d. [c.1838], MIL 26/13, both MP, CA.

33   Women's involvement with the Anti-Corn Law League has recently begun to receive more considered attention, see P.A. Pickering and A. Tyrrell, *The People's Bread: A History of the Anti-Corn Law League* (Leicester, 2000), esp. pp. 116–38; S. Morgan, 'Domestic Economy and Political Agitation: Women and the Anti-Corn Law League, 1839–46', in K. Gleadle and S. Richardson (eds), *Women in British Politics 1760–1860: The Power of the Petticoat* (Basingstoke, 2000), pp. 115–46.

34   M. Priestman [Tanner] to P. Bright, 2 April, 4 April 1843, MIL 31/1(4), MP, CA. Recent research has established the considerable part that women might play during elections, even before 1832, and even though personally disfranchised, see, for example the evidence presented in E. Chalus, 'Women, Electoral Privilege and Practice in the Eighteenth Century'; S. Richardson, '"Well-neighboured Houses": The Political Networks of Elite Women, 1780–1860'; M. Cragoe, '"Jenny Rules the Roost": Women and Electoral Politics, 1832–68', all in Gleadle and Richardson, *Women in British Politics*, pp. 19–38, 56–73, 153–69 respectively.

35   M. Wood to J. Bancroft, 2 February 1840, BAN 1/85, SBCP, SRO. M. Priestman [Tanner] to J. Bright, 28 February 1843, and n. d. [1843], MIL 31/1(2).

36   M. Wood to E. Bancroft, 3 January 1843, BAN 1/13, SBCP, SRO.

37   I discuss the domestic culture of this circle, and more especially the ways in which it promoted and sustained a social network of radical women Friends, in S.S. Holton, 'Kinship and Friendship. Quaker Women's Networks and the Women's Movement', *Women's History Review* (forthcoming, 2005), and see also related discussions in Wright, *Friends in York*, pp. 51–68; Plant, 'Gender and the Aristocracy of Dissent', pp. 61–71, 144.

38   H. Bright to W. Clark, 26 November 1865, 2 January, 31 January 1866, MIL 55/1, MP, CA.

39   H. Bright to W. Clark, 9 February 1866, MIL 55/1; M. Wood to J. Crosland, 18 May 1858, MIL 58/2 (preserved among Helen Bright's letters to Jane Crosland), MP, CA.

40   H. Bright to W. Clark, 17 November 1865, MIL 55/1, MP, CA. On the role of the Clarks in Street, and the paternalism of William Clark, see M. McGarvie, *The Book of Street* (Buckingham, 1987), esp. pp. 123–52; K. Hudson, *Towards Precision Shoemaking: C. & J. Clark and the Development of the British Shoe Industry* (Newton Abbott, 1968), esp. pp. 24–5. See also, anon, *Clarks of Street 1825–1950* (privately published, c.1950); Brendan Lehane, *C. & J. Clark 1825–1975* (privately published, c.1975).

41   H. Bright to W. Clark, 22 November 1865, MIL 55/1, MP, CA .

42   H. Bright to W. Clark, 11 March, 12 April, 13 April, 19 April, 17 May, 18 May 1866, MIL 55/1; Enfranchisement of Women Committee, 'Balance Sheet of Receipts and Expenditure, 1866–67', (with list of subscribers), MIL 28/2, all MP, CA.

43   H. Clark to W. Clark, 2 December 1865, 7 January, 9 January, 11 January, 14 January, 9 February, 13 February 1866, MIL 55/1. On women's work in local government, see P. Hollis, *Ladies Elect: Women in English Local Government, 1865–1914* (Oxford, 1985).

44   On the link between temperance and women's suffrage in this circle see, M. Barrow, 'Teetotal Feminists: the Temperance Leadership and the Campaign for Women's Suffrage', in C. Eustance, J. Ryan and L. Ugolini, *A Suffrage Reader: Charting Directions in British Suffrage History* (Leicester, 2000), pp. 69–89.

45   S.S. Holton, *Suffrage Days: Stories from the Women's Suffrage Movement* (London, 1996), pp. 72, 105–6.

46   Minutes of the Central Education Board, and of the Central Education Committee, FEC/M1, FEC/M2 and M3, Friends' House Library.

47   S.S. Holton and M. Allen, 'Offices and Services: Women's Pursuit of Sexual Equality within the Society of Friends, 1873–1907', *Quaker Studies*, 2 (1997), pp. 1–29; Kennedy, *British Quakerism*, pp. 211–36.

48   H. Clark, Diaries, 29 January–31 February [sic], 19 March, 27 March, 13 April, 3 May, 6 June 1919, 9 January, 27 March 1920, MIL 70, MP, CA.

49   'M.C.G.' [Margaret Clark Gillett], 'Alice Clark', (privately published, n.d. [c.1934]), pp. 4–5; A. Clark, Diaries, 20 February 1893, MIL 91/1; A. Clark to H. Clark, 2 November 1892, MIL 87/2; A. Clark to W. Clark, 12 November 1892, MIL 87/1, all MP, CA.

50   A. Clark to P.B. McLaren, 7 December 1893; 4 February 1894, 13 March 1898, MIL 87/3; A. Clark to W. Clark, 11 May 1905, MIL 87/1; A. Clark, Diaries, 12 August 1895, MIL 91/1; A. Clark to Mary Priestman, 9 July 1900, MIL 87/4, all MP, CA.

51   A. Clark, *Working Life of Women in the Seventeenth Century* (London, 1919), p. lxiii. See also her, 'Elizabeth Fry', *Present Day Papers*, 3 (1900), a journal established by a reforming movement within the Society that sought to promote a greater understanding of liberal theology among Friends, and of the history of their church. On this movement, see Kennedy, *British Quakerism*, pp. 270–311.

52   See, S.S. Holton, '"To Live Through One's Own Powers": British Medicine, Tuberculosis and "Invalidism" in the Life of Alice Clark', *Journal of Women's History*, 11 (1999), pp. 75–96; Holton, *Suffrage Days*, pp. 61–182 looks at Alice Clark's suffrage career in more detail.

53   H. Clark to A. Clark, 23 October 1912, MIL 88/2, MP, CA. Chenies Street Chambers were apartments built especially for working women by the Ladies Residential Chambers Company. On the design and domestic arrangements there, see E. Crawford, *Enterprising Women: The Garretts and their Circle* (London, 2002), pp. 206–17.

54   See S.S. Holton, *Feminism and Democracy: Women's Suffrage and Reform Politics, 1900–1918* (Cambridge, 2002 edn), pp. 97–115 on this aspect of the women's suffrage campaigns; on the Shaw fellowship, see C. Shaw to Mr Reeves, 8 June 1911; on Alice Clark's tenure, see Secretary to Mrs Shaw, 17 December 1913; Mrs Shaw to Miss Mactaggart, 23 October 1914; Secretary to Mrs Shaw, 7 December 1915 [probably should read 1914]; 23 July 1915, 15 December 1915; Alice Clark to Dear Sir, 20 November 1915, all London School of Political and Economic Science Archive, Central Filing Registry, 835.

55   A. Clark to C. Marshall, 29 March 1915, 3 July 1915, D/Mar/45, D/Mar/47, respectively, Catherine Marshall Papers, Cumbria Record Office, Carlisle.

56   See also, 'A Note by Alice Clark', in N. Penney, *The Household Account Book of Sarah Fell of Swarthmore Hall* (Cambridge, 1920), pp. xviii–xxxii, which appears to have been her last historical publication. On Quaker famine relief in Austria, see S. Spielhofer, *Stemming the Dark Tide: Quakers in Vienna 1919–1942* (York, 2001).

57   S.S. Holton, 'Feminism, History and Movements of the Soul. Christian Science in the Life of Alice Clark', *Australian Feminist Studies*, 13 (1998), pp. 281–93.

58   Anon, *Clarks of Street*, p. 43.

Chapter 3

Good Housekeeping: Professionalising the Housewife, 1920–50

Judy Giles

One of second-wave feminism's earliest challenges to mainstream thought was to conceptualisations of 'work'. Women's work, it was argued, did not always take place in the workplace nor was it always waged labour. The work involved in creating a home and rearing children, feminism argued, should be as equally valued as any other kind of work. Moreover, it was claimed, domestic work should not necessarily be the sole responsibility of women, whose potential to be fully contributing members of society could be seriously stunted by domestic responsibilities.[1] Two recent articles in the British media suggest that there is a growing concern about the double burden of paid work and unpaid labour in the home that is currently the lot of many women. This concern is not expressed simply by a patriarchal media anxious to return women to their 'proper' place in the home. Much of the debate is conducted by women – media journalists who themselves are experiencing the hectic juggling required to balance career and domestic commitments.[2] A recent book by the American feminists, Barbara Ehrenreich and Arlie Russell Hochschild reveals, what one reviewer calls 'western feminism's dirty little secret'.[3] The essays in Ehrenreich and Hochschild's book paint a disturbing picture. Behind the so-called postfeminist image of the liberated woman, briefcase in one hand, baby and casserole dish in another, lies an underworld of women who remain oppressed and exploited. The work of domesticity, discarded by affluent, professional women in search of careers and high earnings, has been taken up by an army of invisible women, who look after the children, clean the toilets, cook meals and can be dismissed on a whim. In the United States, these women are all too frequently migrant workers from poorer countries. In Britain there is a black economy of domestic work carried out for unregulated and pitiful wages by less educated and poorer women, sometimes from other countries, who work for professional women. This gendered tension between individual fulfilment and interdependence is key to the experience of twentieth- and twenty-first-century modernity and has, consequently, been a crucial arena for feminist theorising. In order to think through these tensions in the present and for the future, we need to explore how they were understood in the past. In this chapter I argue that, as historians of women, we need to address the fact that for millions of women in the first half of the twentieth century, domestic responsibility was understood as their primary work. At the end, drawing on this historical understanding, I briefly pose questions about how second-wave feminism understood unpaid domestic work and its relation to the world of paid work.

The two articles, mentioned above, appeared recently in Sunday newspapers and concerned what is seen as a growing trend for professional women to abandon their careers in order to stay at home with their children. Both writers suggest that (some, professional) women are looking to the 1950s housewife as an ideal to be emulated. As one article says:

> The stalwart feminists of the 1970s might be horrified but it seems that their daughters – highly educated and driven since birth to be professional high achievers – are reaching their late twenties or early thirties and finding that a career is not all it was cracked up to be. Instead they are getting in touch with their inner housewife, immersing themselves in the joys of flower arranging and cooking.[4]

Should we be concerned about what after all may be media hype? Should we be concerned that professional women want to stay home, bake cakes and bring up their children themselves? Should feminism see this as a frightening return to the conditions of the 1950s? Or can this be understood as welcome evidence that women can now choose between domesticity and career, or a part-time combination of both?

First, it is important to question the 'ideal' that is supposedly being emulated in this trend towards domesticity. In the 1940s and 1950s the figure of the stay-at-home housewife was a stock stereotype for advertisers and other image makers. The standard advertising images of happy housewives, beautifully attired, baking cakes and ironing shirts, existed simultaneously with attacks on suburban housewives who were seen as acquisitive and 'neurotic'.[5] As Joanne Meyerowitz has demonstrated neither of these versions captured the complex realities of the lives of many, so-called 'ordinary housewives'.[6] Women in the 1950s held down part-time jobs, others combined career and domesticity, many of those who stayed at home to care for children played an important and crucial part in local politics or were engaged in demanding voluntary work.[7] The suburban housewife, baking her cake, dressed in crisp white shirt and flowered skirt, with 2.4 children was a cultural myth, rather than a reflection of the real lives of millions of women. What is interesting today is that for the contemporary media, the choice made by some women to stay at home, is represented in terms of the 1950s housewife. Now, as in the 1950s, such representations reduce the very real caring work that such women do and the often diverse ways in which they manage to balance their own needs with that of their children. As one woman says: 'I'm not a cup-cake maker and my tea towels aren't ironed – but I like the idea that my child is eating food I cooked and I've enjoyed motherhood and being at home more than I thought I ever could'.[8] Secondly, the focus in debates about women and domestic responsibilities is all too often focused on how white professional women can combine meaningful work with childcare. It rarely considers working-class or ethnic groups for whom domesticity may have very different meanings. In this essay, therefore, I am arguing that for many women at a specific historical moment (1920–1950), the role of full-time housewife offered a new and attractive identity that bestowed dignity and purpose. Moreover, the material conditions – decent homes, greater affluence – in which that role could be fulfilled were of particular significance for working-class women.

A crucial factor in the formation of the housewife role was the professionalisation or modernisation of housework that occurred in the first half of the twentieth century in Britain. This modernisation was not limited to Britain: North America, Australia and other European nations experienced similar trends, and it was linked to the economic and social transformations that originated in the Western world as a result of new scientific and technological knowledge that have since spread to every corner of the globe. These include: industrialisation, new forms of corporate power, the emergence and growth of urban and suburban environments, geographical mobility, demographic upheavals as a result of mobility, war and improved health, mass systems of communication, and a volatile, but continually expanding, capitalist market.[9] These transformations had far-reaching consequences for the organisation and understanding of domesticity. Home and domestic responsibilities were conceived and experienced very differently in 1950 from 1850. Companionate marriage, smaller families and a consequent child-centredness, suburbanisation, the disappearance of residential domestic service, and the emergence of a consumer culture shaped new forms of domesticity and, in doing so, produced opportunities for change that were beneficial for millions of women. Equally, of course, such changes brought anxiety, loss and insecurity. As Marshall Berman argues 'to be modern is to find ourselves in an environment that promises us adventure, power, joy, growth, transformation of ourselves and the world – and, at the same time, that threatens to destroy everything we have, everything we know, everything we are'.[10] To understand modernity, as many of the classical narratives have done, as simply a masculine project located in the public spaces of politics, the nation, the workplace 'effectively writes women out of history by ignoring their active and varied negotiations with different aspects of their social environment'.[11] The nature and meaning of domestic work was (and is) a highly significant aspect of the social environment with which women negotiated. Moreover, these negotiations were experienced differently by women of different classes.

What I have in mind by the term 'professionalisation' is the upgrading and revaluing of women's domestic work that took place particularly after the First World War and found its apogee in the figure of the wartime housewife whose work on the 'home front' was understood as a crucial factor in the victory over fascism. 'Professionalisation' was a manifestation of modernity, understood through ideas of the 'modern' home. The rhetoric of scientific management and industrial rationalisation advocated by Taylorism and Fordism at the start of the twentieth century was quickly adapted to discussing women's work within the home. 'National efficiency' demanded that the so-called private sphere of motherhood and housework be reconstructed as vital to the survival of the nation; as vital as advances in war technology or industrial production. In the name of efficiency, 'experts' and professionals were called upon to extend the scientific and rational principles inherent in the forces of modernisation to housework, childcare, sexual relations, and nutrition. Kerreen Reiger argues that one of the strategies used to introduce scientific rationalism into personal relationships and domestic organisation was 'to define the housewife as a modern, "efficient" houseworker', working with the medical profession, educators, nutritionists and child psychologists to create a safe, hygienic and ordered space – the 'modern' home.[12] This ideal of the 'professional' housewife, energetically promoted by women's magazines and advice manuals, emerged at a historical moment when middle-class women were losing their role as mistress of a large household of servants, and working-class women were enabled to buy or rent a whole house rather than the rented rooms that had previously constituted home.

In order to understand what was at stake here for working- and middle-class women I have drawn on Pierre Bourdieu's theories of taste and cultural capital. Bourdieu argues that consumption practices, ideals of taste and lifestyle are differentiated by social class and that, rather than simply reflecting class position, what we buy and how we consume material objects are constitutive of class difference.[13] He demonstrates, for example, how in France, what he calls, the new *petit bourgeoisie* use the products of consumer capitalism, but also its cultural forms and practices, to carve out a distinctive area of cultural authority. Thus, not only material objects but also, what Bourdieu calls cultural capital, can be appropriated by different social groups to distinguish them from each other and to lay down markers that clearly identify distinctions. For Bourdieu, cultural capital is that which individuals gain from formal education and family upbringing. For example, a knowledge of and liking for certain 'high art' books, music, films and theatre constitutes the cultural capital of the educated middle class that is passed on, via family upbringing, to each generation. However, cultural assets, as Bourdieu demonstrates, can also be constructed around food consumption. He shows how in France the understanding and meaning of different food choices is classed in that middle-class food became 'cuisine' that required 'proper' methods of preparation while the working classes preferred plain but plentiful food, presented unpretentiously. Although it is important to remain aware that Bourdieu tends to construct rather static class positions, nor does he engage with ethnicity or gender, nonetheless his ideas are richly suggestive for explaining how the (classed) home and housewife were in the process of being constructed in the first half of the twentieth century in Britain.

Significant for the professionalisation of the housewife was the increasing availability of labour-saving devices such as washing machines, refrigerators and electric or gas fires. These commodities had the potential to lessen enormously the burden of hard work carried out in the home and advertising for them often represented the home as a well-ordered machine directed by a 'scientific' housewife. However, economic historians have argued that the new electrical labour-saving devices available in the inter-war years were only taken up very slowly.[14] It wasn't simply the price of electrical appliances that made them less attractive to working-class women consumers but a preference for spending money on display, luxuries and leisure rather than on reducing the time spent on household tasks. Radios, for example, were frequently listened to in the evenings when housewives sewed or knitted and were perceived as luxury items that made housework more tolerable. Curtains, furniture and wallpaper functioned to signify the pride a woman took in her skills as a housewife and in this sense the display was about a 'modern' identity based on hard work in contrast to the Victorian ideal of the ornamental, leisured lady. From the 1920s the bridge-playing, 'parasitical' lady of leisure was a figure much derided in women's magazines both in Britain and America. As one interviewee from Judy Attfield's study of women living in the new town of Harlow in the 1950s commented, 'We were the homeworkers ... We had to get on and make the best of everything that we could. That was taking pride in what you'd got. Everything was polished'.[15] Doris Arthurs who had been a housemaid in the household of the Lord Mayor of Birmingham recalled the suite she acquired on her marriage in 1932:

> We saw this beautiful brocade seven piece suite. It was beautiful, covered in green with pale pink, all pale green little like forget-me-nots all over, it was lovely, and it had one wing chair for the gentleman and another sort of tub chair and the corner of the settee was like a tub but the other was a bolster effort, and we thought it was lovely.[16]

For women like these the pleasure gained from the purchase of furnishings and non-functional household items for display was inextricably linked to a sense of pride both in the work carried out to make a comfortable home and in ownership of those commodities that previously had belonged only to the affluent. Consumption practices were closely allied to their identity as a housewife, an identity that, in Bourdieu's terms, rested on appropriating what had previously been the province of middle-class women – the creation of comfortable, ordered homes.

Pride and self-esteem were important also to middle-class women but in slightly different ways. An unpublished 1930s Mass Observation Report on the Psychology of Housework claims that the majority of complaints about the drudgery of housework came from middle-class women, complaints that had not been alleviated by the availability of labour-saving devices or the continued employment of domestic help. The Report concludes condescendingly that:

> Since these women's trouble is not really overwork but anxiety to prove to themselves their indispensability, then the only effect of increased labour-saving mechanisms, unaccompanied by other drastic social changes, will be to intensify the situation just described. Faced by yet further curtailment of useful work in the home, the more spirited will be even more willing to abandon their homes, and the weaker will be driven to even more neurotic symptoms in the effort to convince themselves that their job at home is a full-time one.[17]

It is easy for us today to condemn the thinking that underpins these assertions but we need to be aware that, at a time when career opportunities for women were limited and generally required a woman to remain childless, if not single, many middle-class women believed that identity and satisfaction could be gained from their roles as wife, mother, and mistress of a home. Modernity, in the form of science and technology, could threaten that identity, at the same time as it promised to remove the burden of drudgery, a burden that it should be noted was never as pressing for the middle-class woman with servants as it was for her working-class counterpart.

In an unpublished manuscript written in 1944, Celia Fremlin, an observer for Mass Observation argues that the work of the middle-class wife has become redundant: restaurants provide good food, laundries can do the washing, clothes are produced by chain stores and tailors, the loss of servants means the role of mistress is no longer necessary, and labour-saving devices have reduced the work involved in the running of a small, 'modern' home. She concludes that the middle-class woman's 'natural job has been taken from her by the triumphs of modern science and modern organisation' and that 'she is left in the most terrifying of all situations ... that of being virtually unnecessary to the society to which ... she irrevocably belongs'.[18] It is not surprising that middle-class women were anxious about maintaining their status at a time when this could be perceived as under threat from a newly emerging suburban culture that was increasingly open to the working class. In addition the decline in residential domestic service diminished the middle-class woman's role from that of mistress of servants to the less class specific role of housewife. According to a survey of the middle classes, published in 1949, the middle-class housewife:

> normally insists upon a rather higher standard of feeding than – at any rate – the urban working-class wife. She may not spend more money on food; she tends to expend more time and care on buying; to prepare and cook more food at home; to produce, with the aid of a stock-pot, more soups and stews, as well as making more jam, bottling more fruit, and so forth. The house or flat which the middle-class housewife has to run is normally larger, and contains more belongings. Often special rooms must be looked after, such as a husband's study, studio, or consulting room, and generally a nursery.[19]

The emphasis on cooking and preparing food is telling. The use of convenience foods was seen as a lower-middle- and working-class habit while preparing and cooking fresh foods was a signifier of a certain cultural capital even though such work had more often than not been performed by a cook or general servant.

Middle-class women may have been pulled in two directions. While they recognised the potential to save time offered by new household appliances, they may have been aware simultaneously of the status attributed to their use of time. Time invested in cooking, sewing, bottling fruit and making jam was, as Lewis and Maude suggest, a signifier of social status. Lewis and Maude go on to distinguish between 'deserving' and 'undeserving' members of the middle class: 'the hard-working professional couple with three children' are the former while the 'rich widow and the successful black marketeer' are the latter.[20] The saving and spending of time were not simply pragmatic considerations; they were symbolic activities that signified in complex ways. In the first half of the twentieth century the idle, leisured life and conspicuous consumption of the Victorian middle-class woman was firmly rejected in favour of hard work and efficiency. This was not simply a product of modern rationalisation but was an important way in which what was perceived as old-fashioned Victorianism gave way to a modern form of living. The creation of healthy, ordered, comfortable homes was at the centre of this with the middle-class housewife leading the way. Thus, the consumption of furnishings, curtains and domestic help was a means by which middle-class housewives could assert, through public displays of their managerial efficiency and hard work, their continued status as *the* arbiters of taste, fashion, good food and comfort.

I want to turn now to the story of a working-class woman. Mavis Kitching, born in 1916, grew up in rented rooms in inner-city Birmingham.[21] Her father was, almost permanently, unemployed due to illness and her mother had numerous jobs as a cleaner in order to supplement the family's meagre income. After her mother's death, Mavis, as the eldest daughter took on her mother's domestic role. In 1948 Mavis married and she and her husband, George, were allocated a new council house in a leafy, pleasant area of Birmingham's growing suburbs. In the story Mavis tells she recalls the shoes and clothing that she received, as a small child, from a local charitable organisation, 'you were given *Daily Mail* clothes, a big D.M. on the side of your boots, and your dresses were like prison dresses'.[22] Throughout her school days, Mavis was tormented as a recipient of charity. The D.M. on her boots marked her out as 'different', an object of charity to be patronised by those whose philanthropy provided the boots and clothes, but equally an object of contempt to her more affluent peers. In adulthood Mavis vowed that 'my kids will never have D.M. clothes' and 'I would work my fingers to the bone rather than them have to have *Daily Mail* clothes'.[23] Mavis's experience and understanding of poverty as a state of exclusion and dependency formed a subjectivity that was historically and socially specific. This included anger and resentment towards those middle-class philanthropists whose words and behaviours defined her. At the same time, anger and resentment mixed with gratitude: for instance, Mavis gratefully recalls how the Girl Guides paid for her to go on holiday with them. The subjectivity formed from dependence, exclusion and gratitude manifested itself in a profound awareness of the significance and power of money. Money and the commodities that signified affluence were, for Mavis, markers of social inclusion. One of her most treasured possessions, acquired in the early years of her marriage, was a treadle sewing machine. The pleasure she took in using the machine to make clothes for herself and her family expresses an acute sense that she has achieved a place where she is safe from the agonies of her childhood, a place in which charitable clothes are replaced by clothes of her own making.

Mavis insists that she loves homemaking and housework, 'people laugh at me – some people say they don't like housework but I love it. I love doing it, knitting, sewing. It's my favourite thing sewing and altering'.[24] Housework, for Mavis, was both personally and socially useful work. Providing comfort, clothing and order for herself and her family offered Mavis a sense of purpose and dignity. The post-Second World War glorification of the housewife, celebrated in women's magazines, inscribed in social policies, for example, family allowances, and confirmed by the increasing availability of domestic commodities and labour-saving devices, legitimated the work involved in creating a home. Mavis who had grown up understanding that she would receive nothing unless she 'earned' it either through hard physical work or through psychological endurance, found herself in adulthood at a specific historical moment when the work she most enjoyed was not only officially validated but, frequently, celebrated. During the Second World War commentators and politicians had praised housewives who maintained the 'home front' for their valiant efforts. J.B. Priestley, for example, elevated the housewife from her position in the frequently invisible and always marginalised, private sphere to one where housewifery is vital to the public world of politics, war and reconstruction:

> Now there's a familiar type of masculine mind that believes that women should have nothing to do with political and public life. Woman's place, they tell us, is in the home. It's largely the same mind, I believe, that then muddles away so that the home is put on short rations and then bombed. Privately I've believed for years the opposite of this – that a great deal of political and public life is nothing but large-scale common-sense housekeeping, and that as women have an almost terrifying amount of common-sense and the ones who are good at housekeeping are very good at it, then the sooner some of our communal and national affairs are managed by women the better … For this is total war; and total war is right inside the home itself, emptying the clothes cupboards and the larder, screaming its threats through the radio at the hearth, burning and bombing its way from roof to cellar. It's ten times harder being a decent

housewife and mother during such a war than it is being a soldier. You have to make a far greater effort to keep going, for you've no training and discipline to armour you. The soldier has his own responsibilities, but when he assumed them he was released from a great many others; whereas his womenfolk know no such release, but have more and more responsibility piled upon them.[25]

For Mavis, and millions of women like her, the celebration of home and housewifery both during and after the war, must have been a tangible and visible marker that they had 'earned' the right to be included in a society that had sought to exclude and denigrate those whose poverty so often made them outsiders.

One of these markers was her new council house which Mavis loved. It represented the better future that she had always dreamed of. As Alan O'Shea reminds us, modernity for many people in Britain was understood in terms of 'betterment' or consumption. The opportunity to acquire a decent home in pleasant surroundings, free from poverty and ill-health frequently constituted the desires and aspirations of those lower-middle- and working-class people who in the early twentieth century became an identifiable market in a changing economy.[26] Council tenancies, home ownership, the ability to purchase a wider range of domestic products, and welfare reforms made possible the dreams of millions of women like Mavis in the years after the Second World War. Modern homes were places not only of safety and belonging but also places where women, like Mavis, could actively work to make spaces of comfort and pleasure through the exercise of their creative skills in homemaking, knitting, and sewing. Many older women condemn the disappearance of housekeeping skills amongst younger women. To understand why, given that housekeeping can be monotonous and arduous, we need to recognise the meanings such skills had for women of this specific generation for whom the opportunity to be a housewife in a home of one's own was a mark of self-worth and belonging; an opportunity to acquire the cultural capital that had so often been denied them.

However, it is equally important to remember that this 'better future' was granted to working-class women on certain terms. Mavis recalled how when she and George first moved into their council house:

A visitor used to come. She would turn your bedclothes back and lift your bed up and look underneath to see if there was any fluff or anything … And they fumigated all your furniture from down town before you come into here. They always made sure you was clean.[27]

Being a 'good' housewife was associated with cleanliness which was itself
a mark of social status: a form of cultural capital that distinguished the
'respectable' working class from those perceived as feckless and undeserving.
According to Mary Douglas, when something becomes 'matter out of place',
for example dirt in the home, when it becomes represented as a threat to order,
stringent efforts are made to exclude and reject it.[28] Such a reaction was
certainly the case with regard to those working-class families that were moved
to the suburbs. Council tenancies required certain standards of housekeeping
that were closely monitored by middle-class visitors and other tenants: those
unable to keep their homes in 'a good, clean condition' ran the risk not only of
losing the tenancy but also the respect of neighbours. The washing of clothes,
bedding and net curtains was one manifestation of this complex relationship
with dirt and cleanliness. When the soap powder Persil advertised itself as
labour-saving because it only required a two minutes soak and a two minutes
boil, many women were disdainful, insisting that the wash must be boiled
for twenty to thirty minutes if it is to 'get them a nice white and all sort of
sterilizing them. When you boil things, you sterilize them. The whiteness is the
important part'.[29] This emphasis on cleanliness and whiteness was linked to
an investment in hard work: women whose washing was grey were perceived
as lazy, 'they should be ashamed, they should change the water more often'.[30]
Poverty was frequently associated with dirt and disorder and represented as
threatening. Hence, washing nets, scrubbing doorsteps, boiling the wash to
achieve whiteness and sweeping under beds were not only practical ways
of combating disease and dirt but were also symbolic demonstrations that,
even if you were not very affluent, you did not belong to the class of people
known as 'the poor'. In order to grasp the particular pleasures that modernity
offered these women, it is necessary to recognise the ways in which dirt,
disease and otherness constituted the elements from which they were so often
invited to create subjectivities. 'Betterment', for them, signified cleanliness,
health and belonging, and was made materially manifest in clean bodies and
clothes, fit, healthy children, the ability to purchase domestic commodities,
and a comfortable house in the suburbs. For many working-class women, the
post-war world offered opportunities to actively create 'modern' homes that
provided this hygienic, ordered and healthy environment. As such it became
possible for them to see themselves as active agents in the creation of a 'better
future' and a modern world through their work in the home.

The relationship of middle-class women to domestic modernity varied
from that of their working-class sisters in that the subjectivities offered were
formed from different elements. By the 1950s middle-class women had lost

their servants, although the more affluent might still be able to afford part-time, non-residential help. With the loss of servants went the loss of a certain authority linked to the supervisory role of the mistress in the middle-class home and this could create anxieties around power and status. Middle-class college educated women who came to adulthood in the 1950s had grown up in a world where servants were taken for granted, and in which the status and authority of the middle-class mistress was still reasonably secure. In 1946 the BBC Home Service broadcast a debate on how to secure domestic help for middle-class women, given the general unwillingness of women to enter domestic service. A number of the women who contributed to this debate spoke 'as housewives and mothers' with a particular role to play in the future of the nation.

> *Mrs. Serpell* [middle-class housewife]: I've got two small children. When you are trying to cope with two toddlers, trying to bring them up to become more or less *rational citizens*, it's almost impossible to cope with all the housework yourself ... I personally feel I don't want to have more than two in my family unless I'm sure of getting somebody to help.[31]

Post-war reconstruction was concerned above all else with restoring social stability at home as the means to increased prosperity and future advancement. The fact that domesticity was such a key issue in the late 1940s and early 1950s enabled many middle-class women to speak confidently and publicly from their position 'as housewives and mothers'. A particular example was the British Housewives League a nationally organised association that protested against the Labour government's policies on food rationing in the late 1940s. This pressure group held marches and rallies that gained considerable attention and offered a space in which middle-class housewives could speak politically from their position as responsible citizens, an identity that had been strengthened by their co-operation on the home front during the war. Many women found a voice 'as housewives' and were able to use this to press their claims that the organisation and spaces of everyday life, in which the rearing of children occurred, should be central concerns of any modern society.[32] Mrs Lovelock, the founder of the BHL, for example, insisted that because women's lives were 'bound up with the home and children, and the simple lasting experiences of life' they were best placed 'to know what's worth preserving in Britain, and what wants changing'.[33] Whilst some working-class women were able to appropriate the identity of housewife as a means of asserting their right to belong, their right to no longer be seen as 'matter out of place', some middle-class housewives were able to use the role to demand the support that would enable them to achieve better conditions in which to carry out their work as wives and mothers.

For all classes the modern home represented a space in which children could be brought up free from the harsh discipline, material deprivation and unhealthy environments of the past. In her autobiography Kathleen Woodward describes her mother's life in the late nineteenth century:

> Six children she reluctantly bore, and she was in the habit of saying in a curiously passionless tone that if she had known as much when her first child was born as she learned by the time she bore her sixth, a second child would never have been ... to me it was clear that if we children had never been born mother's life would have been as an absurd dream of continued ease.[34]

Perhaps the most significant change for women in the twentieth century has been the spread and development of birth control. Kathleen Woodward's mother made no pretences, 'regretting each [child] come to a world filled with anxiety and numberless hours of toil'.[35] The establishment of a Welfare State, the increasing use of birth control and the spread of affluence after the Second World War meant that children, rather than being seen as another unwanted mouth to feed, were seen, in Carolyn Steedman's words, 'as repositories of hope, and objects of desire'.[36] In Britain, in the 1950s, children (and the reproductive capacities of the mothers who bear them) became central to the programmes of successive governments for re-building Britain, not as it had been in the recent past, but as a 'modern' nation. At the same moment young women and men, wearied by the war years of separation and anxiety, began to plan the homes and families that would establish a sense of a future for themselves as individuals. As Lesley Johnson observes with regard to post-war Australia,

> Children as the repositories of hope, for whom safe places – homes with particular characteristics – were needed, represented the focus of a set of gendered desires in the 1950s, not for the past, for tradition, but for a commitment to and an expectation that 'as housewives' women were part of the nation – citizens in the fullest sense – and part of its future.[37]

For millions of women the tasks involved in creating 'safe places' for children were seen as 'work' and valued accordingly. Many older women refer to domestic chores as 'getting my work done'. To conceptually separate unpaid and paid labour, home and work, can obscure the diverse ways in which women understood, negotiated and articulated their relationships to modernity. This is not to celebrate uncritically all aspects of domesticity. All too often homes have been sites of violence, of insecurity, of frustration and tedium. However, in the first half of the twentieth century, modern life for millions of women was about aspiring to and working towards the creation of a space called 'home', in which violence, insecurity, disease, discomfort and pain were things of the past. This could provide women with a sense that they had a stake in the nation and the possibility of achieving, what was believed to be, the project of modern social existence – the right to define their own futures and the capacity to be in control of their own lives.

However, as I indicated at the start, it is important to link this historical shift to a wider conceptual issue. The gendered dichotomies that underpin the distinctions between work and home persist in, and can limit, the ways in which feminist historians have thought about domesticity and housework. I am proposing that rather than seeing domestic work as outside and exempt from the historical narratives of modern Britain that focus on the workplace or the political arena, we need to explore the links that women perceived between domestic work and a sense of belonging to the modern world. To do so not only rescues millions of women from historical invisibility but, more radically, challenges the oppositions that have historically defined woman in the post-Enlightenment traditions of Western culture. I am proposing that if we are to contest those cultural understandings of femininity that link women with domesticity, stasis, the everyday, the private, the traditional and dependency and thereby deny them historical agency, it is vital that the dichotomised and gendered understandings of home/work, private/public are disrupted.

The homologies that construct the meaning of 'home' are organised around certain key oppositions: home/away (journey or voyage), stasis/ movement, everyday/exceptional, private/public, traditional/modern, dependence/independence, feminine/masculine. Contemporary feminism has often deployed these oppositions in its emancipatory narratives. 'Leaving home', for example, is represented by many second wave feminists as a necessary condition of liberation. Marilyn French's *The Women's Room* and Betty Friedan's *The Feminine Mystique* both insist on women's journey from suburban domesticity to liberated autonomy and, although this is not achieved without pain, it is intended to be read as a universally desired feminist aspiration. Equally, feminist histories in the 1970s and 1980s claimed that women were forced 'back home' after operating successfully in the public world of work during the First and Second World Wars. Critiques of consumer culture condemned popular images in advertising and magazines, that bombarded women with 'false' desires for 'ideal homes'. Such histories were written in a cultural framework that envisioned domesticity as something that must be rejected and left behind if women were to become 'modern', emancipated subjects. In terms of the worlds of home and work 'staying at home' was an undesirable option; 'going out to work', entering the public world, was the only valid route for a woman who sought liberation.

Marshall Berman insists that modernity is a journey away from 'home', a journey into the unknown, a 'risky' venture that is, nevertheless, exhilarating and exciting, and one that demands we leave behind the safe haven of the familiar. The spaces of 'modern man' are the city and the street; domesticity, represented in the twentieth century, by the suburban home, is the antithesis of all that is new, alive and modern. In all these formulations home is represented as a place of tradition and stasis from which it is necessary to escape if full selfhood is to be achieved. Hence, the modern self-defining subject, 'unrestrained by private or domestic responsibilities, possessing a rational mind freed from the distorting effects of the emotions and the needs of the body' is understood as an individual characterised by those values historically associated with the public sphere and with masculinity.[38] I am proposing an alternative understanding of home, and the relationship of the work involved in creating homes to modernity, that neither pathologises nor pities the millions of women in the first half of the twentieth century, for whom, as we have seen, the work of domesticity was a primary concern and home an actively created space of pleasure and social belonging.

Modernism and feminism's reliance on emancipatory narratives of 'leaving home', has meant that the profound need of all human beings for the safety, connectedness and continuity for which home is a metaphor, has received little attention in academic scholarship, either feminist or mainstream. Hence, the attempt in this chapter to unravel the complex motivations and meanings that surround the work done by women in the home is part of a wider project that in expanding our understanding of domestic work might enable us to re-think the ways in which we integrate the needs we *all* have for belonging, continuity and comfort with our equally powerful desire for autonomy, movement and the new. How, in other words, women and men can create spaces in which the best values of public and private, home and away are no longer polarised, but can be integrated to produce those safe spaces that are an essential element of modernity's project. Domestic work has historically been carried out by women and continues today to be carried out by the poorest and most exploited women in the global economy.

Notes

1   For example, B. Friedan, *The Feminine Mystique* (Harmondsworth, 1965); E. Malos, *The Politics of Housework* (London, 1980); A. Oakley, *The Sociology of Housework* (London, 1974); S. Rowbotham, *Woman's Consciousness, Man's World* (Harmondsworth, 1973).

2   M. Driscoll, 'Selling Out', *The Sunday Times*, 14 September 2003; F. Weldon, 'Do You Envy the 50s Housewife?', *You*, 31 August 2003.

3   B. Ehrenreich and A. Russell Hochschild, *Global Woman: Nannies, Maids and Sex Workers in the New Economy* (London, 2003); P. Toynbee, *The Observer*, 12 July 2003.

4   Driscoll, 'Selling Out'.

5   Friedan, *Feminine Mystique*; S. Taylor, 'The Suburban Neurosis', *Lancet*, 26 March 1938, pp. 759–61.

6   J. Meyerowitz, 'Beyond the Feminine Mystique: A Reassessment of Postwar Mass Culture, 1946–1958', *Journal of American History*, March (1993) pp. 1455–82; J. Meyerowitz, *Not June Cleaver: Women and Gender in Postwar America, 1945–1960* (Philadelphia, 1994).

7   Meyerowitz, *Not June Cleaver*.

8   Driscoll, 'Selling Out'.

9   M. Berman, *All That Is Solid Melts Into Air: The Experience of Modernity* (Harmondsworth, 1988).

10 Berman, *All That Is Solid*, p. 15.

11 R. Felski, *The Gender of Modernity* (Cambridge, MA, 1995) pp. 17–18.

12 K. Reiger, *The Disenchantment of the Home: Modernising the Australian Family 1880–1940* (Oxford, 1985), pp. 2–3.

13 The discussion following draws on P. Bourdieu, *Distinction* (tr. R. Nice) (London, 1984).

14 S. Bowden and A. Offer, 'The Technological Revolution that Never was: Gender, Class and the Diffusion of Household Appliances in Interwar England', in V. De Grazia with E. Furlough (eds), *The Sex of Things: Gender and Consumption in Historical Perspective* (California, 1996).

15 J. Attfield, 'Inside Pram Town: A Case Study of Harlow House Interiors, 1951–61', in J. Attfield and P. Kirkham (eds), *A View From the Interior: Feminism, Women and Design* (London, 1989).

16 Interview with Doris Arthurs, February 1987.

17 Mass Observation (MO), *Report on the Psychology of Housework*, MO Archive (University of Sussex, 1939).

18 C. Fremlin, 'The Crisis: War in Diaries', unfinished, unpublished manuscript, MO Archive (University of Sussex, 1944).

19 R. Lewis and A. Maude, *The English Middle Classes* (London, 1949), p. 206.

20 Ibid., p. 207.

21 Mavis's story was first commented on in J. Giles, *Women, Identity and Private Life, 1900–50* (Basingstoke, 1995) and, more recently, in J. Giles, *The Parlour and the Suburb: Domestic Identities, Class, Femininity and Modernity* (Oxford, 2004).

22 Interview with Mavis Kitching, February 1987.

23 Interview with Kitching.

24 Interview with Kitching.

25 J.B. Priestley, *All England Listened: the Wartime Postscripts of J.B. Priestley* (New York, 1967), pp. 112–15.

26 A. O'Shea, 'English Subjects of Modernity', in M. Nava and A. O'Shea (eds), *Modern Times: Reflections on a Century of English Modernity* (London, 1996), pp. 16–17.

27 Interview with Kitching.

28 M. Douglas, *Purity and Danger* (London, 1966).

29 Mass Observation, *Clothes Washing: Motives and Methods: Interim Report; Laundry Usage*, MO Archive (University of Sussex, 1939).

30 Ibid.

31 *The Listener*, 11 April, 1946, p. 464.

32 L. Johnson, 'As Housewives We Are Worms: Women, Modernity and the Home Question', *Cultural Studies*, 10, 3 (1996), p. 456.

33 J. Hinton, 'Militant Housewives: the British Housewives' League and the Attlee Government', *History Workshop Journal*, 38 (1994).

34 K. Woodward, *Jipping Street* (London, 1983) p. 7.

35 Ibid.

36 C. Steedman, *Landscape for a Good Woman* (London, 1986), p. 108.

37 Johnson, 'As Housewives we are Worms', p. 459.

38 Ibid., p. 450.

PART II

FACTORY LABOUR

Chapter 4

'Women of True Respectability?' Investigating the London Work-girl, 1880–1900

Emma Liggins

As Clementina Black, a founding member of the Women's Trade Union Association and a tireless campaigner for the rights of women in industry, claimed in 1889:

> There is perhaps no class of whom the wealthy or the educated know so little as of working women. Everybody in these days knows something of the slums, something of the crofter's cottage and the Irish cabin; but the industrious, independent woman who spends her days working at a skilled trade in a factory crosses our path but seldom, and few of us know anything of her thoughts, her aims and her struggles.[1]

By focusing on the 'thoughts, aims and struggles' of the 'industrious independent woman', both novelists and social investigators of the late Victorian period were able to bring to the attention of the middle classes her desperate struggles to survive and her resilience in the face of difficulties, offering a number of perspectives on the unknown lives of factory workers and other women in industry. Black's claim is used to introduce a speech by a married factory worker who set up her own union, printed in *Nineteenth Century*. The article can be seen as characteristic of its time in its framing of the working woman's tale of oppression with the feminist's observations on how the woman worker should be interpreted. Such frameworks of interpretation were a hallmark of the new social investigatory writing by women in the 1880s and 1890s. Based on interviews with working-class women about their work, analysis of their wages, expenditure and budgeting, and careful observation of their domestic habits, they provided a new set of narratives about working-class femininity and respectability. Deborah Epstein Nord has argued that the focus of analysis was primarily 'the domestic plight of working-class women',[2] but their experiences of a 'work culture', whether it be as one of many in a public workplace or completing piece-work in the home to an employer's deadline, were at least as important to their understanding of their own lives. It is also necessary to broaden this limited view of work culture to encompass after-work behaviour and the lifestyles of women workers. As Scott McCracken has pointed out, 'paid employment is an entry ticket to *fin-de-siècle* London', which offers 'multiple stages on which new identities can be rehearsed',[3] not least the new urban femininities which fascinated the East End novelists. According to Philippa Levine, at a time when the sweated labour of women was rapidly becoming a public concern, 'poor pay and monotonous work would certainly not encourage women to invest energy in their identity as workers'.[4] And yet how, where and when they worked, and who with, and what they did after work, were essential to the formation of the identities of women working in industry, raising a series of questions about the respectability they struggled to maintain in both the domestic and the public sphere.

As feminist historians from Ellen Ross to Barbara Harrison have noted, the complex process of accessing working-class women's voices in this period is compounded by the difficulties of interpreting their complaints: as researchers we must be aware that views articulated to investigators and the answers to their questions 'were constituted by a context in which they were given or presented, and this was nearly always for the pursuit of political objectives'.[5] This chapter does not seek exclusively to interpret the views of women in industry, though I do draw on these, but to focus on the ways in which they were interpreted and framed not only by the female investigators but also by contemporary novelists. As Judith R. Walkowitz has demonstrated, a comparison of the uses of narrative across fictional, investigatory and journalistic discourses in this period allows us to consider 'the dynamics of metropolitan life as a series of multiple and simultaneous cultural contests and exchanges'.[6] This interdisciplinary approach has been increasingly recognised as providing a valid and illuminating perspective on Victorian culture, and since the 'literary turn' in history, the uses of cultural history to an understanding of literature, and vice versa, have been acknowledged. In this chapter I shall compare the narratives about the London work-girl in 1880s East-End fiction with those offered by social investigators, feminists and female contributors to the periodical press, drawing particularly on Clara Collet's research on women's work for the fourth volume of Charles Booth's *Life and Labour of the People of London* (1893). Writers such as George Gissing and Margaret Harkness anatomised the 'city girl', exploring the differences between factory workers and women who worked in the home and their varying experiences of London life. Typically in urban fiction fears about the sexualities of factory girls, bar maids and other workers in the public sphere are offset by the cherished respectability of home-workers such as seamstresses, though the character of the industrial worker remains radically unstable.

Investigative research into the lives of female industrial workers both reinforced and challenged prevalent images of the work-girl. According to Carl Chinn, 'the standardised image of the slum woman was of a person whose appearance and habits were commensurate with the miserable, squalid districts in which she lived … she was regarded as a foul-mouthed slut'.[7] Linking drunkenness and carelessness to the problem of unequal pay and the starvation wages many women were forced to accept, Clementina Black was prompted to demand, 'Is it any wonder that those who live thus turn to drink? Is it any wonder if they become coarse and brutal?'[8] However, she evokes the stereotypical image of the drunken, 'coarse' worker with no control over her behaviour only to refute it, going on to register her amazement at the 'virtues' rather than the 'failings' of the poorest workers: 'The good feeling, the moderation, the kindness, ay, and the good manners, of the London working woman are a perpetual source of surprise to me … All the women, for instance, of whom I have spoken as known to myself and many more whom I know as well or better, are women of true respectability, honest, industrious, sober, self-respecting citizens'.[9] Her later interviews with women in industry confirmed this conviction; in the introduction to *Married Women's Work* (1915) she reiterated that, 'a very large majority of the women visited are evidently kindly, industrious, reasonable, self-respecting persons, emphatically good citizens'.[10] 'Self-respecting' workers 'known' well to the investigator could then be used to authoritatively attack damaging cultural stereotypes. However, the statistical work of Black's contemporary, Clara Collet, Booth's researcher who went on to become Labour Correspondent for the Board of Trade, tends to emphasise the failings, rather than the virtues, of women in industry, perhaps because as a highly educated civil servant and former teacher, Collet aligned herself more obviously with the new class of 'professional' women workers. Her section on 'Women's Work' in *The Trades of East London* (1893) questions Black's vision of citizenship by including the rather dubious observation that 'mental activity is not a characteristic of East End working women'[11] and goes on to highlight the 'immorality' of younger, unskilled workers, such as fur-sewers. Collet's involvement with the recently formed Charity Organisation Society perhaps also encourages an unfair assessment of her interviewees, as she even accuses the majority of women of working only 'to make an appearance of industry' in order to obtain charitable assistance.[12] Deborah Epstein Nord has argued that 'a feature of much social-investigative writing by women during this period was the middle-class woman's conviction that her concerns converged with those of working-class women'.[13] Such a conviction may partly explain the motivation of a feminist such as Black for taking up the cause of women in industry – her active involvement with the Women's Industrial Council and the Anti-Sweating League in order to improve working conditions and establish a minimum wage certainly testifies to her determination to achieve economic rights for women workers, a feminist agenda relevant to all classes of women in the workplace.[14] But in Collet's case, her writing often foregrounds her fears of the work-girl's immorality, rather than a shared concern about the difficulties women workers might face in the male-dominated public sphere, as if she prefers to preserve a distance between her own professionalism and the struggles of the industrial woman worker.

East-End novelists borrowed from social-investigative writing in their concerns about immorality and respectability, often making direct comparisons between the identities of female home-workers and those who worked in the public sphere. It has been argued that the realist novels of George Gissing depict pay and working conditions with the same 'accuracy' and familiarity with the East End as statistical reports of the time.[15] In an 1891 lecture to the Charity Organization Society on Gissing's work which she admired, Collet spoke of 'his intimate knowledge of the habits of life and thought of working people'.[16] In his late 1880s novels the home-worker is valued for the respectability she earns through a combination of exhaustive labour and domestic duties. In *Demos* (1886) the seamstresses Emma Vine and her widowed sister, Kate Clay, share their poky and sparse rooms with an invalid sister, Jane, and Kate's young children, restricted to the domestic space by their trade and their caring duties. Signalling the dangers of working outside the home, Jane's ill-health has been brought on by walking long distances to work because she cannot afford any other transport; 'the fifth attack of rheumatic fever was the price she paid for being permitted to earn 10 shillings a week' (p. 35).[17] The inadequacy of this wage is confirmed in Black's study of sweated labour, in which she attests, 'all of us are aware that no young woman can really live, in a large town, the life of a civilised human being upon 10 shillings a week or less'.[18] Although evidence from an 1897 report by the newly established Women's Industrial Council suggested that home-workers were 'probably the most completely wretched workers in our country',[19] fictional representations often painted a different picture in order to shore up the values of domesticity. Richard Mutimer, Emma's sweetheart, a mouthpiece for conservative views about women's work, is glad that his sister does not have to go out to work because 'a girl's proper place is at home' (p. 48). Emma's 'motherly care' of her sister's children, and her 'striving her hardest to restore order in the wretched home' (p. 393) are facilitated by her choice of work culture, though for women caring for young children, home-work is often less of a choice than a necessity. Resourcefully combining the demands of paid work with child-care, the seamstress keeps the children amused until bedtime by '[telling] her stories to the humming of the machine' (p. 395). The moral qualities she is able to develop by working at home are seen as increasingly valuable within the text in marked contrast to those of her sister, who neglects her children in order to spend drunken evenings with disreputable acquaintances in the nearby public houses. In line with arguments about the advantages of working at home, Gissing demonstrates that the domestic sphere is the safest and most appropriate place for the working-class woman, where her morality is least at risk of corruption.[20]

Placing a woman in a factory or work-room may have slightly improved her economic condition, but she had to struggle to protect her moral position in such an environment. By entering the public sphere and mixing with men and other women with different life experiences, she was believed to compromise her respectability. Collet was particularly vehement in her warnings about the 'mischievous influence' of factory women 'brutalized' by marriage on their companions, claiming that their 'coarseness' would have adverse effects on 'respectable girls'.[21] Such fears are illustrated in Emma's brief period of working outside the home:

> She had no companions. The girls whom she came to know in the workroom for the most part took life very easily; she could not share in their genuine merriment; she was often revolted by their way of thinking and speaking. They thought her dull, and paid no attention to her. She was glad to be relieved of the necessity of talking. (p. 396)

Although this reflects Collet's views by characterising the merriment of the workroom as 'revolting', it also suggests that respectable girls can resist the effects of the 'coarseness' of older married women to which they are 'expos[ed]'.[22] Emma's exclusion in the workroom is less important to her than her desire to earn money to support her family: she is driven by her acceptance of her position as a working woman, 'we've got to work ... and to earn our living like other women do' (p. 224). Andrew August has characterised such attitudes in terms of 'a culture of women's work' in poor neighbourhoods, 'consistent with the general expectation of women's behaviour – that they would work hard throughout their lives'. This argument 'challenges the idea that working-class women accepted a notion of the female sphere that did not include paid work'.[23] In this sense Emma may be closer to Black's more positive model of the working woman as 'self-respecting citizen', suggesting that those who worked hard in factories and workrooms, who were to take active roles in the formation and campaigning of the new unions, perhaps had more control over their respectability than Collet accounted for.

In Gissing's later fiction the division between 'typical' and 'respectable' factory girls is explored in more detail. In *Thyrza* (1887) the description of the Lambeth hat factory where the Trent sisters and Totty Nancarrow work privileges respectability over the coarseness often associated with factory culture; the laughing workers who belong to 'the class of needlewomen who preserve appearances' are 'becomingly dressed' and affectionate, trading stories with 'much cheerfulness' (p. 261) as they work.[24] In his more developed account of Whitehead's, the artificial flower factory in Clerkenwell, where *The Nether World* (1889) is set, Gissing systematically delineates the 'various types of the London crafts-girl' (p. 127) distinguished by age, health and expectations, who choose to earn their living in the work-room.[25] Although such types include those broken by ill health and those who have 'outlived their illusions', these are balanced against the girl who is 'already tasting such scanty good as life had in store for her'. Factory work for women is increasingly valorised in the following passage:

> If regularly engaged as time-workers, they made themselves easy in the prospect of wages that allowed them to sleep under a roof and eat at certain intervals of the day; if employed on piece-work they might at any moment find themselves wageless, but this, being a familiar state of affairs, did not trouble them. With few exceptions, they were clad neatly; on the whole, they plied their task in wonderful contentment. The general tone of conversation among them was not high; moralists unfamiliar with the ways of the nether world would probably have applied a term other than negative to the laughing discussions which now and then enlivened this or that group; but it was very seldom indeed that a child newly arriving heard anything with which she was not already perfectly familiar. (p. 127)

Rather than emphasising the monotony of making flowers day in and day out, the passage emphasises the camaraderie and contentment of the neatly dressed workers, who still have the ability to laugh and gossip despite the uncertainty of their employment; significantly Gissing makes no comment on the low level of wages in a 'season trade' considered by Collet to be 'extremely irregular'.[26] Here the low tone of the conversation is shown to contain nothing that a working-class girl might not already know, with Gissing distancing himself from the misconceptions of those 'moralists unfamiliar with the ways of the nether world' who might suggest otherwise. Countering current views about the 'weak emotional natures' of factory girls whose unskilled labour encourages them to 'float along with the stream, losing … their very identity, and becoming as featureless and colourless as the very streets they live in',[27] the passage suggests that the identities of London work-girls are far more colourful than has been imagined in the moral agendas of the social investigators.

However, such generosity is only achieved by the foregrounding of more 'refined' versions of the industrial woman worker. The ray of sunlight which lights up the head of Jane Snowdon, 'the child newly arriving', whose innocence has already been established in her suffering at the hands of her cruel and 'coarse' co-worker, Clem Peckover, symbolises Jane's superiority to most types of the London work-girl; a few pages later this is made explicit in Gissing's more judgmental comment that her laughter is so 'unlike the shrill discord whereby the ordinary workgirl expresses her foolish mirth' (p. 138). In order to atone for the 'shrillness' of the voices of more ordinary women, (a word also used in Collet's descriptions),[28] Gissing consoles himself with the ideal of those who can rise above the vulgarities of their class. With her interest in reading and music, the cultured Thyrza is differentiated from her fellow factory worker Totty; she even looks refined with her golden hair and is thus able to attract the middle-class hero. Significantly, her refinement is nurtured and protected by her sister who recognises its potential value. She seeks to educate Thyrza in the practical qualities their life requires but also to safeguard her domestic virtues, ' I want to keep you away from everything that isn't homelike and quiet' (p. 52). According to one reviewer, this was blatantly unrealistic as the work-girl appeared 'so very much above the average of the East-end hat-liner', that W.T. Stead was forced to conclude that Gissing had uncharacteristically idealised his heroine.[29] East-End novelists usually avoided describing 'the lowest of the low', as Edith Sichel notes, with both Gissing and his contemporary Walter Besant exercising their philanthropic intentions on the 'better sort of work-girl'.[30] Emma Vine, whose brief period working outside the home only serves to reinforce her separateness, also falls into the category of the 'better sort', as she refuses to enter into the banter of the workroom:

> It was her terrible misfortune to have feelings too refined for the position in which fate had placed her. Had she only been like those other girls in the workroom! But we are interesting in proportion to our capacity for suffering, and dignity comes of misery nobly borne. (p. 397)

The authorial intrusion at the end of the passage seems to confirm Gissing's preference for the 'refined', suffering work-girl over the typical factory girl who knows how to enjoy herself, even though he is simultaneously lamenting this difference. The laughter of the ordinary work-girl may gesture to her resistance to social norms through the sense of solidarity she shares with her fellow workers. A slightly later assessment of the factory girl characterised this in terms of her freedom and modernity: 'the modern woman of the poorer classes cannot stay at home, it is too dull, the surroundings too depressing, she likes to get into the lively circle of the factory room'.[31] This raises the larger issue of the working-class heroine, as, perhaps if Emma, Jane or Thyrza had been like 'other girls', they would not have aroused the sympathies of the middle-class reader in quite the same way. In the same way that social investigators edited out of official accounts details of poor women's lives which conflicted with their moral agendas, Gissing cherished the asexual respectability of his work-girl heroines in order to reinforce 'the middle-class investigator's professed conviction that the working-class woman's place was in the home',[32] however dull. Getting into the 'lively circle' of the public sphere, however, remained a desire of the typical factory girl which could not be so easily ignored.

Investigations of the London work-girl also encompassed the crucial issue of her recreation after work, often in order to establish the threatening nature of working-class female sexuality if left unattended. The socialising of pleasure-loving factory girls was singled out by investigators as dangerously immoral and in clear need of middle-class management. At a time when feminists were divided about the need for protective legislation in the workplace, some of them began to argue that women might also need to be protected from the dangers of leisure. In an article on the growing need for clubs for working girls, Maude Stanley, who elsewhere advocated such activities as gymnastics for promoting ideals of citizenship, delineated the specific dangers of unregulated recreation:

> Our work-girls … seek their recreation where alone they can find it, by loitering about the streets after dark when work is over, with some chosen companion; often it is with girls, sometimes in rough play with boys and lads. After a time the walk round, the looking into the shop-windows, the passing by the glaring gas-lit stalls in the evening markets, ceases to have interest. Then comes, according to their means, the visit to the music hall, the cheap theatres, the gin-palaces, the dancing saloons and the wine shop; then follow other temptations, the easy sliding into greater sin, the degradation and the downfall of all womanly virtue.[33]

Identifying the streets as a heterosocial space, where 'rough play with boys and lads' signifies the courting rituals of the working classes, the passage suggests that the 'temptations' attendant on other enclosed heterosocial spaces may seduce work-girls into 'greater sin', either casual sex or its commodified form, prostitution. The inclusion of the wine shop and the gin-palace underlines cultural concerns about the degradations of drinking, often associated with popular forms of working-class entertainment such as music hall and theatre, and linked later in the article to other forms of 'foul behaviour' like swearing, fighting and smoking. August offers a more positive picture of women's participation in 'the vibrant cultures of leisure in poor neighbourhoods', which may be closer to the social reality but he ignores the attendant difficulties of women's 'relaxation outside their homes'.[34] The prevalent fear is that women 'loitering about the streets after dark' are effectively trespassing on male territory, and moreover, adopting male habits, which will quickly ensure 'the downfall of all womanly virtue'. The provision of clubs and entertainments for working women by new unions such as the Women's Protective and Provident League and the Women's Industrial Council was an attempt to protect the womanliness of industrial workers by keeping them off the streets. This can be seen as an interventionist measure certainly but it is worth considering Levine's view that 'these important provisions … gave women access to activities and spaces from which they were often excluded', thereby encouraging 'the autonomous development of a women's culture'.[35]

Despite the sympathetic tone of some investigative accounts, feminists who genuinely appeared to want to help their less favoured 'sisters' at times seemed unable to edit out their disgust with the pleasure-seeking (and by implication, sexually curious) work-girl. The easy acceptance of male company was felt to be the particular province of factory girls, who were increasingly characterised by feminist investigators in terms of the sexual dangers of their after-work behaviour. Collet's description of the factory girl is typically double-edged, half admiring and half condemning:

> She can be recognised on ordinary days by the freedom of her walk, the numbers of her friends, and the shrillness of her laugh. On Saturday evenings and Sunday afternoons she will be found promenading up and down the Bow Rd, arm in arm with two or three other girls, sometimes with a young man, but not nearly so frequently as might be imagined. On these occasions she is adorned and decked out, not so much for conquest as for her own personal delight and pleasure, and for the admiration of her fellow women … She goes to penny gaffs if nothing better is offered her; she revels in the thrilling performances at the Paragon or the music halls; and only too often she can be

seen drinking in the public-house with a young man with whom she may or
may not have been previously acquainted.[36]

Not to be confused with the 'thousands of quiet, respectable, hard-working
girls' who also work in factories, this street-wise young woman enjoys her
leisure, which ranges from the relative innocence of window-shopping to
the dangers of drinking. Although she happily accepts what is offered to her
by men, she dresses for 'her own personal ... pleasure', rather than for them
and her 'fellow women' seem at least as important to her sense of identity.
Collet downplays her sexuality by emphasising that she is more likely to be
arm in arm with other girls than men. Going to public-houses with men is,
however, a sure sign of immorality and roughness for the single work-girl;
Chinn claims that it was only acceptable for older, married women to frequent
such spaces.[37] And yet the sexual knowledge passed on in the workroom may
have a positive side. A few pages later Collet asserts that the fear of unwanted
pregnancy protects the work-girl from 'the worst forms of immorality'.[38] By
the late 1890s, when more clubs had been established for working girls in
order to teach them acceptable womanly behaviour, factory girls were still
being vilified for their 'freedom' on the streets. These women who 'go off in
shoals to a crowded thoroughfare' and are 'always on the look-out for a lark'
are shown to 'fall prey to every kind of bad influence, with no better guide
than a weak emotional nature, and no higher interest than the pleasure of the
moment'.[39] Perhaps more significantly, this article notes that the low earnings
of factory girls actually prevent them from frequenting 'places of amusement
except on rare occasions', compelling them to remain on the streets where
they are 'learning no good'. Social investigatory writing clearly then drew
on stereotypical views about pleasure-loving work-girls, but perhaps also
acknowledged its own failure to fully account for their sexual identities, as
investigators such as Collet appeared to admire, as well as condemn, the work-
girl's capacity to control her relationships with men. To adapt Ross's arguments
about these 'mixed texts', this may be an example of poor women speaking
and behaving in ways which their better-off sisters secretly envied.[40]

   The hierarchical relationship between the female investigator and the
working woman is a fraught one, raising questions about the conditions
necessary for cross-class identification and the agendas that may have driven
individuals to undertake specific areas of feminist enquiry. In her discussion
of Mary Higgs' account of the destitute women she observed in women's
lodging houses in *Glimpses into the Abyss* (1906), Nord has perceptively
argued that, 'the female social investigator's connection to the woman of the

streets is a harder, more unsettling link to sustain than her affiliation with her working-class housewife double'.[41] Women in industry appeared to be similarly unsettling to Collet, perhaps because rather than focusing on family life and maternity, she, like Higgs, was forced to confront issues around sexual respectability which may have made her uncomfortable. Her decision to base her construction of the typical factory girl on those in 'the lowest grade of factory workers' predominant in jam, rope and match factories is interesting, given the investigator's usual choice of case studies whose views would tally with their political agendas. In a revealing aside about the differences between typical and respectable industrial workers, she reflects that 'the East End investigator does not so easily find these [respectable] girls who "keep themselves to themselves"',[42] implying either that more respectable girls prefer not to be interviewed or that she prefers not to include them in her research. Jane Miller's account of Collet's early career and work for the Civil Service shows a woman who sometimes disliked interviewing and whose knowledgeable reporting for Booth is punctuated by moments of rage, 'even if that rage seems almost to be directed at the women themselves rather than at the society which thrives on their exploitation'.[43] Her conclusion is that the investigator's concern with women's issues 'became a professional concern, from which she distanced herself'. This distance may be rooted in Collet's views on female professionalism and her perception of herself as a professional woman worker with very different priorities to industrial workers. Her later research, published in a collection significantly titled *Essays on Educated Working Women* (1902), engaged much more sympathetically with the financial deprivations of higher paid workers in the respectable professions, such as journalism, clerical work and teaching, women whom she saw as 'fitted' by their education to become truly self-supporting. The operation of the marriage bar in certain professions (as in Collet's own) also deterred such women from seeking marriage, thus minimising risks to their respectability. In contrast, Clementina Black had no difficulties in identifying with women in industry, continuing to campaign for their rights throughout her long career. Unlike Collet who seemed rather contemptuous of shop girls for their desire for male company and public entertainments, Black expressed her sympathy for these 'shut in' women whose endurance of the restrictive living in system was as problematic as their ill health and exhaustion.[44] It is perhaps significant that both Collet and Black later chose to investigate married women's work, perhaps finding in the married woman worker, whose concerns were more to do with family life than amusement and attracting men, a more respectable interviewee.

East-End fiction is often less judgmental about the work-girl's enjoyment of public entertainments. In *Thyrza* more than his other fiction, Gissing seems to celebrate rather than attack the 'air of freedom and joyousness' (p. 39) attached to this figure of the street-wise work-girl. Collet's description seems to fit the representation of the fun-loving Totty Nancarrow, who is distinguished by her laughter and her independent walk, 'that swaying of the haunches and swing of the hands with palm turned outwards ... characteristic of the London work-girl' (p. 113). Totty snatches kisses with Luke Ackroyd in the street, talks in a 'merry, careless way' and is at her ease in the mixed company of pubs and music halls. In an exuberant early scene, Thyrza accompanies her to a 'friendly lead' at the local pub, at which money is donated to a needy barber in exchange for an evening's entertainment. Peter Bailey's argument that the late Victorian pub 'provided [a] social space within which a more democratised, heterosocial world of sex and sociability was being constituted'[45] is borne out in Gissing's descriptions of the pub as a respectable arena for mixed-sex pleasure, which admits thirsty women with babies and companies of 'neatly dressed' girls, as well as 'liquor-sodden creatures whose look was pollution' (p. 38). Like Totty, 'the girls who sat with glasses of beer before them, and carried on primitive flirtations with their neighbours, were honest wage-earners of factory and work-shop, well able to make themselves respected. If they lacked refinement, natural or acquired, it was not their fault' (p. 41). Unlike Collet who believed that 'their great enemy is drink',[46] Gissing suggests that single women can retain their respectability in the pub, refuting stereotypes in his portrayal of Totty, who might enjoy a glass of ginger-beer with friends but disapproves heartily of Ackroyd's increasing drunkenness. However, the scene in the pub is also designed to reinforce Thyrza's distance from her unrefined fellow workers: refusing to drink but agreeing to sing in a public place, she advertises her sexual availability, horrifying her sister who exclaims, 'If you go on and sing in a public-house, I don't know what you won't do' (p. 48). Contradicting his earlier remarks, Gissing seems to imply that entering a pub is seen to jeopardise any aspirations to refinement on the part of working-class women, whose need for recreation must be satisfied in more cultured ways. Although August has argued that 'women were integral parts of the lively pub and street culture in [poor] neighbourhoods',[47] their status needs qualifying, as the urban narrative persistently warns of the dangers of entertainment outside the home.

Theatres and music halls were also identified as disreputable spaces for single women, linked to sexuality and prostitution by the need for poorly paid women to be accompanied and paid for by men, what Kathy Peiss has described as the practice of 'treating'.[48] An 1884 edition of the *Fortnightly Review* containing two articles on 'Social Reforms for the London Poor' identified the problem of finding 'legitimate and desirable pleasure' for young working women. Excluded from the more respectable and expensive theatres and generally denied the reading-rooms, clubs and coffee-houses which are 'as a rule inaccessible to women and children', women instead have 'plenty of inducements to vice' and the 'excitement of low theatres and dancing saloons'.[49] In Margaret Harkness's *A City Girl* (1887), the pleasure-loving 'masher' and seamstress Nellie Ambrose aligns herself with the frivolous factory girl by choosing a blue feather for her hat before agreeing to go to the theatre with the married philanthropist Arthur,[50] though in the last chapter after her unplanned pregnancy she realises 'what a heavy price she had paid for a few hours' amusement ... she had no wish now for theatres and outings' (p. 185).[51] The London work-girl's 'fondness' for the theatre is generally perceived to be dangerous, though this is usually more to do with the intentions of the required male escorts than the immoralities of modern drama. In *Demos* Mutimer forbids his sister Alice to accompany her admirer Keene to the theatre and the barmaid Clara in *The Nether World* loses her job and her respectability when she accepts Scawthorne's offers of entertainment; her mother tells Sidney, 'she's been going to the theatre and such places with a man as she got to know at the bar, and Mrs Tubb says she believes it's him has tempted her away' (p. 91). As a relief from the drudgery of labour, recreation was clearly essential – Nellie 'sorely wanted a little diversion, a little amusement ... [she] longed for a change before she set about a new patch of trousers' (pp. 62, 63) – but the dangers of entering heterosocial spaces and the casual encounters with men they necessitated offered many kinds of temptation. An artificial flower maker interviewed for the *Fortnightly* article admitted that she sometimes accepted 'a music-hall treat' in preference to walking the streets or going back to her lodgings, but did not like the late hours or the fact that 'they make me drink'.[52] Significantly, when Totty agrees to go to a music hall with Ackroyd, she refuses to drink and asserts, 'I pay for myself, or I don't go at all. That's my rule' (p. 193). Without such rules to protect them, women's wishes for theatres and outings often yield undesirable consequences, as they remained vulnerable to the economic and sexual power concealed behind 'the tacit legitimacy of treating'.[53]

So what are the implications of the work-girl's restricted freedoms in the heterosocial world of leisure? Peiss has usefully commented on the dangers of overemphasising the 'liberation' of working women at the turn of the century, pointing out that 'understanding working women's culture calls for a doubled vision, to see that women's embrace of styles, fashion, romance and mixed-sex fun could be a source of autonomy and pleasure as well as a cause of their continuing oppression'.[54] Whilst feminists continued to advocate the importance of girls' clubs and the need for the combination of 'recreation and culture',[55] the stereotype of the pleasure-loving work-girl remained culturally pervasive. The knowing awareness of such representations by work-girls and investigators testifies both to the pervasiveness of the stereotypes and the part they may have played in the 'continuing oppression' of the working woman. In an 1896 edition of the *Girl's Own Paper*, an article on the life and work of factory girls compiled from letters sent into the magazine included the comment by a dress-maker that 'girls in work-rooms get the name of being very careless in religious matters and of spending all their leisure time in the pursuit of pleasure, and some of it of a questionable character, but I am sure it is not so with the majority of work-girls'.[56] The list of preferred activities which includes reading, evening classes and church attendance may say more about the magazine's religious agenda and socially aspirant readership than actual changes in working-class leisure,[57] but the evidence in the article does point towards a deconstruction of the dominant image of the pleasure-loving work-girl. Similarly, as proof for the feminist desire that East London girls 'value' their club rooms, Violet Greville quotes from one of the converted who claims, 'Since we have had a place to spend our evenings in we are ashamed to be seen standing about the streets'.[58] But not all London work-girls were ashamed to enjoy the freedoms of the streets where their 'showy attire' could be seen to best advantage. In 1908 the related figure of the 'flash girl' is compared to the physically active New Woman by the investigator May Craske, who pleads, 'When you see her coming out of her factory, laughing loudly and romping roughly in the streets ... forgive the working girl her noisiness and all her faults, and try to see beneath the rough exterior the same charm of the natural girl'.[59] By coupling the factory girl's independence with the urban freedoms of the New Woman, investigators were also able to offer an alternative perspective on their 'rough' sisters whose 'noisiness' (or 'boisterous[ness]', as Collet termed it)[60] they may have secretly envied.

Narratives about the work cultures of women in industry in the 1880s and 1890s can then be seen to present an ambiguous picture of the London work-girl and the solidarity of factory culture, oscillating between admiration for respectability and disgust for immorality. The social investigators were instrumental in producing identities for the work-girl, though Black's vision of industrious citizenship is clearly a different image from Collet's descriptions of showily-dressed streetwise revellers. Gissing's focus on more refined working-class heroines allows him to downplay the dangers of working in industry. Whilst both kinds of writing often seek to reinforce the working woman's place in the home, or at least in the new girls' clubs, this is destabilised by the insistence on women's presence on the streets and in public places in a culture seen as hostile to the idea of working-class women's leisure. Notions of respectability are contested as the work-girl's enjoyment of the freedom of the streets and heterosocial public space may be a sign of her enviable independence rather than a 'questionable' failing. By the early twentieth century, urban freedom, particularly in fiction, is much more associated with the modernity and respectability of the working woman, as Deborah Parsons' readings of the *flâneuse*'s confident occupation of public space in modernist women's writing have shown,[61] though by this time investigators' interest in the East-End industrial worker is increasingly being replaced by what Ross refers to as 'the "discovery" of the mother', heralding a renewed focus on domesticity.[62] This development of attitudes towards 'women's requirements in the worlds of work and leisure'[63] shows how the standard image of the immoral work-girl, defined by her roughness, outspokenness and capacity for pleasure, can then be revalued, if not entirely reclaimed, in a more accommodating vision of women's work culture at the turn of the century.

Notes

1   Clementina Black, 'A Working Woman's Speech', *Nineteenth Century*, 25 (1889), pp. 667–71 (p. 667).

2   Deborah Epstein Nord, *Walking the Victorian Streets: Women, Representation and the City* (New York, 1995), p. 208.

3   Scott McCracken, 'Embodying the New Woman: Dorothy Richardson, Work and the London Café', in Avril Horner and Angela Keane (eds), *Body Matters: Feminism, Textuality, Corporeality* (Manchester, 2000), p. 63.

4   Philippa Levine, *Victorian Feminism, 1850–1900* (London, 1987), p. 111.

5   Barbara Harrison, *Not only the 'Dangerous Trades': Women's Work and Health in Britain, 1880–1914* (London, 1996), p. 216. See also Ellen Ross, *Love and Toil: Motherhood in Outcast London, 1870–1918* (New York and Oxford, 1993), pp. 18–20. Ross's discussion of social investigatory works as 'mixed texts', where the voices of working-class women 'mingle' with those of the feminists, is particularly useful.

6   Judith R. Walkowitz, *City of Dreadful Delight: Narratives of Sexual Danger in Late-Victorian London* (London, 1992), p. 10.

7   Carl Chinn, *They Worked all their Lives: Women of the Urban Poor in England, 1880–1939* (Manchester, 1988), p. 18. He contests this image by arguing for the importance of 'a hidden matriarchy', in which the mother wielded power as 'the pivot of the working-class family' (p. 20).

8   Clementina Black, 'The Organization of Working Women', *Fortnightly Review*, 52 (1889), p. 699.

9   Ibid.

10   Clementina Black, 'Introduction', in Ellen Mappen (ed.), *Married Women's Work*, (1915; London, 1983), p. 15.

11   Clara Collet, 'Women's Work', in Charles Booth (ed.), *Life and Labour of the People of London, Vol IV: The Trades of East London* (London, 1893), p. 267.

12   Ibid., p. 281. Collet was involved with the COS from 1884 to at least 1906, contributing regularly to its *Review*. This long involvement may 'be partly explained by her willingness to make use of those channels which were hospitable to women writers'. See Jane Miller, *Seductions: Studies in Reading and Culture* (London, 1990), p. 89.

13   Deborah Epstein Nord, *Walking the Victorian Streets: Women, Representation and the City* (Ithaca, 1995), p. 216.

14   For more information on Clementina Black's life and work, see Mappen, *Married Women's Work*, pp. xi–xv.

15   See Ruth M. Adams, 'George Gissing and Clara Collet', *Nineteenth-Century Fiction* (1956), pp. 72–7.

16   Clara Collet, 'George Gissing's Novels: A First Impression, *Charity Organization Review* (1891), p. 377. It was through this lecture that Gissing first became aware of Collet and her work. They met for the first time in 1893, after which they became friends and correspondents, frequently exchanging stories and reports.

17   George Gissing, *Demos: A Story of English Socialism*, ed. Pierre Coustillas (1886; Sussex, 1982).

18   Clementina Black, *Sweated Industry and the Minimum Wage* (London, 1907), p. 42.

19   Cited in Black, *Sweated Industry and the Minimum Wage*, p. 2.

20   Harrison, *Not Only the Dangerous Trades*, p. 96.

21   Collet, 'Women's Work', p. 313.

22   Ibid.

23   Andrew August, *Poor Women's Lives: Gender, Work and Poverty in Late-Victorian London* (London, 1999), pp. 118, 119.

24   George Gissing, *Thyrza*, ed. Jacob Korg (1887; Sussex, 1974).

25   George Gissing, *The Nether World*, ed. Stephen Gill (1889; Oxford, 1992).

26   Collet, 'Women's Work', p. 294.

27   Albinia Hobart-Hampden, 'The Working Girl of To-Day', *Nineteenth Century*, 43 (1898), p. 727.

28   Collet, 'Women's Work', p. 322.

29   Review of *Thyrza*, *Whitehall Review*, 12 May 1887, p. 20; [W.T. Stead], 'George Gissing as a Novelist', *Pall Mall Gazette*, 28 June 1887, p. 3.

30   Edith Sichel, 'Two Philanthropic Novelists: Mr Walter Besant and Mr George Gissing', *Murrays Magazine* (1888), pp. 506–18. Quoted in Pierre Coustillas and Colin Partridge (eds), *George Gissing: The Critical Heritage* (London and Boston, 1972), p. 116. Predictably, this review contrasts Besant's optimism to Gissing's pessimism, though ultimately Gissing's realism wins out over Besant's 'Bowdlerised Whitechapel … [his] family edition of the East End' (p. 118).

31   Mr Wheatley, 'Drunkenness amongst Women: Reported Alarming Increase', *Birmingham Daily Post*, 1 January 1901. Quoted in Chinn, *They worked All Their Lives*, p. 84. Wheatley was the Superintendent of a Church Mission amongst the poor, concerned that women were now enjoying the same freedoms as men.

32 Nord, *Walking the Victorian Streets*, p. 219. She argues that Maud Pember Reeves' *Round about a Pound a Week* (London, 1913), based on the visiting of poor Lambeth women by the Fabian Women's Group, used evidence selectively in order to promote an 'image of competent and devoted maternality' (p. 224).
33 Maude Stanley, 'Clubs for Working Girls', *Nineteenth Century*, 25 (1889), p. 76.
34 August, *Poor Women's Lives*, p. 127.
35 Levine, *Victorian Feminism*, pp. 113, 115. The WPPL was formed in 1874 and helped to provide women with 'invaluable services' such as banks, a Swimming Club and a Seaside Holiday House. The WIC, formed in 1894, 'placed considerable emphasis … on the recreational facilities it aimed to provide'.
36 Collet, 'Women's Work', pp. 322–3.
37 Chinn, *They Worked All Their Lives*, p. 120.
38 Collet, 'Women's Work', p. 325.
39 Hobart-Hampden, 'The Working Girl of To-day', pp. 726, 727.
40 Ross, *Love and Toil*, p. 20. Ross argues that poor women were able to articulate views about men, particularly abusive husbands, about which their observers had to remain silent, as they were 'prohibited from vulgar language, talk of sex or open man hating'.
41 Nord, *Walking the Victorian Streets*, p. 233.
42 Collet, 'Women's Work', pp. 322, 278.
43 Miller, *Seductions*, pp. 78, 100.
44 Black, *Sweated Industry and the Minimum Wage*, p. 54.
45 Peter Bailey, 'Parasexuality and Glamour: The Victorian Barmaid as Cultural Prototype', *Gender and History*, 2, 2 (1990), p. 167.
46 Collet, 'Women's Work', p. 325.
47 August, *Poor Women's Lives*, p. 128.
48 Kathy Peiss, *Cheap Amusements: Working Women and Leisure in Turn-of-the-Century New York* (Philadelphia, 1986), pp. 51, 54.
49 Violet Greville, 'The Need for Recreation', in 'Social Reforms for the London Poor', *Fortnightly Review*, 35 (1884), pp. 20, 22, 24.
50 Collet, 'Women's Work' mentions the factory girl's love of luxuries such as brightly coloured hats and feathers. See p. 323.
51 John Law [Margaret Harkness], *A City Girl: A Realistic Story* (1887; New York and London, 1984).
52 Greville, 'The Need for Recreation', p. 22.
53 Peiss, *Cheap Amusements*, p. 54.
54 Ibid., p. 6. Peiss's reading of leisure for working women in New York does highlight the working woman's similarity to the New Woman in her new-found independence and sexual expressiveness. She links the emergence of heterosocial culture to 'a sense of modernity, individuality and personal style'.
55 Greville, 'The Need for Recreation', p. 26.
56 See 'Girls who work with their Hands: Insight into the Life and Work of Factory-Girls Given by Themselves', *Girl's Own Paper*, 16 May 1896, pp. 517–18. The request for letters issued six months earlier asked for 'a description of the daily round … together with any note of satisfaction or aspiration that may describe the state of mind of the writer'. See *Girl's Own Paper*, 26 October 1895, p. 63.
57 This best-selling magazine was published by the evangelical publishing house, the Religious Tract Society, and had a 'wide cross-class appeal' to its intended juvenile audience. See Hilary Skelding, 'Every Girl's Best Friend? The *Girl's Own Paper* and its Readers', in

Emma Liggins and Daniel Duffy (eds), *Feminist Readings of Victorian Popular Texts: Divergent Femininities* (Aldershot, 2001), pp. 37, 40–41.

58 Greville, 'The Need for Recreation', p. 24.

59 May Craske, 'Girl Life in a Slum', *Economic Review*, 18 (1908), p. 189. Quoted in Nord, *Walking the Victorian Streets*, p. 217.

60 Collet, 'Women's Work', p. 325.

61 See Deborah L. Parsons, *Streetwalking the Metropolis: Women, the City and Modernity* (Oxford, 2000), pp. 116–22 for her discussion of the working girl's occupation of women-friendly public spaces such as cafés and restaurants in 1910s fiction by Dorothy Richardson and Virginia Woolf.

62 Ross, *Love and Toil*, p. 22. She argues that 'mothers and their domestic needs were in many ways the key to the order and pattern that observers began to find in the noisy, bustling, streets of the East End'.

63 Levine, *Victorian Feminism*, p. 117.

Chapter 5

'It was Just a Real Camaraderie Thing': Socialising, Socialisation and Shopfloor Culture at the Rowntree Factory, York

Emma Robertson

It just … bred camaraderie really, because … everybody was so good with everybody else. It was just helping everybody else to get what they needed to do – some working harder to help others to catch up. It was just a real camaraderie thing … They were just good people I think. It just made people good people … (Janet)[1]

Janet began work at the Rowntree confectionery factory in York at the age of 17 in 1956. She was employed in the Card Box department, making gift boxes for chocolate assortments such as Black Magic. In narrating her oral history, the 'camaraderie' of the factory was a recurring theme.[2] Indeed the quotation above illustrates a struggle to really capture in words the importance of relationships between workers. The theme of friendship and camaraderie as part of enjoying work for women recurs in numerous studies of women factory workers. Sue Bruley's study of female munitions workers in the Second World War, for example, demonstrates how friendship was a key element in enjoying factory work, even where the work itself was felt to be monotonous: 'They did not look for satisfaction in product terms, but were more socially orientated'.[3] In this chapter I will look at women's workplace cultures – broadly defined as 'a way of life, a set of shared meanings with specific symbols' – in the context of the Rowntree firm, particularly with regard to relationships between women.[4] My study will draw on 13 oral history interviews conducted with women who worked at the factory between 1936 and 1989.[5] They varied in age from 60 to 88 years and had worked at the factory for anything between six months and 46 years on various shifts. All the women were white, could be defined as working class and all but one had been born in York.[6] Although this is essentially a local study, I will also consider how York women's experiences contribute to broader historical understandings of workplace cultures.

Feminist analyses of women's employment in factories have realised the vital importance of shopfloor culture in women's working lives. By 'shopfloor culture' I am referring to the actions of the women themselves rather than the officially constructed 'culture' of the factory as an institution. I include practices such as: the forming of friendship groups; talking and singing; rituals and celebrations; as well as subversive acts such as stealing and sabotage. However, the workplace practices of women workers were constructed in relation to, and as a reaction to, the official policies of their employers. Their autonomy in creating a shopfloor culture was constrained by factory rules by which they could lose their jobs, as well as by other gendered frameworks that shaped their family and community roles. Workplace cultures do not exist in isolation from cultures outside the factory. Women's actions in the capitalist workplace were culturally embedded in terms of class, regional and ethnic identity as well as in the culture and structures of patriarchy (such as heterosexual marriage and unequal pay). Pollert, for one, feels that working women's culture is a matter of 'style' rather than substance[7] whilst Westwood locates the relative failure of working women's resistance in the collusive nature of a 'culture of femininity' with 'patriarchy'.[8] Celebrating forthcoming weddings, for example, may reinforce the commitment of women to the institution of heterosexual marriage within which they are under the control of both their husband and the state. However, Westwood also recognises the 'oppositional, energetic and potentially very powerful' aspects of women's culture.[9] Using Rowntrees as a case study, I want to consider the extent to which interactions between women and their cultural practices on the shopfloor served the official policies of the firm, and the extent to which they were a site of resistance and struggle.

Of the existing historical and sociological studies of women's labour, few are fully relevant to York women. As Tilly and Scott observe, 'York was isolated from changes which took place elsewhere in England. Even its appearance changed little'.[10] York remained relatively unindustrialised throughout the twentieth century, though the railway and confectionery industries were strong. In 1951 and 1971, confectionery alone accounted for over half the employment in manufacturing in York.[11] The Rowntree firm, founded in 1862 by the Quaker industrialist Henry Isaac Rowntree, was therefore a key source of employment for women in York for several generations. Women often made up more than half the Rowntree workforce: they numbered 3,557 as compared to 3,468 men in 1950 and this figure did not include seasonal or part-time workers.[12]

Like other Quaker-run businesses (such as the confectioners Cadburys and Fry), Rowntrees became renowned for its advanced policies of industrial welfare such as the provision of a company doctor and dentist, and the establishment of pension schemes. Although the management of the business passed out of the hands of the Rowntree family by the 1960s, and the direct influence of Quakerism had long since declined, the ethos of respectful treatment of workers remained strong.[13] Joseph Rowntree (who joined the firm in 1869) and his son Benjamin Seebohm have become famous in their own right for their forward-thinking approach to issues of poverty, and the trusts set up by Joseph from the profits of the business still influence life in the city. However, the charitable projects of the Quaker businessmen were largely dependent on the labour of York workers. The history of these workers remains largely unwritten, except as a reflection of the 'enlightened' labour policies of the Rowntree family. The firm certainly maintained its reputation as a 'good' employer long after the direct involvement of the Rowntree family had ceased. This may be due partly to the formalised, 'systematic' approach to industrial welfare formulated by the Rowntrees.[14] Although the factory began as a paternalist organisation in which Joseph is said to have known his entire workforce by name, the Rowntree firm of the twentieth century did not rely on a culture of individualised paternalist philanthropy. Management aimed to foster a workplace culture in which the workers were committed to the smooth running of the business. This was to be achieved through workers' councils and an encouragement of trade unionism (although the relationship with trade unions was not always easy) as well as through profit sharing schemes. Workers were not to be referred to or thought of as simply 'hands' but to be respected as individuals.[15] The Rowntree firm also encouraged workers to become involved in social activities at the factory. Through sports, music and drama, workers were to use their leisure time in a rational and improving manner. Very few of the women I spoke with had an involvement with these 'official' activities, particularly when they were married and had children; either they had insufficient time or they preferred to keep their leisure time to themselves. However, it is in this relatively enlightened context that women workers at the factory created their own shopfloor cultures. Of course, the factory was far from a democracy and in the hierarchy of the factory, women operatives, especially part-time workers, held the least power.

The earliest date of employment for my narrators was 1936, at a time when Rowntrees was developing its most successful products: Black Magic, Kit Kat, Smarties and Aero. The latest date at which any of the women interviewed were still at the factory was 1989, a year after the dramatic and highly controversial takeover by Nestlé.[16] This chapter will, however, focus on the 1950s as the time when most of the women were in employment. The

Second World War and its aftermath significantly altered the position of women at the factory. During the course of the war itself many were taken off their work to be recruited as munitions workers, sometimes within Rowntrees. To meet demand for confectionery after the war they were needed in such large numbers that Rowntrees experienced a shortage of female labour in the 1950s. Whereas before the war married women had been excluded from permanent employment at the factory and could only obtain work as seasonal workers, now they were encouraged to apply, particularly for part-time work; all except one of the women I interviewed had married and had subsequently worked at the factory.[17]

Jobs at Rowntrees were still highly gender segregated in the second half of the twentieth century, meaning that women spent most of their working lives with other women; this was (and is) typical of many areas of work. They were employed to sort, pack and decorate the confectionery, often sitting side by side on assembly lines, with female supervisors. This raises the question of whether there was a specifically 'feminine' work culture. From women's testimonies it is clear that men were on the margins of their work spaces: moving chocolate and materials in and out of the workrooms or mending machinery. This is not to suggest a homogenous or consistent 'feminine' culture but clearly women were working in a female-dominated social space. This raises immediate questions about the relationships between women on the shopfloor.

On starting work at the factory, many of the women I spoke with soon discovered that mixing with others was not always easy.[18] As Eva remarked, 'You don't get on with everyone'. Marital status, respectability, age and race were all identified by the women as areas of difference and conflict between them.[19] For example, Mary, taking on seasonal employment in the late 1930s, remembered how working with older married women with very different life experiences and outlooks proved traumatic:

> I went and I was very upset because I wasn't used to working with married women. They used to pull my leg because I was more or less innocent ... When I went home at night I used to cry and my husband said, 'for goodness sake, give your notice in, we'll manage'. And I said no, it's only for a few weeks, I'll have to learn to stick up for meself.

Shopfloor culture excluded certain women as even common experiences, such as marriage, could be a source of conflict. Women did not, in contrast to Glucksmann's assertion, constitute a 'homogenous group ... united as a gender'.[20] What emerged particularly strongly, however, was a very individual subjectivity. Women believed that their experience of work was very personal and were often loath to speak for others: 'Well, they didn't all think the same way', Mary reminded me. Yet friendship could overcome such differences to a degree.

Those who went into the factory later in life, or from other jobs, were often shocked by the behaviour of their colleagues. Glenda recalled, 'I didn't think I'd last a week there with different types of girls which you had to cope with in a factory but, then, I was one of 'em at finish [laughs]'. Many of the women I interviewed implicitly accepted the stereotype of female factory workers as 'rough', even though they also emphasised the diversity of women they encountered and the basic goodness of their co-workers. Although the figure of the 'factory girl'[21] was never mentioned explicitly, Janet implied that the stereotype was present in contemporary thought and discourse: 'Everybody used to think 'cos it was a factory you were rough. And you always get odd ones, don't you? But it wasn't like that at all – that was the very minority. They were good people …'. In their oral histories, several women reflected on, and often challenged, discourses of female factory labour as not quite 'respectable'.

Notwithstanding the acknowledgement of diversity by the women, the spirit of 'camaraderie', as illustrated by Janet in the epigram to this chapter, was strong. Andrew Phillips has noticed the importance of friendship in his oral history-based research. He astutely observed: 'the community spirit achieved within their workplace … represented a real ownership by the women of their working lives'.[22] The physical position of women workers in many departments, particularly as the practice of assembly line production became more common, was often conducive to the making of close friends. This spirit of friendship underpinned the oral histories of many of my interviewees. Women told me of their 'special' friends whom they sat next to for long periods. For those who were not on the lines, perhaps as room examiners or check-weighers (positions of marginally increased status, with responsibility for monitoring the quality of work), the isolation from the other women could prove hard to bear at times. These women often take a different, more detached perspective of women's friendships within the factory. Joyce, working the evening shift as a room examiner, was one who felt left out: 'Being on my own I wasn't so involved with all the tales they used to come out with …'. If we interpret 'tales' as gossip, Patricia Spacks's work is helpful in theorising Joyce's sense of exclusion: gossip can 'solidify a group's sense of itself by heightening consciousness of "outside"… and "inside" (the temporarily secure territory of the talkers)'.[23] For many, the difficulties of leaving the community of the 'girls' for a more solitary job which involved the implementing of factory discipline were not worth the extra prestige. As Kathleen told me, 'I didn't want to be bossing people about … I liked working with the girls as a group, not as one individual'. Yet even for those who felt excluded to some extent, the activities of the other women could be a source of strength in getting through the shift. Joyce, for example, liked to hum along with the songs of the women on the line. These informal, spontaneous aspects of their culture were more important for most women than trying to change conditions through formal mechanisms such as the Central Works Council and Trade Union.

Strict rules on movement around the factory, general conduct, and the pressures of production could be negotiated and sometimes directly resisted by women uniting in their friendship groups. Women would cover for each other to allow friends to go to the toilets (often for cigarettes), help each other to reach production targets and support each other in playing practical jokes or 'being cheeky'. The language of 'girlhood' alongside explicit statements of 'it was like being at school', could be seen to bolster a discourse of women as immature, yet it also gave women access to the power coterminous with the liminal state of childhood. However, women were also keen to perform well at their jobs, often having a strong sense of their working identity as, for example, packers. When asked what her favourite memory of Rowntrees was, Nancy responded, 'To get a good start for the next day we used to hide our work in the shavings' drawers'. The element of secrecy here was obviously exciting, yet by 'getting a good start' (hiding packing materials in drawers meant for the shavings used to fill up boxes) Nancy and her friends were also increasing production. Corbett suggests that, 'many adaptive work behaviours, whilst "against the rules", may actually be functional to the extent that they help the organisation's overall performance'.[24] Where women were able to help each other in their work without antagonism, they played an important role in socialising new workers into the factory regime. As Dublin commented in his work on mill workers in nineteenth-century America, 'the larger work group played a crucial role in the socialization of women workers …'.[25] For the uninitiated, the 'old hands' were to be looked up to as those who knew their way around the system. Although a challenge to existing institutional structures of training and management, it was clearly to the advantage of management if workers 'knew the rope to everything' (Glenda).[26]

The issue of helping each other out, thereby avoiding any loss of wages or reprimands from the supervisors, is balanced by the more negative forces of 'collective self-disciplining'.[27] As Joyce recalled, if someone was felt to be not pulling their weight, they would become the subject of abuse: 'Many a time I used to listen to arguments [puts voice on] "Hey! Pull your weight, pull your socks up and, you know, get on with it. I'm taking it all off at the back and you're doing all the talking, chattering. Stop it, or else we" …'. This was particularly an issue in those departments where wages and bonuses were on a group basis. Enforcing a group identity could therefore effectively fracture any broader potential unity on the basis of common oppressions.[28]

Those working around the conveyors were able to talk and even sing, though this was regulated to some extent if it was seen to interfere with productivity. Women's narratives indicated that such activities were not simply ways of relieving the monotony of factory work. Talking was a particularly highly-contested activity and there is confusion in accounts of whether or not it was allowed. Joyce remembered: 'We used to have little chatters on the quiet but we weren't supposed to'. Rather than stop talking, women had to become 'sly', as one woman put it, and continue conversations with their heads down.[29]

Quaker-influenced rules aimed to enforce decorum at all times: for instance the directive 'That packers conduct themselves in a decorous fashion especially in the matter of loud talking'.[30] Oral accounts suggest that not everyone conformed. As Joyce told me, 'Some were a bit rough and they used to swear to each other – you used to hear them shouting across to each other [laughs]. You used to close your ears to a lot of things'. There is a sense that this was expected behaviour from women who worked in a factory, even as the speaker subverts such expectations in discussing her own actions. Again, we see women negotiating with gendered perceptions of factory workers. The issue of swearing and of being cheeky remains an important aspect of women's sense of self according to whether or not they joined in; it was a challenge to the 'respectability' with which some women identified.[31] Joyce distances herself but, for others, learning to talk like the 'old school' was an aspect both of coming to terms with work in the factory itself and with the development of increased self-confidence. This was particularly marked in the narrative of Mary, who told me, 'I was getting more broad-minded than what I was before. So, I thought, I would stand up for myself and be cheeky, talking back to other people'. Gladys, meanwhile, vividly remembered an 'eye-opening' incident of an older woman defying factory rules on eating chocolates:

> Her jaws were going and t'overlooker passed and she said, 'Are you eating Mrs So and So?' But she was one of the old school, been there years, and she said, 'Yes, do you want one?' She offered her this big tray – she didn't know where to put herself …

The increased confidence gained at work could be carried on into a woman's home life, as she felt more able to talk back to her family. Shopfloor cultures may, therefore, have provided cultural resources for women outside the factory walls.

In gossip, the supposedly separate worlds of work and home life could intersect as women talked about their personal lives over the production line. Joyce remembered, 'Everybody used to talk about their boyfriends or their families or where they'd been, and what they did ...'. The outside world could even make literal inroads into the world of production, 'unknown to the charge-hand', in the material form of photos, letters and other items. In one sense this liberated the women from a sole concern with the products they were dealing with and encouraged the development of solidarity between them as they shared experiences. However, some women became the subject of gossip if they transgressed social rules. One woman remarked how, 'if anybody left because she'd got into trouble, you know, having a baby and that – Ooh, it was a big thing in those days, you know, it had to be hushed up more or less'. Speaking about the unspeakable gave some women power over others whilst reinforcing the hegemonic discourses of unmarried motherhood as shameful. A more obvious strategy of resistance involved talk that attempted to aid transgressions such as theft. There would be a 'buzz on', as Valerie described it, if an inspection was likely, in order to warn would-be thieves. In this way, as Patricia Spacks comments, gossip could be an effective 'resource for the subordinated'.[32]

Having a laugh and playing jokes had their serious side. Mary remembered the time when she got locked in the men's toilets, making her late for work, as simultaneously terrifying and ridiculous. Retelling the story in dramatic mode, she makes us acutely aware of the impact of being laughed at by other women:

> 'Where have you been?'
> 'Oh', I said, 'I can't tell you'
> 'WHERE HAVE YOU BEEN?'
> I said, 'Well, I can't tell you'.
> So, overlooker came, 'You're wanted at the desk'.
> When I went –
> 'Where have you been? Where have you been – for forty minutes?'
> 'Well', I said, 'I went upstairs and I went through a door and it locked on me and I couldn't get out and it was gents' toilets'.
> Well –
> She said, 'You won't do that again!'
> Mind they made fun of me for ages.

Reinforcing Mary's embarrassment by laughing at her mistake, her co-workers mitigated the need for any real punishment; the humiliation was punishment enough. Laughing at those who did not conform tended to reinforce hegemonic discipline rather than effectively subvert it. Nevertheless, as Paul Willis notes, 'the "laff" is the privileged instrument of the informal, as the command is of the formal'.[33] 'Having a laugh' allowed breaking out of the factory routine. In the form of being cheeky, it could also break down the institutional hierarchies which governed women's work.

Singing was generally an accepted and worthy activity in the eyes of the firm.[34] The phenomenon of a room of around 500 girls singing in unison was retold with pride by a young worker, Madge Munro, in a 1932 radio broadcast: 'they hear us all singing cheerfully at our work. You know the kind of song – "My gal's a Yorkshire gal" … with its kind words to the "factory lass". The line which makes many visitors smile is "Eh by goom she's a champion"'.[35] The song quoted is richly suggestive of regional, gendered discourses at play in its potentially ironic performance by women workers; as women singing about 'My Gal', they subvert the apparent heterosexual context of the song.[36] Singing was apparently the sign of a happy workforce whilst music was seen to encourage a better rhythm beneficial to the repetitive actions of conveyor line work. Indeed most women spoke of singing as 'part of liking it' (Kathleen) – something which contributed to their sense of enjoyment of work and to their conception of Rowntrees as a good firm. However, 'Music While You Work' – playing music over speakers in the workrooms – which was intended to keep up workers' spirits (and productivity) in wartime, was later stopped by some overlookers who felt it was distracting.[37] There seems to have been an implicit hierarchy here, with spontaneous outbursts of unaccompanied singing valued far more highly by management than simply singing along to the popular music of the post-war era. For the workers, however, popular music at work provided an opportunity to perpetuate the linkage of music and romance. Valerie recalled that 'a lot of the girls and boys that worked in the department were like boyfriend and girlfriend … if they knew it was their song they used to be waving to each other, stop work and just wave. We used to have a bit of good fun then'. Music could effectively disrupt production, yet it also aided the production of heterosexual romance. McRobbie and Garber recognise that girls' cultures may 'symbolise a future general subordination – as well as a present one'.[38] Whilst flirtations carried on during working hours were a method of resistance, heterosexuality could equally play a part in women's oppression both outside the factory, and in the sexual politics of the working world.[39]

Ruth Cavendish, in *Women on the Line*, remarked of her own time on the shopfloor that, 'Working on the line changed the way you experienced time altogether'.[40] Hours were re-divided with relation to the work she had to get through and rituals such as payday 'divided up the week'.[41] Celebrations of marriage, birthdays, retirement and leaving to have a baby provided a welcome break for the women at Rowntrees from the monotony of the factory routine, with 'privileges' such as being able to entertain friends in the canteen. Valerie described what happened when a woman left to get married: 'you would buy their lunches – so you would order it from the canteen and it would be sent up and you would have a little lunch with them in the work area. And that was given to you like a privilege'. The mass of presents received on such occasions was fondly remembered by all the women who had been at the factory: 'I had a really good start to me bottom drawer'. Marriage rituals also provided the opportunity for practical jokes. As Valerie recalled: 'by mischief, they would do something to you, or to your coat or whatever … They tied me up and they put all balloons on me coat'.[42] It is clear that these rituals were simultaneously disruptive and displays of conformity. The myths of romance and marriage, perpetuated through shopfloor rituals, were a distraction, but an accepted one, from the monotony of work. Women were being socialised into the patriarchal culture which existed both outside and inside the factory walls.

The ideal of leaving work on marriage was pervasive, encouraging women not to see their work as a long term part of their lives. As Kathleen told me, 'I said I was going to finish Rowntrees when I married but I didn't. I went back to buy two bikes and I was there 46 years after that'. There is a tension here between expectations of married life and the reality.[43] The ease with which Kathleen seems to have fallen back into work after her marriage in 1947 suggests that women workers were in demand at this time. Yet Rowntrees always perpetuated gendered ideologies of being good wives and mothers in the home through, for example, its school and journal. Such contradictory messages from the firm, reflecting the complex interaction between the demands of capitalism and patriarchy, have been internalised by the women themselves, emerging as a sense of wonder at the length of time they spent at Rowntrees despite their initial intentions. Of course, in the late 1940s and 1950s, women were also receiving conflicting messages about their roles from outside the factory. The pronatalism of the post-war period coincided with an increased demand for women workers in industry to rebuild the economy. As Bruley states, 'the biggest change in women's employment in the post-war years was the growth in numbers of married women workers'.[44] Yet this was not accompanied by a change in the perception of women's primary role as being in the home.

To conclude, it is clear that friendships and interactions with other women were central to these women's experiences of paid employment. Other studies of women workers have drawn similar conclusions. As friends and co-workers, women engaged in cultural practices such as gossip, singing, practical jokes and wedding rituals. Such actions were embedded in the gendered, classed and raced society in which they lived at the time and are (re)interpreted within the cultural context of the oral history interview. As members of shopfloor communities, women were reacting to the monotony of their work and the restrictions of factory regulations; but they also found genuine enjoyment in their tasks and exercised creativity and agency in their workplace cultures.

However, despite an overwhelming emphasis on the importance of camaraderie at the factory, the women I spoke with did not have an uncomplicated relationship to their co-workers. They had an explicit awareness of differences between them that worked against any attempts to categorise them as a homogenous group on account of their similar positions on the shopfloor. These differences were employed in the construction of their own identities, often to emphasise their 'respectability'. There was thus no consistent, unified version of a 'feminine' work culture, although socially-defined 'female' concerns relating to heterosexual romance, marriage and childbirth were important (working both to include and exclude). The recognition of 'difference' and the meanings this has for women workers clearly has resonance for any study of women's labour.

Keeping the issue of 'difference' in mind, friendship could have both positive and negative connotations. On the one hand, the actions of some women were a force in socialising others into an acceptance of the factory regime. On the other, socialising gave women the potential for solidarity in uniting against oppression, as well as providing strategies for resistance learnt from the 'old hands'. 'Socialising' thus has at least two related but different meanings: one repressive, the other liberating. In the oral histories I recorded, it is the positive aspects of 'camaraderie' that are emphasised in the women's narratives. I would not want to dismiss this as simply nostalgia but to recognise it instead as an affirmation of the agency of women themselves in managing work experiences. Workplace friendships have often continued into retirement, facilitated by these women living in York for most if not all of their lives. The importance of the Rowntree factory in York, not simply as a place of employment but as a symbol of the city itself, was reflected in women's engagement with discourses of company loyalty; in cities with a broader industrial base, this commitment to one firm as part of local pride is unlikely to be so pronounced. The locally-specific trope of Rowntrees as a 'good firm', which was so dominant in the majority of women's narratives, was often elided with memories of old friends. As Glenda commented, 'I loved working at Rowntrees, well, I loved the people there'.

Notes

1   This is an extract from one of 13 oral history interviews conducted in June and July 2000. All names have been changed to guarantee anonymity. All quotations in this chapter are taken from these interviews, unless otherwise indicated.

2   I use the term 'narrating' to highlight the ways in which meaning is being actively created during the oral history process. As Portelli asserts, 'memory is not a passive repository of facts, but an active process of creation of meanings'. A. Portelli, *The Death of Luigi Trastulli and Other Stories* (Albany, 1991), p. 52. I follow Caroline Daley in the use of the term 'oral history narrators' (as opposed to 'informant' or 'interviewee') as I agree that it 'recognises that the individual has some control over what they tell and how they shape their past'. Daley, '"He Would Know, but I Just Have a Feeling": Gender and Oral History', *Women's History Review*, 7, 3 (1998), p. 354. Of course, as the interviewer and the author of this chapter, I am also implicated and active in this creation of meaning; as is the reader of this chapter.

3   Sue Bruley, '"A Very Happy Crowd": Women in Industry in South London in World War Two', *History Workshop Journal*, 44 (1997), pp. 66–7. I would suggest, however, that some women at Rowntrees did indeed find satisfaction in the products they were producing. Ethel, for one, took great pride in making the patterns on individual chocolates for Black Magic, telling me how it was 'quite artistic'. The Rowntree management, unlike the wartime employers Bruley describes, also believed in educating workers as to the whole process of production, rather than simply their fragmented roles, and this may have facilitated greater engagement with the work itself.

4   S. Westwood, *All Day Every Day: Factory and Family in the Making of Women's Lives* (London, 1984), p. 89. Like Westwood, I am studying the way of life of women on the shopfloor: their workplace practices both as directly related to the work itself and in terms of their actions within work time more generally.

5   I contacted the women through family, friends and acquaintances. To make the interviews as relaxed as possible, I conducted them in the women's own homes on a one-to-one basis, spending a morning or afternoon with each woman (the interview itself lasting between an hour and an hour and a half). I adopted a life history approach, which allowed each woman to direct the interview to a certain extent, although I also had themes to cover such as 'rules' and 'wages'. The oral histories quoted in this chapter are all based on one interview with each woman; I have since been in contact with several of the interviewees on a less formal basis.

6   I would make no claims to having a representative sample of all the women who worked at Rowntrees. The research I am currently undertaking involves interviews with women who migrated to York from Europe and Asia before working at Rowntrees.

7   A. Pollert, *Girls, Wives, Factory Lives* (London and Basingstoke, 1981), p. 151.

8   Westwood, *All Day Every Day*, p. 22. The term 'patriarchy' needs to be used with care to discuss women's position since it may imply a rather one-dimensional power structure.

9   Westwood, *All Day Every Day*, p. 90.

10 Louise A. Tilly and Joan W. Scott, *Women, Work and Family* (New York, 1978), p. 79.

11 For detailed statistical analysis see Charles Feinstein, 'Population, Occupations and Economic Development', in C. Feinstein (ed.), *York 1831–1981* (York, 1981), pp. 140–41.

12 R. Fitzgerald, *Rowntree and the Marketing Revolution, 1862–1969* (Cambridge, 1995), p. 413.

13 See also Carol Kennedy, *Merchant Princes: Family, Fortune and Philanthropy* (London, 2000). Kennedy discusses the long-lasting influence of the Cadbury family and the Quaker ethos at the Bournville factory.

14 Fitzgerald, *Rowntree and the Marketing Revolution*, p. 223.

15 Benjamin Seebohm Rowntree, *The Human Factor in Business: Further Experiments in Industrial Democracy* (London, 1938), p. 99.

16 It was the Nestlé takeover, rather than the 1969 merger with Mackintosh, which figured most prominently in women's narratives despite the fact that all but one had retired by then.

17 Labour historians and sociologists have analysed extensively the increase in part-time, married workers after the war. See, for example, J. Lewis, *Women In Britain Since 1945* (Oxford, 1992) and V. Beechey, *Unequal Work* (London, 1987).

18 The extent of social divisions amongst factory workers is also apparent from testimony relating to work in wartime. Despite the assertion of class solidarity from official sources, women themselves have highlighted where there were conflicts between different groups, often based on notions of 'respectability' linked to regional identity as well as class. See Penny Summerfield, *Women Workers in the Second World War* (London, 1984), p. 56.

19 Given my focus here on white workers, this chapter is unable to examine the experiences of women who would not identify as such. However, it is also important to problematise 'whiteness' as a racial category, as discussed in H. Brown, M. Gilkes and A. Kaloski-Naylor (eds), *White?Women* (York, 1999).

20 Miriam Glucksmann, *Women Assemble: Women Workers and the New Industries in Inter-War Britain* (London, 1990), p. 261.

21 See Carl Chinn, *They Worked All Their Lives: Women of the Urban Poor in England, 1880–1939* (Manchester and New York, 1988), p. 91. L.A.G. Strong believes the 'Rowntree Girls' had a reputation as 'a rough crowd' in the past, a discourse which York women may have been working against. Strong, *The Story of Rowntree* (unpublished manuscript, 1948), p. 19. See Emma Liggins, this collection, for a study of the 'factory girl'/'work-girl' in the nineteenth century.

22 A. Phillips, 'Women on the Shopfloor: The Colchester Rag 1918–1950', *Oral History*, 22 (Spring 1994), p. 62.

23 Patricia Spacks, *Gossip* (New York, 1985), p. 5.

24 J. Martin Corbett, *Critical Cases in Organisational Behaviour* (London, 1994), p. 33.

25 Thomas Dublin, *Women at Work: The Transformation of Work and Community in Lowell, Massachusetts, 1826–1860* (New York, 1979), p. 73. Male workers, who may have been the fathers and brothers of young women workers, could also play a part in this. For those women whose family members worked at the Rowntree factory, family discipline often literally translated onto the shopfloor. The supposed boundaries between home and work disintegrated as misdeeds at work could be punished at home.

26 Cavendish has also commented on how informal training actually worked to the benefit of management. Ruth Cavendish, *Women on the Line* (London, 1982), p. 20.

27 Glucksmann, *Women Assemble*, p. 173. However, Glucksmann's assertion that 'the response was engendered by the system itself rather than by the women's personalities …' (p. 174) denies women agency in their response to collective discipline.

28 The group payment system had, however, been a response in some cases to the demands of the workers themselves: see Rowntree Archives, Borthwick Institute, University of York: R/DL/LS/1, Labour Research Reports, No. 1, c.1930.

29 Rules on talking at Rowntrees were by no means as strict as those at some factories, such as the Ford car manufacturing plants. Corbett highlights the 'Ford whisper' as one means of covert communication on the assembly lines, but suggests that even this was limited due to fear of disciplinary action. Corbett, *Critical Cases in Organisational Behaviour*, p. 129.

30 Rowntree Archives: R/DP/PC/23, Cream Packing Department, 'General Instructions for Overlookers, Chargehands etc., c.1929–1938', p. 6.

31 See Iris Marion Young, *Justice and the Politics of Difference* (Princeton, 1990), p. 137.

32 Spacks, *Gossip*, p. 5.

33 P. Willis, *Learning to Labour: How Working-class Kids Get Working-class Jobs* (Farnborough, 1977), p. 29.

34 In contrast, see Marek Korczynski on the banning of singing and music in factories influenced by Taylorism. M. Korczynski, 'Music at Work: Towards a Historical Overview', *Folk Music Journal* (2003), pp. 314–34.

35 'Madge Munro Talks to 2,000,000 People', *Cocoa Works Magazine* (hereafter *CWM*), Christmas 1932, p. 845. This magazine was given free to all employees four times a year.

36 Gill Valentine, 'Hetero(Sexing) Space: Lesbian Perceptions and Experiences of Everyday Spaces', in L. McDowell and J.P. Sharp (eds), *Space, Gender, Knowledge* (London, 1997).

37 The BBC broadcast 'Music While You Work' was a programme aimed at factory workers. Gramophone records were also used in a number of factories, including Cadburys and Horlicks.

38 Angela McRobbie and Jenny Garber, 'Girls and Subcultures', in Stuart Hall and Tony Jefferson (eds), *Resistance through Rituals: Youth Subcultures in Post-war Britain* (London, 1998), p. 221.

39 The issue of sexual harassment was not discussed by any of the women and this silence needs to be investigated.

40 Cavendish, *Women on the Line*, p. 112.

41 Ibid., p. 113.

42 Similarly, Westwood, *All Day Every Day*, describes the elaborate 'bride's rituals' which took place at the paternalist hosiery factory where she worked in the early 1980s.

43 Pollert, *Girls, Wives, Factory Lives*, p. 105, recognised that women's expectations of marriage held them back from dealing with injustices in the workplace.

44 Sue Bruley, *Women in Britain since 1900* (Basingstoke, 1999), p. 122.

PART III

YOUTH

Chapter 6

'You'd the Feeling You Wanted to Help': Young Women, Employment and the Family in Inter-war England

Selina Todd

Entering paid employment was a fact of life for most young women reaching the end of their compulsory schooling in inter-war England, with approximately 85 per cent of those who left elementary school going straight into paid work.[1] Over 60 per cent of young women between the school leaving age – 12 prior to 1921 and 14 thereafter – and 25, the average age of first marriage for women, were in full-time employment. Despite this, few studies of young women's work in inter-war England have been undertaken.[2] This is largely explained by women's short working lives. Their entry to employment was frequently attributed by contemporaries to their own lack of discernment and desire for spending money; young women allegedly treated their employment as, in the words of J.B. Priestley, 'a dreamy interlude between childhood and marriage'.[3] That young women's employment patterns were shaped primarily by personal consumption patterns has not been questioned by the limited historiography on youth, which has concentrated on the emergence of the youthful consumer, preceding the development of mass youth culture in the 1950s.[4]

This chapter questions that representation, suggesting that employment profoundly shaped social, economic and cultural aspects of young women's lives. It focuses particularly on the importance of familial need in shaping young women's entry to the labour force and employment choices, the impact of their employment upon their family relations and household role, and on the importance of wage-earning in the construction of youthful culture and identity. It suggests that young women's labour force participation and employment patterns were primarily shaped by household need; it argues that the transition from school to work did not mark a simple shift from dependency to independence; and it builds on local case studies undertaken by Alexander, Roberts and Sarsby in arguing that the demands of the labour market on the working-class household shaped a distinctive, working-class, youthful, feminine identity.[5]

In illuminating the links between economic conditions and the creation of cultural and social identity, this chapter draws on employment and earnings data provided by the Census and government records, on contemporary social surveys, and on 59 testimonies of women who were themselves young workers in inter-war England. Distinctions are drawn between juvenile girls and boys (those aged above the school leaving age but below 18) and young adult women and men (aged between 18 and 24) where necessary, although the majority of the study is concerned with young women across this age range. Personal testimonies have been selected from published autobiographies and archival life history collections, in order to construct a national sample. While the historian must engage as critically with life history as with other source material – and conclusions presented here are never exclusively based upon these testimonies – they are nevertheless valuable, both for the vivid recollections of youthful experience that they offer, and because they demonstrate that to many women, paid work retrospectively appeared central to their life experience.

Optimistic surveys of inter-war England imply that the economic importance of young wage-earners diminished over this period,[6] pointing to rising real wages, a narrowing of the earnings gap between skilled and unskilled manual workers as the latter's earnings rose, an accompanying fall in prices, increasing state welfare and the extension of unemployment insurance to almost all manual workers. Yet while such material improvements were highly significant, social surveys suggest that between 4 and 20 per cent of working-class households continued to live in poverty.[7] The major causes of this were adult males' low wages and unemployment,[8] indicating the potential value of supplementary earners to many households. The importance of young workers in this respect was highlighted by Rowntree, whose poverty cycle demonstrated that households' vulnerability to poverty declined significantly when children began work.[9]

Young wage-earners were thus of particular importance to households lacking a wage-earning, male household head, continuing a trend noted by Horrell and Oxley in the nineteenth century.[10] The sexual division of labour meant that paternal absence or unemployment generally increased economic pressure on their sons to a greater extent than on their daughters, as Eichengreen found in inter-war London.[11] However, daughters' ability to make a valuable economic contribution to working-class households increased over the inter-war years, particularly in urban labour markets. While poorly paid domestic service remained young women's largest employer, Table 6.1 shows that their opportunities for relatively well-paid factory, shop and clerical work rose. Moreover, the gender pay differential was far less significant among young workers than among adults, indicating that a child's earning potential, and thus decisions about their labour force participation, were not determined exclusively by their sex. In 1935 women over 18 had mean weekly earnings of 31s 3d, just 48 per cent of adult men's (64s 6d), whereas younger women earned 71 per cent of young men's weekly earnings (16s 4d compared with 22s 11d).[12] While sons were often a greater long-term economic asset to households, gender did not exert a decisive influence on short term earning power.

Young women were also less vulnerable to unemployment than adults or young men. In November 1931, 13 per cent of girls were unemployed compared with 16 per cent of boys, and this differential increased over subsequent years, as girls' unemployment fell at a faster rate.[13] Young women's lower medium- and long-term earning potential was, then, at least partially compensated for by a greater likelihood of obtaining and retaining a job. In the late 1920s and early 1930s, paternal unemployment raised the value of a daughter's paid work. The establishment of a household means test, which assessed an individual's benefit entitlement in the context of all household earnings, increased this pressure. An investigation into the survival strategies of 2,354 disallowed unemployment benefit claimants across England in 1931 found that 83 per cent of them were supported by other people, mostly relatives.[14] Peggy recalled that when, as a teenage factory worker in the mid-1930s, she received a wage rise, means test regulations meant that her unemployed father's dole money was stopped: 'he cried like a baby and so did I, he fetched me out of work to tell me … and I said "It don't matter daddy, it don't matter, we'll get through somehow, we'll get through somehow"'.[15] Contemporary investigations, such as that undertaken by Beales and Lambert, indicate that Peggy's example was typical, and highlight that by forcing paternal dependency on children the means test could severely strain familial relations.[16]

While their presence was often essential in households living on the poverty line, relative affluence did not necessarily reduce young women's labour force participation. Married women's paid employment was frequently a short-term response to particular hardship, and only 10.4 per cent were recorded in the labour force in 1931.[17] Conversely, daughters' economic contribution was considered essential to the everyday running of many working-class households, explaining their higher rate of labour force participation. From

Table 6.1 Age distribution of women workers in selected occupations, 1931

Occupation	Total women	Girls	Girls as % total	Young adult women	Young adult women as % total	% Young women occupied	Change in % young women occupied, 1921–31[a]	Change in % young women occupied, 1931–51[b]
Metals	96120	20403	21.23	41255	42.92	1.61	–.31	.31
Textiles	574094	62327	10.86	166122	28.94	5.97	–1.98	–2.51
Textile goods	542809	101714	18.74	171703	31.63	7.15	.02	–.99
Paper/printing	63994	16555	25.87	23516	36.75	1.05	–.86	.28
Transport/communication	68899	18112	26.29	20765	30.14	1.02	–.05	.73
Shop assistants	394531	86624	21.96	171873	43.56	6.76	1.26	2.01
Domestic service	1332224	210376	15.79	428681	32.18	16.71	2.33	–12.92
Other personal service	594754	49054	8.25	120857	20.32	4.44	1.53	–.08
Clerks/typists	579945	86710	14.95	239726	41.34	8.54	.85	13.35
Warehousemen/packers	155784	45517	29.22	63328	40.65	2.85	.47	–.55
Occupied	5606043	848737	15.14	1772913	31.63	68.56	5.43	3.23
Unoccupied	10804851	477028	4.41	725102	6.71	31.44	–5.43	–3.23
Total	16410894	1325765	8.08	2498015	15.22	100.00	.00	.00

Notes

a 'Girls' refers to 12–17-year-olds in 1921
b 'Girls' refers to 15–17-year-olds in 1951

the mid-1930s, young workers' earnings became increasingly important in enabling households to engage in luxury consumption. The economic recovery meant that by 1936, Bowley recorded the average weekly income of working-class families as 76s. This included a margin of 20s for leisure and luxury consumption.[18] Yet this margin was too large to be entirely accounted for by mean adult male earnings, which were under 65s per week.[19] Many households clearly relied upon supplementary earners to achieve Bowley's margin, highlighting that household breadwinning strategies continued to be 'pluralistic and multifaceted',[20] and challenging the correlation of femininity with domesticity implied in many existing studies of inter-war gender relations.[21]

Entering employment did not grant young workers full independence, but it was recognised as a transition from dependent schoolgirl to breadwinner by many women. Fowler has suggested that by the 1920s, the main appeal of work was the opportunity to earn some spending money,[22] and this certainly was an attraction for many. Nellie Hilton recalled that she voluntarily became a half-time mill worker at the age of twelve in the early 1920s, although her mother told her she did not need to, because: 'I saw these [mill] girls, being, "oh, I'm getting so much money"'.[23] However, the great majority of my sample recognised the need to earn their keep, and many welcomed the opportunity to 'repay' their parents for their childhood dependency, expressing the reciprocity of familial relationships. Many, like Dolly, who began factory work in Manchester in 1938, viewed wage-earning as an opportunity 'to put something back into the house'.[24] Mrs Hevness was aware that when she entered residential service in the mid-1920s her family 'were glad to get rid of me, because I had four other sisters and two brothers, and times were very hard'.[25] Most young women felt that their contribution of earnings was a necessity for their own and their household's welfare.

Entering employment was considered a step towards adulthood for young women in most communities. The reciprocal relationship that was established between wage-earning daughters and their parents is demonstrated by the operation of the family economy. The widespread practice of young workers 'tipping up' their weekly earnings to the household budget, and receiving in return a proportion as spending money, recently highlighted by social historians, is recalled by my own sample.[26] Household need and level of earnings primarily determined the amount of spending money they received.[27] Juveniles were expected to contribute the majority of their earnings to the household economy, receiving between 6d and 5s weekly spending money.[28] In their late teens and early 20s young workers' earnings rose, and the proportion they retained as spending money generally increased, enabling young women to become 'relatively privileged consumers of leisure',[29] although they were frequently expected to pay for clothes and travel expenses out of this. As Rowntree noted of working-class York households, family composition was also important, with younger siblings benefiting from the ongoing contributions of older brothers and sisters.[30] However, gender was less important in determining levels of financial independence. Although the family budgets presented in Rowntree's study indicate that many young men received slightly more spending money than young women of the same age, this reflected the gender differential in earnings rather more than parental bias towards sons. As Claire Langhamer has stressed, leisure was a reward for paid work.[31] Granting young workers some personal independence helped to build a reciprocal relationship that could bring long term benefits for parents, encouraging young earners to remain resident in the household until marriage, and to continue to offer economic and emotional support even after they had left home.

The relative value of a young woman's financial contribution to her household, her choices of work and the longevity of her working life were all clearly shaped by household need. However, they were also strongly affected by her regional location, demonstrating that no uniform sexual division of labour existed. Hatton and Bailey's study of the 1931 Census demonstrated that local male employment and earnings opportunities, together with family size, strongly influenced married women's labour force participation rates.[32] Young, single women's higher rate of labour force participation, which exhibited more limited regional variance, and was less affected by such variables as paternal unemployment or family size, means that this type of comparative, county-level quantitative analysis would be of limited value to the current study. However, close scrutiny of local case studies can offer some indications of the household and county-level factors which influenced young women's labour force participation and shaped their limited choices of jobs, as well as providing more insights into their economic value to different households.

Three provincial case studies are presented here, of Northumberland, Blackburn and Coventry, drawing on Census data from 1921 and 1931. They demonstrate that local labour demand not only affected young women's employment and earning patterns, but also shaped social and cultural gendered and age-specific roles in the household and wider community. Northumberland's strong sexual division of labour was typical of many rural localities, and indicates how the interaction of domestic responsibilities with the needs of the family budget shaped girls' labour force participation.

Blackburn, conversely, recorded the highest rate of adult female labour force participation of any English county in both Censuses and provides information on how mothers' labour force participation affected girls' employment patterns. Finally, Coventry offers an example of a relatively buoyant city, where young women's earnings were crucial to the expansion of working-class leisure and luxury consumption. Juvenile girls are the focus, since the Census offers detailed records of their employment at local level.

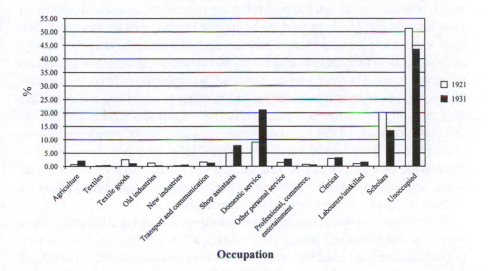

Figure 6.1   Occupational distribution of girls, Northumberland, 1921 and 1931

Source: Census of England and Wales, 1921, County Table for Northumberland (London, 1923), table 18; Census of England and Wales, 1931, Occupation Tables (London, 1934), table 18.

In rural and mining communities, limited local employment for women and the traditionally high wages of miners increased reliance on male breadwinners. In Northumberland, where 34 per cent of men were employed as miners, just 7 per cent of women were engaged in employment, and 43 per cent of girls compared with 78 per cent of boys. The strong sexual division of labour in many mining and agricultural areas reduced the incentive to send a daughter into the workforce, a major reason why 21 per cent of girls who had left school were unoccupied in 1931 across England, compared with just 6 per cent of boys. In such communities maintaining a daughter at home denoted respectability, which in this localised context signified male breadwinning but also a maternal need for domestic help in large households. Forty-nine per cent of Northumberland girls were unoccupied in 1931, but personal testimonies and social surveys indicate that most enjoyed less leisure time than employed siblings, with some becoming 'the family drudge'.[33]

Despite this, few households could afford to support a large number of non-earners, and the relatively large size of mining families encouraged daughters' employment as residential domestic servants, a low paid occupation but one which provided board and lodging, relieving spatial and financial demands on poor households. The long working hours and low pay of servants meant that they were unable to make a very significant contribution to the family economy, and did not benefit from spending money or experience the increasing amount of leisure enjoyed by young office, shop and factory workers, who, by the mid-1930s, were benefiting from reductions in working hours, rising wages and the proliferation of cinemas and dance halls.[34] As domestic service declined as an employer in the 1930s, and more young women entered employment, due to an increase in industrial, retail and clerical jobs, so a more homogeneous experience of youth began to emerge, but it remained fractured by social class, and was characterised for working-class girls by economic and social responsibility as well as a degree of independence.

In communities where households required more than the adult male wage, women's and juveniles' labour force participation was higher. This pattern prevailed in many Lancashire textile towns, like Blackburn. In 1931, the largest employer of men was the textile industry (22 per cent) and unskilled labouring (14 per cent). As a result, 62 per cent of women and 79 per cent of both girls and boys were engaged in paid employment. Most girls entered the textile industry where there was greater gender equality in earnings than in most other industries, and many expected to remain in full time employment after marriage.[35] One lace worker from Nottingham, where a similar employment pattern prevailed, explained that she continued working after her marriage in the 1930s, with the support of her spouse, because, 'if you're a lace worker, you're a lace worker, its in you and that's it'.[36]

Here, as in Northumberland, the value of girls' earnings to their households changed over time. Young textile workers were vulnerable to unemployment in the late 1920s and early 1930s, but the fact that they *had* to work for economic reasons is highlighted by the concurrent increase in the proportion employed in personal service, from 2 per cent in 1921 to 6 per cent in 1931. The decline in the proportion of unoccupied girls over the same period strongly suggests that the unemployment of other household members prompted girls to enter the

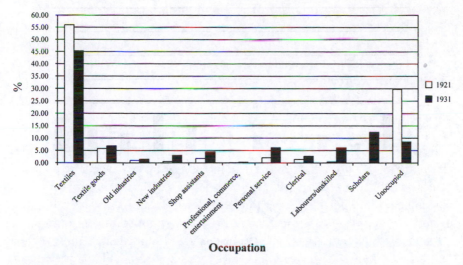

Occupation

Figure 6.2   Occupational distribution of girls, Blackburn, 1921 and 1931

Source: Census of England and Wales, 1921, County Table for Lancashire (London, 1923), table 18; Census of England and Wales, 1931, Occupation Tables (London, 1934), table 18.

labour force in areas where jobs were available; the rising proportion employed as shop assistants and factory workers testifies to the gradual expansion of light industry in the north west, which accelerated in the late 1930s, and to the attractiveness of cheap girl workers for employers.

In areas where a significant proportion of men were skilled workers, young women often ceased full time work upon marriage, but their earnings still had great short term value. In Coventry, 38 per cent of men were metal workers, earning relatively high wages, and only 22 per cent of adult women were in the workforce. However, 75 per cent of girls and 90 per cent of boys were in the labour force. The largest employer of Coventry boys was the metal industry, but most of those employed were engaged on apprenticeships, entry of which was restricted to 15- or 16-year-old boys. Many boys who left school at 14 entered 'blind alley' employment – 14 per cent were messenger boys – to mark time before competing for an apprenticeship, leaving girls, 75 per cent of whom entered employment, to occupy secure, relatively lucrative, semi-skilled jobs in the textile industry (19 per cent) and clerical sector (17 per cent). The low wages of metal apprentices enhanced the value of a daughter's employment. The increase in light manufacturing jobs and particularly in

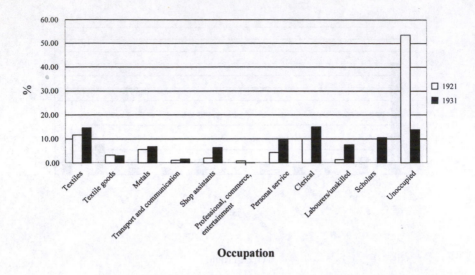

**Figure 6.3   Occupational distribution of girls, Coventry, 1921 and
1931**

Source: Census of England and Wales, 1921, County Table for Warwickshire (London, 1923),
table 18; Census of England and Wales, 1931, Occupation Tables (London, 1934),
table 18

retail and clerical work from the mid-1930s meant girls' earning potential
continued to increase.

The relatively high labour force participation of girls in Coventry reflects
a pattern identified by Horrell and Oxley in late nineteenth-century England,
where rises in the standard of living did not reduce, but were in fact largely
dependent upon, children's employment. Their dataset recorded high rates of
juvenile participation among certain relatively well paid groups of industrial
workers, indicating that economic security and material improvements in the
standard of living were frequently valued more than an adherence to a sole,
male breadwinner model which frequently could not deliver affluence.[37]
This trend clearly continued as socioeconomic aspirations rose in the 1930s.
Young women's employment thus helped to shape and realise working-class
material aspiration by the late 1930s. The ways in which it influenced and
was shaped by their own personal hopes and identity formation will now be
examined in greater depth.

Personal consumption did not prompt young women's entry to
employment, but how far did personal aspiration interact with the needs of

the family economy and with labour demand in shaping the occupational choices of this group? While state involvement in the juvenile labour market increased over the inter-war period, its effects remained limited, with less than 35 per cent of school leavers finding a job through an employment exchange by the late 1930s.[38] Kinship networks remained the most common form of occupational recruitment throughout the period.[39] Employers supported this practice, which enabled them to select workers according to family background and income level. Young women were aware that they 'had to be a good type' to obtain popular, secure, semi-skilled employment and attributed a failure to get such jobs to a lack of family contacts, suitable clothing or travel expenses.[40] Such demands, and the wider influence of relatives on the job search, shaped young women's own choices of and perspectives on employment, with paid work becoming increasingly central to their aspirations. The testimonies cited here cannot provide exhaustive explanations for the occupational choices of this group, but the examples given do nonetheless provide insights into the subjective motivations of individuals, from which a number of common themes emerge concerning attitudes towards employment and the interaction of work with gender and class in the formation of a youthful, feminine identity.

Mothers were particularly influential in shaping a daughter's occupational expectations and experiences.[41] Mothers made daughters aware from an early age that social distinctions were denoted by cleanliness and behaviour;[42] consequently cleanliness was valued in the workplace, one Coventry factory worker commenting 'Nice girls didn't work in factories but Courtaulds was different, it was a women's factory'.[43] Security was also of importance; a Ministry of Labour investigation into vocational training highlighted that by the mid-1920s long-term security was often valued more than skill or wages due to employment.[44] Another consideration was a daughter's safety, both physical and moral. Janet, who grew up in a Nottinghamshire village, wanted to enter shop work in a Nottingham store, but this was too far from home for her mother's liking: 'when I was going to work in Nottingham she says, "I'm sure you're not, you're going to factory or else!"'.[45] Such testimonies emphasise the youth of these wage-earners and the fact that decisions about employment were not entirely directed by norms of respectability. Sarsby's conclusion that in the Potteries, working women and their communities adopted a pragmatic and flexible approach to respectability and conformity can be applied to many of my sample, for whom it is clear that job choices involved a careful evaluation of the consequences of a job for a daughter's welfare and for her family's income, as well as for a household's social standing.[46]

As this suggests, definitions of respectability varied according to local employment opportunities and a family's social status. The concern that Roberts found amongst women from relatively affluent, skilled working-class families regarding respectability and the establishment of collective, fairly inflexible, moral values,[47] is not evident among Sarsby's poorer sample, nor among many of my own, particularly those affected by unemployment or low wages. Poverty inspired pragmatism. Generally, however, both poor and more affluent working-class women viewed respectability as closely allied with escaping poverty, rather than with attaining middle-class status – an important difference. While clerical work was generally considered the pinnacle of respectable employment, other occupational distinctions were ambiguous. Marion Kent's mother sent her into domestic service because she considered local factories 'rough',[48] a typical rationale for such a choice.[49] In contrast, as Roberts has shown, mothers in areas offering relatively clean light manufacturing work, or non-manual employment, might favour this over residential service because it offered higher wages, meant that daughters could remain in the parental home, offering domestic help and companionship, until marriage; and was considered socially superior to service by many urban women.[50]

As daughters grew older, marital considerations became more important. Maternal concern to secure a daughter's happiness could be combined with the knowledge that an economically secure child might offer financial as well as emotional support to ageing parents. A 'good match' could mean a middle-class marriage – Dolly Scannell's mother was one of many to view her daughter's office job as a 'wonderful opportunity' partly because it enabled Dolly to meet middle-class men[51] – but more usually meant finding a man who had the ability to be a good provider. Hilda Ashby, who grew up in a Northumbrian mining village, recalled that in the early 1930s:

> if you went to a dance and you met a boy, the first thing you'd ask – 'Are you working?' Oh, if you could get a boy friend who was working you knew you were quids in! … when I started going with Jock Marshall, my father said 'What are you doing with him? He's not working.' You had to look for a man who was working.[52]

The wage packet alone did not define a good provider, however. As Davies and Roberts have noted, women were aware that male expenditure on drink or gambling could be as detrimental to the family economy as low wages, and many of my sample cited a commitment to finding and keeping a job, and to household saving, as qualities that attracted them to their husband.[53] Mrs Hughson almost left her fiancé because although he was relatively well paid he rarely took the initiative in such matters as saving for marriage and 'he wasn't making a more business-like a method of [flat-hunting]'. She believed that her ultimatum, combined with her decision to move from full-time domestic service to part-time charring in order to help flat-hunt, prompted her fiancé to set a date for their wedding and to participate more actively in planning for the future.[54] A man's occupation was only one of several criteria that defined his worth.

Daughters' aspirations were influenced by maternal hopes, but also by a desire to escape the poverty their mothers endured. Expanding earning and employment opportunities became increasingly central to the realisation of such hopes. Many young women attributed their employment choices to a desire for financial independence.[55] Doris Knight, for example, took up a vocational scholarship rather than attend an academic high school because she believed dressmaking would give her independence and satisfaction, while enabling her to make ends meet more satisfactorily than her mother had done.[56] But aspirations were also nebulous. Histories of youth have tended to divorce the worlds of work and commercial consumption, foregrounding the latter in analyses of identity formation. In reality, clothing, courtship and earning a living were closely intertwined, as Alexander's study of inter-war London indicates.[57] Nellie Oldroyd aspired to office work because 'I did want to sit in an office, in a white shirt and black skirt, and be somebody, not work in a mill'.[58] Ann Smith, herself a mill-worker, emphasised the importance of her own move from a mill where workers wore clogs and shawls to one 'a bit cleaner' where workers 'could wear coats and hats … it was much nicer then'.[59] The expansion of relatively clean, secure, well-paid work was thus an important factor in the emergence of the modern, independent young woman, defined by a degree of social and financial independence unknown to many of her mother's generation.

Young women's ability to achieve these aspirations changed over time, pointing to a generational shift in employment patterns and expectations, and in the wider social and cultural experience of youth. Many of those who began work in the 1920s found that their aspirations, raised by industrial expansion during the First World War, were thwarted by inter-war employment contraction and by poverty. A large number articulated disappointment that the family economy had had to take precedence over their ambitions. Many domestic servants, including Lavinia Swainbank and Mrs Cleary, recognised that their occupation was primarily determined by lack of alternative employment and household poverty.[60] In the early 1920s Winifred Cotterill was unable to take up a desired Post Office job because factory work paid more and her family required the wages.[61] The family economy continued to constrain girls' personal aspirations into the 1930s. The Ministry of Labour found that low income households prioritised sons' work-related expenditure over daughters' in areas where young women's employment was low paid or unlikely to continue into adulthood, limiting their options to jobs not requiring travel or smart clothes.[62]

Women who worked in the later 1930s benefited from employment expansion, but their choices remained constrained by social background. Many presented their increasingly varied employment pathways as a successful struggle against the odds. Eileen worked in factories, offices and a hairdresser's salon in Nottingham during the 1930s; she viewed this as 'making ends meet, its trying to push on a bit better, to try to get a better standard of living each time'. Stress was placed in her account as in many on the need for 'ingenuity and economy',[63] grounded in a recognition that, in Dolly's words, 'a lot is where you're brought up – the little narrow place you see, what your parents have done. You're expected to go into a certain little niche'.[64]

Unsurprisingly, given their low earnings, and the sexual division of adult labour in many communities, young women continued to focus aspirations for independence on marriage and courtship. However, their own wages were increasingly considered important in achieving material aspiration and making a good match. Young women increasingly equated marriage with buying or renting their own home by the late 1930s[65] due partly to large scale housing development,[66] but also to their expanding earning opportunities. For Dolly, as for many young women, 'My ambition was to have a nice home, more than ever when I started work'.[67] Many of these women clearly felt more strongly than their future husbands about the value of acquiring 'a home of their own', as Giles and Whitworth have highlighted.[68] Many Coventry factory workers recalled long engagements because 'you had to go courting a few years to save' for a deposit on a house.[69] But an increasing number of women did not have to wait until marriage to realise some material aspirations. While histories of youth have often emphasised generational conflict, the testimonies studied here indicate that collective and consensual strategies for family improvement were common. Dolly's aspiration for a home of her own was shared by her mother, and was realised while Dolly was still living with her parents because 'several of us were out at work by then'.[70] Girls were brought up to value reciprocity in family relationships and to relieve their mothers' responsibilities. This obligation constrained their choices, as the experiences of Lavinia Swainbank and Winifred Cotterill suggest, but could also benefit strategies for self improvement, particularly as access to leisure and luxury consumption expanded from the mid-1930s.

The relationship between young women's employment and the emergence of the modern, independent young woman demonstrates the importance of economic factors in shaping age and gender specific social roles. Entering employment did not mark an escape from parental constraint into personal affluence, but led to the establishment of a reciprocal social and economic relationship between children and parents which has been overlooked by existing histories of youth which frequently emphasise generational conflict. However, the value of their employment, and the lived experience of youth, varied according to locality as well as household need, shaping distinct age and gender specific roles. What most young working women did share was an awareness that their employment and wider lifestyle choices were limited by their household's needs and by their expectation of short working lives. Consequently, while most enjoyed the social and financial independence increasingly available to them as young, single workers, this was accepted as a temporary life stage, with marriage promising the fulfilment of their major social and cultural aspirations.

Notes

1   Report of the Board of Education for the year 1926–27 (PP 1928, ix, Cmd 3091), p. 121; Report of the Board of Education for the year 1937 (PP 1937–38, x, Cmd 3776), p. 96.

2   Those which have been invaluable local case studies include: S. Alexander, 'Becoming a woman in London in the 1920s and 1930s', in S. Alexander (ed.), *Becoming a Woman and Other Essays in 19th and 20th Century Feminist History* (London, 1994); E. Roberts, *A Woman's Place. An Oral History of Working-class Women 1890–1940* (Oxford, 1984), pp. 39–80; J. Sarsby, *Missuses and Mouldrunners: An Oral History of Women Pottery-workers at Work and at Home* (Milton Keynes, 1988), pp. 50–81; and on Scotland, J. Smyth, '"Ye never got a spell to think aboot it." Young Women and Employment in the Inter-war Period: A Case Study of a Textile Village', in E. Gordon and E. Breitenbach (eds), *The World is Ill Divided* (Edinburgh, 1990), pp. 95–116.

3   J.B. Priestley, *English Journey* (London, 1934), p. 133.

4   J. Bourke, *Working-class Cultures in Britain 1890–1960* (London, 1994), pp. 45–6; A. Davies, *Leisure, Gender, Poverty: Working-class Cultures in Manchester and Salford, 1900–1939* (Buckingham, 1992), pp. 83–9; D. Fowler, *The First Teenagers: The Lifestyle of Young Wage-earners in Inter-war Britain* (London, 1995), pp. 99, 110–11; C. Langhamer, *Women's Leisure in England c.1920–1960* (Manchester, 2000), pp. 101–3.

5   Alexander, 'Becoming a Woman', pp. 213–15; Roberts, *A Women's Place*, pp. 68–70; Sarsby, *Misuses and Mouldrunners*, pp. 71–6.

6   J. Stevenson, *British Society, 1914–1945* (Harmondsworth, 1984), p. 116; Fowler, *The First Teenagers*, p. 111.
7   A.L. Bowley and M. Hogg, *Has Poverty Diminished?* (London, 1925), pp. 12–17; H. Llewellyn Smith, *New Survey of London Life and Labour*, 9 vols (London, 1932), III, pp. 78–96 (hereafter *NSLL*); D. Caradog Jones, *The Social Survey of Merseyside*, 3 vols (Liverpool, 1934), I, pp. 156–60; P. Ford, *Work and Wealth in a Modern Port: a Survey of Southampton* (London, 1934), pp. 114–16; B.S. Rowntree, *Poverty and Progress* (1941, London), pp. 30–31; H. Tout, *The Standard of Living in Bristol* (Bristol, 1938), p. 21.
8   Rowntree, *Poverty and Progress*, p. 51; Tout, *Bristol*, p. 44.
9   Rowntree, *Poverty and Progress*, pp. 155–71.
10 S. Horrell and D. Oxley, 'Breadwinning, Family Employment and Household Resource Allocation', in C.E. Nunez (ed.), *The Microeconomic Analysis of the Household and the Labour Market, 1880–1939* (Seville, 1998), p. 53.
11 B. Eichengreen, 'Juvenile Unemployment in Twentieth-century Britain: The Emergence of a Problem', *Social Research*, 54, 2 (1987), p. 288.
12 Ministry of Labour, 'Average Earnings and Hours Enquiry', October 1935, published in *Ministry of Labour Gazette* (February–July 1937).
13 M. Thomas, 'Labour Market Structure and the Nature of Unemployment in Inter-war Britain', in B. Eichengreen and T.J. Hatton (eds), *Inter-war Unemployment in International Perspective* (London, 1988), p. 116.
14 C. Cameron, A. Lush and G. Meara, *Disinherited Youth: A Report on the 18+ Age Group Enquiry Prepared for the Trustees of the Carnegie United Kingdom Trust* (Edinburgh, 1943), p. 70; Rowntree, *Poverty and Progress*, pp. 188–9; A. Deacon, *In Search of the Scrounger* (London, 1976), p. 66.
15 Nottingham Local Studies Library (hereafter NLSL), Making Ends Meet Oral History Collection, transcript no. A66/a, interview with Peggy.
16 H.L. Beales and R.S. Lambert (eds), *Memoirs of the Unemployed* (London, 1934), pp. 20, 40–41, 82–7; W. Hannington, *The Problem of the Distressed Areas* (London, 1937), pp. 46–8; Pilgrim Trust, *Men Without Work* (Cambridge, 1938), pp. 147–8; Cameron et al., *Disinherited Youth* (Edinburgh, 1943), p. 75; J. Beauchamp, *Working Women in Great Britain* (New York, 1937), p. 51.
17 'Occupation Tables', *Census of England and Wales 1931* (London, 1934), Table 5.
18 A.L. Bowley, *Wages and Income in the United Kingdom since 1860* (Cambridge, 1937), p. 39.
19 Ministry of Labour, Average Hours and Earnings Enquiry, October 1935, *Ministry of Labour Gazette* (February–July 1938).
20 S. Horrell and J. Humphries, 'The Origins and Expansion of the Male Breadwinner Family: The Case of Nineteenth-Century Britain', *International Review of Social History*, 42 (1997), p. 64.
21 See for example D. Beddoe, *Back to Home and Duty: Women Between the Wars 1918–1939* (London, 1989).
22 Fowler, *First Teenagers*, p. 29.
23 Lancashire Record Office (hereafter LRO), North West Sound Archive (NWSA), 1999.0340, interview with Nellie Hilton. See also East Sussex Record Office (ESRO), Archive of the University of the Third Age: Lewes and District Branch, Lewes in Living Memory Collection, AMS 6416/1/7/51, interview with Joan Perry.
24 Lifetimes, *Something in Common: A Group Biography* (Manchester, 1975), p. 35.
25 NLSL, Making Ends Meet collection, A78/a/1, interview with Mrs Hevness.

26   Davies, *Leisure*, p. 91.

27   NLSL, Making Ends Meet, A14/a/2, interview with Eileen; see also A66/a/1, interview with Peggy.

28   Langhamer, *Women's Leisure*, pp. 100–101; Rowntree, *Poverty and Progress*, p. 27.

29   Davies, *Leisure*, p. 81.

30   Mass Observation Archive, Worktown collection, Saving and spending, 28/B, Untitled family budgets; Rowntree, *Poverty and Progress*, pp. 78–93, 127–42; Davies, *Leisure*, pp. 84–5; Smyth, '"Ye Never Got a Spell Tae Think Aboot it"', p. 106.

31   Langhamer, *Women's Leisure*, p. 50.

32   T.J. Hatton and R.E. Bailey, 'Female Labour Force Participation', *Oxford Economic Papers* (Oxford, 1988), pp. 711–12.

33   R. Roberts, *The Classic Slum* (Harmondsworth, 1973), p. 53; L. McCullough Thew, *The Pit Village and the Store* (London, 1985), p. 124.

34   On this point see S. Todd, 'Young Women, Work and Leisure in Inter-war England', *The Historical Journal* (forthcoming).

35   J. and S. Jewkes, *The Juvenile Labour Market* (London, 1938), pp. 16–17; Roberts, *Woman's Place*, p. 36; NLSL, Making Ends Meet, A85/c/1, interview with Edna.

36   NLSL, Making Ends Meet, A85/c/1, Edna.

37   S. Horrell and D. Oxley, 'Crust or Crumb? Intra-household Resource Allocation and Male Breadwinning in Late-Victorian Britain', *Economic History Review*, 52, 3 (1999), p. 496.

38   Ministry of Labour, *Report of the Committee on Education and Industry*, 2 vols, I (London, 1926), p. 221; J. Gollan, *Youth in British Industry* (London, 1937), p. 244.

39   Ministry of Labour, *Education and Industry*, I, p. 221; Jewkes, *Juvenile*, p. 34.

40   NLSL, Making Ends Meet, A14/a/2, Eileen.

41   R.L. Miller and B.C. Hayes, 'Gender and Intergenerational Mobility', in G. Payne and P. Abbott (eds), *The Social Mobility of Women: Beyond Male Mobility Models* (London, 1990), pp. 61–3.

42   Roberts, *Classic Slum*, pp. 125–35; E. Ross, 'Survival Networks: Women's Neighbourhood Sharing in London Before World War I', *History Workshop Journal*, 15 (1983), p. 14.

43   Modern Records Centre, University of Warwick (MRC), Coventry Women's Work Collection, Interview with Elsie, MCS 266/6/5.

44   Ministry of Labour, *Report of an Enquiry into Apprenticeship*, 8 vols (London, 1928), VII, p. 166.

45   NLSL, Making Ends Meet, A80/a/1, interview with Janet.

46   Sarsby, *Missuses and Mouldrunners*, p. 4.

47   Roberts, *Woman's Place*, pp. 163–201.

48   LRO, NWSA, 1999.0060, Marion Kent.

49   Tameside Local Studies Library (hereafter TLSL), Manchester Studies Tapes, tape no. 36, interview with Edith Edwards; Roberts, *Woman's Place*, p. 54.

50   Roberts, *Woman's Place*, p. 62.

51   D. Scannell, *Mother Knew Best* (London, 1974), p. 163.

52   H. Ashby, 'Wait till the Banner Comes Home!', in K. Armstrong and H. Benyon (eds), *Hello, Are You Working?* (Whitley Bay, 1977), p. 42.

53   See for example D. Bailey, *Children of the Green* (London, 1981); Scanell, *Mother*; Elsie, in Lifetimes, *A Couple from Manchester* (Manchester, 1976).

54   TLSL, Manchester Studies, tape 26, interview with Mrs Hughson.

55 Lifetimes, *Something in Common*, p. 11; Lifetimes, *A Couple From Manchester*, pp. 36-40.
56 D. Knight, *Millfield Memories* (London, 1976), pp. 12 and 34.
57 Alexander, 'Becoming a Woman', pp. 213–15.
58 N. Oldroyd, 'Sweetmaking', in R. Van Riel (ed.), *All in a Day's Work* (Wakefield, 1985), p. 7.
59 LRO, NWSA, 1995.0125, interview with Ann Smith.
60 TLSL, Manchester Studies, tape 28, interview with Mrs Cleary; L. Swainbank, 'Housemaid', in J. Burnett, *Useful Toil* (Harmondsworth, 1974), p. 221.
61 MRC, Coventry Women's Work Collection, MSS 266/6/2, letter from Winifred Cotterill to J. Castle, 1982.
62 T. Young, *Becontree and Dagenham* (London, 1936), pp. 121–2.
63 NLSL, Making Ends Meet, A14/a/2, Eileen.
64 Quoted in Lifetimes, *Something in Common*, p. 35.
65 J. Giles, *Women, Identity and Private Life in Britain 1900–1950* (Basingstoke, 1995), pp. 62–8.
66 J. Burnett, *A Social History of Housing 1815–1970* (David and Charles, 1978), p. 246.
67 Lifetimes, *Something in Common*, p. 15.
68 Giles, *Women, Identity and Private Life*, pp. 64–78; L. Whitworth, 'Men, Women, Shops and "Little Shiny Homes": The Consuming of Coventry, 1930–1939' (PhD, University of Warwick, 1997), pp. 126–31.
69 MRC, Coventry Women's Work collection, MSS 266/6/4, interview with Mrs Johnson.
70 Quoted in Lifetimes, *Something in Common*, p. 16.

Chapter 7

'Be Yourself': *Girl* and the Business of Growing Up in Late 1950s England

Stephanie Spencer

Girl, a weekly illustrated paper for the 12 to 15 age group, offers an insight into the discourse concerning the teenage girl about to enter the world of work and adulthood in late 1950s England. Published by Hulton press, it was a sister publication to the popular boys' paper *Eagle*. In the late 1950s the image of the average reader offered by *Girl* was a pony-tailed, pleated-skirted, innocent but adventure-loving young adolescent. Closer reading suggests that the wider prevailing representation of adult femininity was a fragile one which required a degree of commitment and work, both by those who wanted to achieve the status of 'woman', and by those with a vested interest in maintaining it. Representations of accepted images of womanhood are powerful and can be difficult to challenge and as such, images within popular culture should be taken seriously by historians.[1] The recognition that all representations are cultural constructions enables the historian to interrogate the transparency or superficiality of apparently simple images and to analyse the complexity of their production. Representations of the adult woman, the adolescent girl or the schoolgirl must be acceptable both to those who produce the image (the editors and advertisers) and to those who buy and consume the product. Both parties will draw on familiar contemporary discourses and both are then implicated in the process of production through a process of dual authorship.

This chapter provides a detailed analysis of *Girl* magazine, focusing on three forms of representation: advertising, advice features and fictional narratives. More broadly, it explores the way that growing up and becoming a 1950s woman was constructed as a business, not only in terms of the financial implications of the rising teenage consumer market identified by Mark Abrams,[2] but as a full-time occupation with its own rules, standards and expected remuneration of husband and family. If work is understood as an activity that supports living, learning a femininity acceptable to post-war society was necessary for the ultimate formation of a family unit of male breadwinner and non-working wife discussed later in this chapter. As Judy Giles argues elsewhere in this book, the role of domesticity for women in the 1950s must be understood as part of a general commitment towards building a better future. Women's and girls' part in this process cannot be read simply in terms of false consciousness or hidden agenda forcing women back into the private sphere of the home. How were concepts of independence and autonomy, once the privilege of the waged worker, built into the 1950s domestic model? A review of the different representations of the teenage and young adult female in the pages of *Girl* offers an insight into the complex business of achieving adult femininity in the late 1950s.

The feminist literary historian Sandra Gilbert states 'I believe that all work around gender is cultural, political and theoretical'.[3] Conceptualisations of gender cannot be isolated within one academic discipline but draw on theoretical perspectives from within history, sociology and cultural studies. In addition, definitions of 'work' which depend upon binaries of public and private, paid and unpaid are unsatisfactory explanations in terms of women's experience. Girls' magazines as one aspect of popular culture offer a snapshot of teenage concerns on entering adulthood. Through fiction, advice and advertising these ephemeral publications reflect the negotiation into the world of work and the construction of adult identity. Becoming a woman was not something which simply happened to teenage girls in the late 1950s; it required a period of apprenticeship and instruction.

I have written previously on the relationship between imagined and everyday experience in teenage girls' formation of adult identity.[4] The following discussion of *Girl* also focuses on the interrelationship between the reader and the representation. The transient nature of a girls' comic suggests that the textual and visual images drew on contemporary, easily recognisable and above all, uncontested constructions of the female teenager. By interrogating these representations it is possible to identify the multiplicity of agents which produced the monolithic *Girl* without forgetting the individual girl herself. Research into popular culture recognises the relationship between the individual and the media text in contrast to a radical post-modern view which would argue that meaning is only locally produced.[5] The role of the reader as an individual and as an imagined group is integral to the formation of these representations. The comic and the women's magazine were a significant part of 1950s popular culture and should not be read merely as quasi-educational texts which 'conned' young girls and women into the role of housewife and mother. Neither are they only a vehicle for increased consumerism in the form of advertising. Anna Gough Yates is adamant that women's magazines, and I would add, teenage publications, are firmly in the cultural realm. They may be market-led but also depend heavily on 'social and cultural processes for effective operation'.[6] Joke Hermes has offered a stringent critique of some feminist readings that emphasise the reactionary nature of women's magazines. She argues that readers are 'the producers of meaning rather than the cultural dupes of the media institutions'. The following chapter reflects a similar approach towards *Girl* in the 1950s.[7]

William Beveridge's blueprint for the Welfare State in 1943 declared that the women of Britain had 'important *work* to do in ensuring the adequate continuance of the British race and British ideals in the world'.[8] As Jane Lewis has observed, 'Beveridge clearly highlighted the needs of race and nation for women's work as wives and mothers, rather than the needs of women as individuals'.[9] The type of woman required for this work, was assumed to privilege her domestic duties above paid employment; she assumed a 'new identity' upon marriage and was ideally able to depend economically upon a sole male breadwinner. A large part of her adult life may not have been spent in paid employment, but domesticity was clearly constructed as work, in terms of duties, expected parameters, and as part of the Beveridge notion of the married couple as a 'team'. Such a construction was implicitly middle class and Martin Pugh has noted how magazines promoted the hegemony of the middle-class values of domesticity, which confirmed a fairly unchanging view of the adult woman's gender role.[10]

With such clear-cut expectations for adulthood, the period of the teenage years became one of apprenticeship for the imminent work of full-time housewife and mother. However, co-existing images of rebellious youth demonstrate that this domesticity was under threat and by no means taken for granted.[11] Following the raising of the school leaving age to fifteen in the 1944 Education Act and a demographic trend towards early marriage and child-bearing, the time between school-leaving and motherhood was reducing dramatically. Indeed it was a major impetus behind the Crowther Report on the development of education between 15 and 18 in 1959.[12] Girls in Secondary Modern schools received a curriculum weighted towards the domestic. Grammar school girls, following a more academic curriculum, nevertheless generally devoted some time to domestic science classes. At the same time the advent of the Youth Employment Officer and the widening of employment opportunities for school leavers did present an alternative future. The ideals of paid employment in terms of status and autonomy were integrated with domesticity within the pages of *Girl*, most of whose middle-class readers were ultimately likely make the choice between career and family.[13]

The relationship between the readers and the producers of women's magazines is one that has been explored at length by Marjorie Ferguson, Janice Winship and Cynthia White.[14] The 1950s saw the readership of women's magazines peak with five out of every six women reading a magazine by 1958, indicating that these publications are worthy of consideration.[15] For most of the 1950s there were few publications aimed directly at older teenage girls as consumers and as mini-adults although periodicals such as *Valentine* and *Roxy* focused on fiction cartoon strips, films and the emergent pop music business. Connie Alderson's research on *Trend*, *Jackie* and *Valentine* in the late 1960s highlighted the significance of these teen publications in informing the teenager how her personality could be improved by changes in her outward appearance of 'dress, hairstyle, make-up, speech and jargon'.[16] The varied content of *Girl*, in contrast to that of *Valentine* and *Roxy*, allows for a wider analysis of the way that this important information was conveyed. *Girl* focused less on pop music and film and explicitly romantic story lines; the fiction ranged from adventure stories to boarding school escapades, the heroines were themselves clearly middle class as demonstrated by the homes they lived in, the language used and the schools they attended. Mothers in the stories reflected the domestic priorities of Judy Giles's analysis. Alderson notes the rigidity of the social class structures within the comics; fictional heroines do not stray beyond their immediate social circle. The middle-class nature of *Girl* may be particularly useful as a case study given Pugh's recognition of the hegemony of middle-class values promoted in women's magazines. Acceptance of a future focused on domesticity clearly did not preclude *Girl* from a representation of careers and paid work for young women as part of their entry to womanhood.

It might initially appear that *Girl* target readership was younger than that of *Roxy* or *Valentine*. This may reflect difference in social class more than chronological age. Whereas working-class readers may have left school and entered employment by the age of 15, middle-class readers of *Girl* were likely to have several years left in formal education. The readers' letters pages and the problem pages of *Girl* give some idea of the age of the readership and these demonstrate that the 14 to 16 age group were regular readers. Dawn Currie has suggested that teenagers read magazines in a different way to adults, using them as vehicles for their own constructions of femininity.[17] Early work on teenage magazines considered that girls might be somewhat passive in their reception of instruction from the publications.[18] Recent studies indicate that girls are more proactive in their reading, but nevertheless use periodicals to inform their construction of femininity.[19] Currie's research amongst teenagers shows that girls read the questions in the problem pages in order to confirm their own construction of the 'norm' and are less interested in any answers. Although her work focuses on current reading habits, her general comments are pertinent for considering the teenage readership of the 1950s. To what extent did the magazines merely reflect the business of growing up, and to what extent did they in any way influence the individual?

Currie, like Penny Tinkler, suggests that the 'map of adolescence' was not as simple as it might appear.[20] Using content analysis and interviews it became clear in Currie's research that teenagers negotiated with these texts, and did not unquestioningly absorb the views promoted in the magazines. She concludes that 'teenzines' provided a 'frame of intelligibility' within which girls could make sense of their world.[21] The frame of intelligibility in *Girl* contained various representations, most of which could also act as instructions or guides to the workplace of middle-class womanhood.

The *Journal of Education* discussed 'good' adolescent periodicals in September 1957. At a 'Comics to Classics' conference, Marcus Morris (editor of *Girl*) commented that the lack of a 'good' periodical was due to lack of awareness on the part of advertisers that teenagers might be a substantial target marketing group.[22] The author of the article suggested that adolescents did not relate to the notion of a gap between childhood and adult status, being content to move from comics to adult magazines, although Abrams's 1959 research on the teenage consumer would seem to make this a somewhat problematic statement.[23] Again there may well have been a class difference between working-class teenagers with earned disposable income (for purchasing *Valentine* and *Roxy*) and middle-class girls still at school, reliant on 'pocket-money' and parental approval for their purchases. The middle-class values apparent in *Girl* may therefore reflect the existing expectations of the adult role rather than a rebellious challenge to the established order.[24]

Advertising

It was revenue from advertising that supported the publication of *Girl* for the apprentice 'woman'. Advertising therefore had to reflect the expectations of a specific age group as well as to 'educate' them into the ways of the consumer. Advertisements varied between whole page spreads that almost crossed the boundaries into feature articles, to small inserts for stamp clubs, geometry sets and chocolate bars. Two advertising features, chosen for discussion here, focus on choice of clothes and represent the young teenager as an embryonic adult. In the third advertisement for toffee we are offered the reader-as-child, still primarily interested in school and hockey. Hence the advertisements also reflected different ages of readership. The first, an advertisement for Harlee coats and suits was presented in terms of a competition.[25] Readers were presented with drawings of eight coats for girls up to 12, and four for girls between the ages of 12 and 15. The first prize for putting the coats in the 'correct order of merit' was £50, a not inconsiderable amount of money in 1956 when chocolate bars cost 2d and the publication itself only cost 4½d. Readers were told 'You may get your Mummy to help you', offering the mother an opportunity to educate her daughter in the ways of established fashion sense. It is immediately striking just how similar these coats were to the adult fashions of the time. Only the young facial features present the models as anything other than middle-aged women. Three pictures offer jackets and pleated skirts and all the models wear gloves. The girls are posed in an adult stance and, although their hairstyles reflect their young age, they are very similar to the formal adult styles popular at the time. When exactly were the girls to have worn such garments? They appear to presuppose formal shopping trips or church-going, constrained activities which would not impair their elegance. The phraseology is also couched in adult terms; 'elegant', 'smart', 'impeccably styled', 'three-way swagger' (would a 12-year-old today even recognise a three-way swagger?). Indeed these girls bear more resemblance to their older sisters going to work than the off-duty school girls who were also candidates for the *Girl* Adventurer of the Week prize.

Two other advertisements highlight this apparent ambivalence between educating girls to be 'grown up' and appealing to their identity as youngsters still interested in toffee and hockey. The first, an advertisement for the Berlei Teen Form Bra reflects the expectations of the Harlee advertisement, encouraging girls towards the construction of their adult identity. The boundary between identity and appearance is blurred, 'See how the other girls envy your grown-up look! You'll be thrilled at how gorgeously "grown-up" you *feel*'.[26] The girls were still expected to be young as it was assumed that they would be accompanied by their mothers on shopping expeditions. The design on the Teen-Form is interesting as it features 'embroidery with dainty dancing dolls' appealing to the woman and the (female) child at the same time. The suspender belt is called 'hey day' and in the picture, presumably for modesty, is shown worn *over* the petticoat, but it might have been somewhat confusing for the young teenage reader. However, the underlying message is that the adult female figure needs care, control and consideration. The advertisement also offered readers the opportunity to send for a free booklet offering '25 secrets of good grooming', a workshop manual for the novice apprentice.

A Palm Toffee advertisement, offered a very different representation from the previous two.[27] A very young girl, with bow in hair, rosy cheeks and wide innocent eyes declares 'after hockey my goal is Walkers Palm Toffee'. As 'Peggy Palm' she is cast in the mould of the schoolgirl heroines of the picture strips. Her face has lost none of its childish round features, and clearly her preoccupations are sport and team games over boys and grooming. In the background, stylised hockey players sprint towards a goal, all still managing to look neat and tidy and very much the women of tomorrow. The advertisement is placed next to a half page feature 'What's Your Worry?' which tackled readers' queries on hairstyles, relations with adults, friendships and outings. The ambivalent transitional nature of teenage girlhood is apparent in this juxtaposition, suggesting uncertainty but also conformity to prevailing norms.

Currie highlights the importance of magazines as sources, not simply because of their reflection of social mores as participants in popular discourse but 'because they are produced in the service of capitalist production'.[28] The advertisements' place in initiating the young readers, not only into the expectations of social roles but into the 'norm' of capitalism also shaped women's relationship to the means of production from an early age. Janice Winship noted how magazines as ideological constructions work at both conscious and unconscious levels to 'smooth over experiential contradictions of women's lives'.[29] The advertisements in *Girl* that are discussed briefly here offer an example of these contradictions for teenagers, as they sought to make the transition from childhood to adult.

Advice Features

The advice features in *Girl* often lay on the borders between advertising and editorial copy. During this period the number and size of the advice features on personal appearance and problems increased, with a specific fashion page being introduced from June 1958. Two regular features were drawn picture strips 'Mother Tells You How' and 'Concerning You'. Both were engaged in instructing the teenage reader into her expected adult role. On 14 November 1956 the seven-frame picture strip in 'Mother Tells You How' illustrated a conversation between mother and daughter. Daughter has admired her grandmother's lacy shawl and mother informs her that it is made in daisy work and shows her how to make a fascinator (in the form of a triangular scarf). The setting is highly domesticated; daughter is unpacking her suitcase (presumably after visit to granny) helped by mother. They are almost indistinguishable in terms of dress and hair, both impeccably groomed, mother perhaps with ear rings to denote her status. The sense of identity and continuity between generations is perhaps surprising to a modern reader as first, mother's advice is actively sought (and taken!) but in addition, granny's daisy shawl is to be admired and imitated. The depiction of leisure time as usefully employed is another reflection on the domestic destination of the heroine.[30]

In 'Concerning You', another picture strip placed on the bottom half page of 'Mother Tells You How', the 12–15-year-old is presented as a mini-adult, working at her figure in a way that was repeated dozens of time in the adult magazines *Woman* and *Housewife*. The focus for the same week as the daisy work discussed above was good posture. Readers were told 'no single factor is more important as a help to health and good looks'. Again granny was set as an example, 'In grandmother's day, young ladies practiced walking with books on their heads. It's still good advice!' The feature instructed the reader not to wear high heels too early and not to stand with her shoulders forward with her weight on one hip. An exercise which 'straightens your spine, flattens your stomach and gives you a trim waistline' followed and the final advice was 'Do remember that whatever sort of figure you have, if you hold yourself properly you will always curve in at the waist. Quite a thought, isn't it?' There is a degree of ambivalence between the highly constructed and instructed nature of femininity implicit in the two features discussed and the headline of the feature which forms the title of this chapter which proclaimed 'Be Yourself!'[31] In this feature a teenage girl was warned not to copy older sophisticated women's looks but at the same time the constructed nature of approved young femininity is clear in the sub title 'Virginia Grey tells you how to find the REAL you!' The 'real' you had also to conform to accepted ideals of teenage girlhood.

Page-long features on the problems of growing up focused the reader on the business in hand. The problems of adolescence in terms of clashes with parents, the right age to have boy friends and 'infatuation or love?' all presupposed a burgeoning heterosexuality in a reader who bought a comic largely full of fiction strips about air hostesses, nurses and school girl heroines.[32] The assumption of future roles is clearly stated:

> Obviously at any age from about 9 onwards, girls start picking their favourites from among the boys they see around them ... Finally – going steady. There can be no doubt that most girls today want to start going steady too young.[33]

Although the feature advised girls *against* getting too serious too young, the underlying message was more to do with developing judgement about boys' characters (so that girls would be ready when the time for a relationship came) than challenging the prevailing expectations of early marriage and settling down.

Fashion features, like the Harlee advertisements, offered girls a scaled down version of their mothers' fashions. When advising readers on a new dress for autumn Marjorie Elliot wrote:

> A dress, like a chameleon, can change its appearance according to the accessories … It can be worn coatless on warmer days, with a hat and gloves for church or shopping expeditions – or, plus a stiff petticoat and some simple jewellery for an informal party.[34]

A nod in the direction of youth is given when the article continues 'Most girls don't follow fashion in the way that some adults do, but all the dresses I have selected this month have an up to date look'. But again, nothing came easily to the girl involved in the metamorphosis to adult:

> Do practice good deportment, so that you stand and move gracefully; these models are just not for slouchers and bouncers … Hardy Amies once said that if a girl has a neat waist then the size of her hips is immaterial. Consequently it is worth cutting out sweets and doing a few posture exercises daily to ensure that your waist is as neat as you can make it. A becoming and well-cut dress is certainly worth a little discipline on the part of its owner.[35]

The didactic tone of the advice offered contrasts with later teen magazines, which seek to collude with the reader using teenage language and phraseology. Alderson notes how the teen magazines in the 1960s created their sense of community by speaking in the same vernacular as their readers. In *Girl* the advice offered is much more hierarchical. The (male) editor wrote a letter each week to the readership telling them of new developments. The editorial staff may have been sympathetic to teen attitudes but they were emphatically not one of the group. This reflects the status of the young reader – she still had a long way to go before she successfully completed the construction of her adult persona. One device for keeping the reader aware of her lowly status was in terms of highlighting the mistakes she might make. Virginia Gray the beauty editor admonished Susie for her negligent attitude in a way not dissimilar to an end of term school report. Despite being fair and slender with sparkling eyes and a sense of fun 'Susie had somehow overlooked the fact that even natural good looks have to be worked at ... she seems sublimely unconscious of tousled hair and uncared for complexion ...'.[36]

Fictional Narratives

It seems that before getting anywhere near the world of paid employment, girls were introduced to the ongoing nature of the work of being a woman, which would continue in addition to periods of paid employment, or in their roles as wives and mothers. Fictional narratives in *Girl* that appeared alongside the advertisements and features ensured that the heroines reflected appropriate ideals of femininity whether at school, at work or even on safari in deepest Africa. Advertisements and features presented a fairly sophisticated representation of the 1950s teenage school girl, yet the fiction appears to draw from a different discourse of youth; less that of an embryonic adult, more a specific space for learning, not only the outward appearance of a woman but also an educative space for character building. The heroines of the stories exhibit characteristics which might appear to be ungendered but they have a resonance with the British ideals implied by Beveridge in his description of the role of post-war womanhood; stiff upper lip in the face of adversity, pluck, daring, a sense of fair play and good always triumphing over evil. These ideals had been present in girls' schoolgirl fiction from Angela Brazil to the *Chalet School* stories and the contemporary Enid Blyton's *Mallory Towers* series. The heroines of the picture stories in *Girl* are shown at school, preparing for work, in work and some are fortunate enough not to have to work (like Vicky and her father Professor Curtiss who faced 'the Vengeance of the Incas' in January 1956).

The schoolgirl heroines whose adventures were chronicled weekly in *Girl*, like Wendy and Jinx of Manor School, invite reader identification. Whatever tight fixes they get into, they are usually wearing their school uniform and clearly not part of the adult world. They solve mysteries and problems without help from well meaning but usually meddling adults, always triumphing in the end. Lettice Leafe, 'the greenest girl in the school', is a more humorous version of the young school girls and the accompanying tribulations and pre-occupations of that role, 'Gosh, it's a wizard dinner uncle, we've got chicken, trifle, jellies, the lot!'[37] These stories are nearly always set against a school background and boarding school was, judging from the letters' page, not an unusual experience for the reader. Even for those without personal experience of boarding school, the genre was familiar enough to offer a comfortable background to adventure and daring exploits.

Massoni confirms that even today 'we know almost nothing' about the relationship between teen magazines and occupational aspirations.[38] The following comments offer some tentative suggestions for a historical approach to this debate. The role of paid employment for middle-class girls presented the editors of *Girl* with a dilemma. Representations of paid employment demonstrated how these learned characteristics might be put to good use upon school leaving but the end of the 1950s also witnessed an increasingly short amount of time between girls leaving school, marrying and starting a family. If *Girl* was to draw on recognisable cultural expectations as I argue earlier in this chapter, presenting a heroine who did not conform to type might not find favour with the readers. *Girl* readers might not have attended a boarding school but the depictions of school life would have been recognisable and familiar given the popularity of boarding school fiction. A storyline which challenged the ultimate goal of domesticity was more problematic. The variety of employment opportunities for women of all social classes expanded rapidly in post-war Britain against an economic background of full employment. At the same time the increased availability of labour saving and consumer goods together with luxuries like foreign package holidays encouraged housewives into the workplace in exchange for 'pin money'. The notion of a full-time continuous 'career' was still contentious in the face of prevailing literature which stressed the need for full-time mothering but a part-time job to supplement the family income was an acceptable expectation.[39]

The Association of Headmistresses was especially concerned at the number of girls leaving grammar school before taking O'levels or progressing into the sixth form and frequently discussed ways in which to encourage girls to take their future careers seriously.[40] According to the pages of *Technical Education* young girls in the late 1950s had a difficult balancing act to perform '[T]he modern girl is expected to earn her own living, which may involve entering almost any occupation on a competitive basis with the opposite sex ... she is also expected to retain her womanliness, to dress with taste, and eventually marry and organise a household'.[41] *Housewife* a glossy magazine aimed at the middle-class market ran a series 'Careers' intended to offer advice to their readers' daughters. The necessary link between a brief spell in employment and eventual domesticity was emphasised in this description of medical auxiliary work, 'A girl who takes up a medical auxiliary career, any one of which is eminently worthwhile, feels such a sense of vocation, that the monetary rewards will be a secondary consideration'.[42]

The publishers of *Girl* were not slow to see the opportunity presented by changes in middle-class job expectations and published the *Girl Book of*

Careers. This was a small publication which offered information on different types of job alongside a picture strip which illustrated a girl engaged in that profession. The careers or jobs covered the whole spectrum from beauty salon work to medicine. The pull of domesticity was dealt with in the editorial preface, 'The aim of many girls when they leave school, is to take up work which will be 'useful' in one way or another, when they get married. This is a good thing to do, but sometimes it leads to a great many possible careers being overlooked'.[43] It is perhaps unsurprising that the careers followed by the *Girl* heroines do reflect traditional expectations. Jobs are shown as being hard work but still remain sites for the representation of femininity. Susan of St Brides as trainee nurse was one of the main storylines of the paper. It was made clear that Susan was not simply filling in time before marriage; she took her job seriously and is often shown studying in favour of socialising. However, despite being depicted as a very good and conscientious student it is significant that Susan is training to be a nurse and not a doctor like her father. While the story writers were happy to establish a family tradition of medicine, the role of nurse as carer and supporter was more in keeping with notions of femininity than the long term commitment of a career in medicine.

Improvements in education and employment prospects led to a number of sociological surveys of school children and their attitude to work and career choice in the 1950s.[44] The pattern of career choice appeared to change from fantasy glamorous occupations (ballet dancers) to more realistic jobs (nurses) as children grew older. Thelma Veness's observation on girls' career choice was clearly reflected in the fiction of *Girl*:

> [T]here is little doubt that marriage and maternity is the central objective of the 'average' girl and that all other ambitions are centred around this central objective in an entirely rational way. She sees herself leaving school to take a job in which she can 'keep neat and tidy' and enjoy companionship. (She is not greatly attracted to the needle trades in which there is a sexual imbalance in the labour force.) She marries at 21, and often returns to her job which she must relinquish when her children come. When these children can be taken off her hands for most of the day she may again return to work.[45]

One popular representation in *Girl* fiction was the glamorous young adult heroine of the picture stories who followed the 'heterosexy' model of the career novel characters identified by Liladhar and Kerslake.[46] I have discussed elsewhere the way that these novels worked out the tension between career and domesticity in terms of plot lines which included boyfriends conveniently posted overseas and the *Girl* stories employed similar conventions. Having confirmed their heroines' undoubted heterosexual femininity, boyfriends stay in the background or rescue them from the distraction of unsuitable male companions.[47] *Girl* heroines act as independent young women, again demonstrating pluck, fair play, integrity in the face of adversity, but there is never any doubt that they will ultimately conform to the discourse of domesticity. The central characters are unremittingly (upper) middle class, young and attractive; Air-Hostess Angela returns home to a large house complete with maid, Susan of St Brides' father is a GP in a very pleasant leafy suburb (and Susan inevitably wins the 'nurse of the year' medal). They are always immaculately dressed in either an attractive feminine uniform which shows off their curves or the type of clothes promoted in the fashion pages.

The career of air-hostess in the 1950s was one filled with glamour and a world outside the mundane, yet it was also one which might be within the reach of the readers of the magazines. It still confirmed feminine attributes of service and the importance of feminine appearance was as necessary as any academic qualifications. More difficult for readers to identify with were the stories about girls of the same age but in far-away or unlikely circumstances. These were represented by Claudia of the Circus (an orphan who lives with Count Boselli and his wife) and Belle of the Ballet and her friends at the Arenska Dancing School. Perhaps these stories were designed to appeal to the younger readers who were still at the fantasy stage of their career expectation. Valerie Walkerdine also highlights the significance of these fantasy narratives for younger girls as a way for them to 'engage with difficult emotions' in their psychic development.[48] Despite their distant and somewhat fantastic settings the heroines still demonstrate the desirable traits of their home-bound sisters.

Conclusions

Good sense and fair play always triumph in the stories. The boundary between fantasy and reality was a fluid one but the advice pages were on hand to clarify the distinction. In 1956 a reader, perhaps unsettled by some of the more bizarre adventures in the fiction wrote to 'What's Your Worry?' 'I am rather a romantic and would very much like to have an exciting kind of job. What do you suggest I do?' The answer brought the reader straight back to earth, 'What makes life exciting is the attitude we have to it, and whether or not we take the opportunities that come along. It does not always have to depend on finding a really romantic and exciting job'[49] and that is the message loud and clear at the end of each storyline; it is girls' character, self reliance and moral values which are universal whether in Timbuktu or nursing in a provincial hospital. By default these admirable characteristics are also those which may be carried seamlessly into the domestic world of the mature woman.

The problem page 'What's Your Worry?' introduced topics that were later covered by more extensive features. Girls' concerns covered areas of female friendship, boyfriends, career choice and the angst of changing from teen to adult. Readers were also invited to send in letters of general interest about their pets, hobbies and day-to-day incidents. 'Adventure Corner' featured 'girls who lead interesting lives' and the *Girl* 'Adventurer of the Week' could be awarded for anything from helping regularly at home to saving a little boy from drowning. Competitions, often sponsored by manufacturers, were another device for involving the readership in the content of the paper and ensuring that the girls were educated into their adult role as consumers by close reading of advertising material. Coates cotton sponsored the sewing competition which, readers were told, attracted numerous entries. The editors were quite overt about the cooperation between readers and publishers: 'We want *Girl* to be your paper so please go on writing to us about it, even if you want to complain'. They did not however, attempt to break down the barrier between the producers and consumers in the same companionable tone that magazines like *Sugar* use today. It was a paper produced *by* adults *for* young girls and as such contained necessary information for their social and cultural education. One who did complain to *Girl* was Mary Tandy who wrote 'I'm Sorry I Was Born A Girl', a full length feature for 28 May 1960. Her article illustrates the strength of the representation of femininity at the time:

> Who would take seriously an announcement that the University Boat Race would take place this year between the women's colleges of Oxford and Cambridge? We aren't supposed to be able to think as well as boys either. Perhaps, in a hundred years time, when we have women bishops, women Prime Ministers and women road workers, things will be different.[50]

In August the paper printed a selection of responses, some agreeing with Mary and some not:

> I think men should be respected because they help the woman and work for her, manufacturing clothes and household needs ... a woman should find out her mistakes and correct them so that her man will love her more.

> If we get married, the man has most of the money worries.

> Now that I am growing up I have to care more about my appearance. Although
> I do not want to bother about clothes, I must, because after all, we must keep
> up with the times.[51]

What is striking about those selected for publication is that the correspondents do not challenge the prevailing notions of femininity, only articulate whether they like having to conform to them. It should not be assumed that girls were passive consumers of advice; they also contributed towards and confirmed the prevalent discourse of femininity.

Dorothy Smith notes that: 'In exploring femininity I do not view it simply as an effect of patriarchal oppression. Apart from avoiding the treatment of women as passive victims, it is important I believe, to recognise women's active and creative part in its social organisation'.[52] I have explored some of the representations of femininity which were present in *Girl* in the 1950s and suggested that, in all their diversity, they combined to demonstrate to their young readership the work that was involved in becoming a woman, who had a valued part to play in post-war British society. Nevertheless, readers themselves contributed to and were implicated in this construction. The work involved in finding a coherent and acceptable identity within the apparently diverse representations on offer was one that clearly found a resonance with the readership. There was a great deal of interaction between the paper and the readers; readers' contributions were encouraged and there were a great many competitions for drawing, sewing and writing. The *Girl* Adventurers' Club and letters' pages all actively sought readers' complicity within the maintenance of the discourse. For a payment of 1s 6d readers could become members of the *Girl* Adventurers' Club with its special offers, competitions and birthday presents, all of which contributed to a sense of belonging to a corporate identity. They also of course ensured a weekly purchase of the club paper. *Girl* even offered weekends away and local table tennis tournaments, another indication that the readers were assumed to be at least in their mid-teens. Membership lasted until the reader's seventeenth birthday, indicating the range of readership. It is significant that the readers' contributions did address the diversity of the representations offered by the copy.

Little has been written about *Girl* since Hemming's analysis of the problem pages.[53] It is apparent that the readers did indeed engage with the discussions on these pages; Hemming confirms that the letters were both genuine and numerous. Women's magazines have come under scrutiny for the part they play in maintaining and creating the icon of femininity identified by Marjorie Ferguson and this analysis has recently been extended to include 'teenzines'.

Dawn Currie's research suggests that care must be taken not to assume that teenagers use magazines as instruction manuals in the same way as adult women. The teenage magazine's role in either challenging or confirming current representations of femininity is becoming a popular area of debate.[54] The extent to which these analyses may be used as theoretical frameworks for a 1950s publication so palpably different from *Girl* may be questionable. They do however, highlight the active relationship between the reader and the text and the significance of using them as source material. This chapter has addressed three aspects of *Girl* in the 1950s; the advertisers, features and fiction together with an overview of the readers' contributions. Although there is wide diversity in the superficial representation of the adult or young adult in these pages, it becomes apparent that the expectation of domesticity and an unchanging assumption of the nature of femininity underpinned a vast majority of the copy. However all-pervasive this may have seemed, the paper clearly intimated to its young middle-class readership that before they could contemplate entering the world of paid employment they had a considerable amount of work to do in ensuring that they conformed adequately to the prevailing discourse. In doing so, of course, they also worked to maintain its dominance into the next decade.

Notes

1   Kimberley Oliver highlights how hard it is to persuade adolescent girls to challenge images of 'ideal' womanhood in magazines in 'Images of the Body from Popular Culture: Engaging Adolescent Girls in Critical Inquiry', *Sport, Education and Society*, 6 (2001).

2   M. Abrams, *The Teenage Consumer* (London, 1959).

3   M. Demoor and K. Heene, 'State of the Art. Of Influences and Anxieties. Sandra Gilbert's Feminist Commitment', *European Journal of Women's Studies*, 9 (2002).

4   S. Spencer, 'Schoolgirl to Career Girl: The City as Educative Space', *Paedagogica Historica*, 39 (2003).

5   J. Hermes, *Reading Women's Magazines* (Cambridge, 1995), p. 13.

6   A. Gough-Yates, *Understanding Women's Magazines: Publishing, Markets and Readerships* (London, 2003), p. 6.

7   Hermes, *Reading Women's Magazines*, p. 5.

8   Report on Social Insurance and Allied Services, Cmd 6404 (London, 1943).

9   J. Lewis, *Women in Britain since 1945: Women, Family, Work and the State in the Post-war Years* (Oxford, 1992), p. 92.

10 M. Pugh, *Women and the Women's Movement in Britain, 1914–1959* (Basingstoke, 1992), pp. 292–3.

11 T.R. Fyvel, *The Young Offenders: Rebellious Youth in the Post War Welfare State* (London, 1963). Fyvel noted how troublesome 'Youths' were predominantly male. See

also S. Weiner, *Enfants Terribles, Youth and Femininity in the Mass Media in France, 1945–1968* (Baltimore and London, 2001).

12   Ministry of Education, *15–18, A Report of the Central Advisory Council for Education (England) (The Crowther Report)* (London, 1959), vol. 1.

13   Despite the rhetoric of secondary education for all, the grammar and secondary moderns divided along the lines of social class. G. McCulloch, *Failing the Ordinary Child? The Theory and Practice of Working-class Secondary Education* (Buckingham, 1998).

14   M. Ferguson, *Forever Feminine: Women's Magazines and the Cult of Femininity* (London, 1983); C. White, *Women's Magazines, 1693–1968* (London, 1970); J. Winship, *Inside Women's Magazines* (London, 1987).

15   Pugh, *Women and the Women's Movement*, p. 292.

16   C. Alderson, *Magazines Teenagers Read with Special Reference to* Trend, Jackie *and* Valentine (Oxford, 1968), p. 105.

17   D.H. Currie, *Girl Talk, Adolescent Magazines and their Readers* (Toronto, 1999).

18   A. McRobbie, 'Jackie: An Ideology of Adolescent Femininity', in B. Waites, T. Bennet and G. Martin (eds), *Popular Culture Past and Present* (Buckingham, 1982).

19   K. Carrington and A. Bennett, '"Girls Mags" and the Pedagogical Formation of the Girl', in C. Luke (ed.), *Feminisms and Pedagogies of Everyday Life* (Albany, 1996); D. Currie, 'Dear Abby. Advice Pages as a Site for the Operation of Power', *Feminist Theory*, 2 (2001).

20   P. Tinkler, *Constructing Girlhood: Popular Magazines for Girls Growing Up in England* (London, 1995).

21   Currie, *Girl Talk*, p. 9.

22   *Journal of Education*, September 1957, p. 394.

23   Abrams, *Teenage Consumer*; J. Springhall, *Coming of Age: Adolescence in Britain 1860–1960* (London, 1986).

24   Tension between existing constructions of womanhood and perceived change in social order is explored for an earlier period in L. Delaney, 'Little Women, Good Wives: Victorian Constructions of Womanhood in the *Girl's Own Annual 1927*', *Children's Literature in Education*, 34 (2003).

25   *Girl*, 29 February 1956, p. 15.

26   *Girl*, 26 March 1960, p. 13, author's italics.

27   *Girl*, 25 January 1956, p. 13.

28   Currie, *Girl Talk*, p. 57.

29   Winship, *Inside Women's Magazines*, p. 135.

30   C. Langhamer, *Women's Leisure in England, 1920–60* (Manchester, 2000).

31   *Girl*, 23 May 1959, p. 14.

32   *Girl*, 12 September 1959, p. 14; 2 May 1959, p. 14; 7 November 1959, p. 14.

33   *Girl*, 2 May 1959, p. 14.

34   *Girl*, 5 September 1959, p. 14.

35   Ibid.

36   *Girl*, 27 February 1960, p. 14.

37   *Girl*, 3 January 1959, p. 8.

38   K. Massoni, 'Modelling Work. Occupational Messages in *Seventeen* Magazine', *Gender and Society*, 18 (2004).

39   Growing disquiet over the general application of Bowlby's theories of maternal deprivation did not stop an overall expectation that mothering was ideally a full-time occupation.

40   University of Warwick, Modern Records Centre, Association of Headmistresses' Papers, MSS.188/4/1/17.

41   M. Woollett, 'The Technical High School for Girls', *Technical Education* (October 1959), pp. 4–6, p. 4.

42   *Housewife*, October 1956, p. 157.

43   *I Want to Be. A Girl Book of Careers* (London, 1957), p. 8.

44   M. Wilson, 'The Vocational Preferences of Secondary Modern School Children', *British Journal of Educational Psychology*, 23 (1953); R.V. Clements (1958) *The Choice of Careers by Schoolchildren* (Manchester, 1958); W. Liversidge, 'Life Chances', *Sociological Review*, 10 (1962).

45   T. Veness, *School Leavers: Their Aspirations and Expectations* (London, 1962), p. xx.

46   E. Kerslake and J. Liladhar, '"Jolly Good Reading" for Girls: Discourses of Library Work and Femininity in Career Novels', *Women's History Review*, 8 (1999) pp. 489–504.

47   S. Spencer, 'Women's Dilemmas in Post-war Britain: Career Stories for Adolescent Girls in the 1950s', *History of Education*, 29 (2000).

48   V. Walkerdine, *Schoolgirl Fictions* (London, 1990), p. 91.

49   *Girl*, 21 March 1956, p. 15.

50   *Girl*, 28 May 1960, p. 15.

51   *Girl*, 20 August 1960, p. 12.

52   D. Smith, 'Femininity as Discourse', in R. Christian-Smith, and E. Ellsworth (eds), *Becoming Feminine: The Politics of Popular Culture* (London, 1988).

53   James Hemming analysed the letters written to *Girl* between 1 April 1953 and 31 March 1955. J. Hemming, *Problems of Adolescent Girls* (London, 1960).

54   M.J. Kehily, 'More Sugar? Teenage Magazines, Gender Displays and Sexual Learning', *European Journal of Cultural Studies*, 2 (1999); K. Massoni, 'Modelling Work' (2004).

PART IV

SCIENCE AND MEDICINE

Chapter 8

'Union is Strength': The Medical Women's Federation and the Politics of Professionalism, 1917–30

Kaarin Michaelsen

At a January 1916 meeting of one of the branches of the Association of Registered Medical Women (ARMW), its attendees raised two intriguing questions regarding the establishment of a new organisation, the Medical Women's Federation (MWF): first, 'why should such an association be formed at all'? And second, 'why now'?[1] That female physicians felt compelled to voice those specific queries at that particular juncture initially appears somewhat incongruous, as British medical women were then experiencing unprecedented professional success. Since their emergence in the mid-1860s,[2] sustained, public recognition of their professionalism and technical skills had eluded female physicians, but the advent of the First World War afforded them an unparalleled opportunity to demonstrate their capabilities to both their male colleagues and the general populace. In fact, until 1918, articles appearing in the national press routinely lauded the wartime activities performed by medical women, praising the 'excellent work done by those at the front'[3] and declaring that 'at this hour, the woman doctor is a vital need of the State'.[4]

Yet, as early as 1916, many individuals within the medical women's community encountered significant professional problems, most notably sex discrimination on the part of government bodies, while engaged in war-related work. Subsequently, female physicians began agitating en masse for the creation of a larger and more nationally visible association than the old ARMW, one explicitly charged with intervening in professional and political debates 'where women's interests are seriously at stake' and directed to 'express its opinion'[5] regarding solutions to matters particularly affecting them. In its heyday, 1917–30, the MWF did indeed come to fulfil an overtly political function, acting as a prominent, vocal, and, increasingly, influential advocate for female physicians in all aspects of social and medical policy. More critically, the Federation's founders consciously intended the organisation to play an integral part in shaping medical women's professional identities in the immediate post-war period by serving as a vehicle for professional assimilation with their male peers, while still ensuring that medical women's distinct perspectives were preserved and protected. By the early 1930s, the Federation[6] had achieved moderate success in its efforts to alleviate some of the most pressing professional difficulties facing medical women, such as pay disparities and inequitable working conditions in public heath posts, thereby demonstrating that for female physicians, 'union [wa]s strength in a very real sense'.[7]

Throughout the late nineteenth and early twentieth centuries, female physicians consciously and continuously strove to answer a fundamental question – what, precisely, did it *mean* to be a 'medical woman'? That endeavour proved exceedingly complicated and highly contentious, both within and outside the nascent community of female physicians, primarily because their dual identities as women and doctors necessitated defining themselves 'in relation to constructs of gender ... and to the ideas surrounding the occupation – professionalism'.[8] During this period, female physicians drew heavily on the rhetoric of the social maternalist strand of Victorian feminist thought – which stressed women's innate differences from men, ascribing to them unique talents for healing and nurturing – first to justify their claims for entry to medicine and, later, to expand the boundaries of women's 'sphere' within it. Operating in perpetual tension with this ideology was the notion that as members of 'a corporate body, units of a great profession',[9] medical women should be regarded by themselves, the public, and their male colleagues as equal to male physicians, indistinguishable from them in their training and adherence to the 'masculine' ethos of the disinterested expert. But, as scholars such as Joan Scott have argued, positioning 'equality' and 'difference' as purely oppositional concepts is not a useful means of analysing the history of feminism. Instead, she suggests adopting 'a new way of thinking about difference',[10] of embracing the idea that inherent in the notion of equality exist assumptions about difference, and vice versa. Female physicians definitely did not regard the process of defining themselves professionally as a simple case of deciding whether they wished to identify as either 'physicians' or as 'women', as equal to or different from their male colleagues. Rather, members of the MWF actually practised what Scott advocates, in that at the very heart of their identities as 'medical women' lay their firm belief that equality and difference were not mutually exclusive strands between which they had to make a permanent choice, that they could develop their own distinct articulation of 'professionalism' by seeking true professional equality expressed through feminine difference. In time, however, this notion of 'professionalism' became subject to a sustained critique by a younger generation of female physicians.

After qualifying as physicians, medical women faced the difficult challenge of situating themselves as female practitioners within a profession still gendered as male. The generally hostile atmosphere they encountered from both their male colleagues and the public, their miniscule numbers – even on the eve of the First World War, women comprised only 0.024 per cent of all actively-practising doctors in Britain[11] – and the fact that they often found themselves practising in isolation from their female colleagues all combined to ensure that medical women's professional lives became extremely trying. Another factor contributing markedly to their difficulties in establishing professional identities for themselves was their lack of any viable means to acquire what Pierre Bourdieu has called 'cultural capital'; Hilary Sommerlad and Peter Sanderson – who use the concept to discuss the situation of women lawyers – define it as the 'kind of social knowledge and ability which is a sign of eligibility for' professional assimilation and success.[12] According to Sommerlad and Sanderson, 'this sort of cultural capital cannot be accumulated simply through formal study but requires participation in complex forms of socialisation and "initiation rites", many of which revolve around masculine culture'.[13] Unfortunately for medical women, the traditional routes to accessing cultural capital, participating in postgraduate clinical training at major teaching hospitals and joining professional organisations like the British Medical Association (BMA),[14] remained largely beyond their purview until the final decade of the nineteenth century.

To alleviate these problems, nine medical women met in London in 1879 to form Britain's first all-female medical society, the ARMW,[15] which expanded by 1916 to include 230 female physicians in a loose network of regional branches stretching across the country. One of the ARMW's primary goals was to create a forum for celebrating medical women's distinctive interests and feminine culture and generating collegiality between them. In that respect, its founding aligns neatly with the broader late Victorian and Edwardian trend which historians have termed 'female institution building'[16] by feminists and their supporters, who created separate enclaves where women could improve their minds, develop their own communities, and take advantage of opportunities for feminine leadership and social networking denied them elsewhere. The convivial atmosphere at meetings encouraged medical women whose paths would not ordinarily cross to socialise with their colleagues, creating alliances that frequently yielded substantial personal and professional rewards in later years. Further, branch meetings helped to foster an ethos of sympathetic 'sisterhood' among female physicians, for they offered members a safe, confidential milieu in which to air their frustrations and discuss the often thorny professional issues they encountered in the course of practising with the only individuals who truly shared their perspective.

The ARMW struck a delicate balance between the emphasis it placed on promoting their feminine identities as women and their feminist ones as doctors struggling to achieve professional equality, privileging neither at the expense of the other. As Ellen More has pointed out, women's medical societies also functioned in another, equally important, manner, 'as an effective instrument of professional integration and legitimation'.[17] For medical women, the ARMW provided a non-threatening venue for engaging in more traditionally 'professional' pursuits, like the exchange of the latest scientific information. Joining an all-female medical association thus reinforced women's identities as physicians and offered them material benefits that they could not acquire elsewhere, such as the opportunity to keep abreast of the latest clinical and technical developments affecting their profession, information that they needed to assimilate in order to sustain their claims to equality with their male colleagues. The ARMW also made a concerted effort to demonstrate its members' professionalism, collegiality, and, most notably, their equality to their male colleagues, which they hoped would enable them to acquire more of the cultural capital vital to professional success. In that spirit, ARMW members often invited male physicians to attend meetings for presentations on special topics relevant to medical practice, the instance first being in December 1899, when Mr Stanley Boyd and the eminent surgeon, Sir James Berry, were invited to deliver papers.[18] Through these actions, female medical organisations like the ARMW operated as 'agents of [both] feminism and professionalization', and, more crucially, as a method of 'reconciliation and mediation between the two'.[19] For their part, medical women themselves largely accepted the way the ARMW interpreted the meaning of their professional identity, combining gendered activities and 'feminist equality interests at the same time – the feminine and the feminist together'.[20]

Though excellent at promoting professional fellowship and sisterly support, the ARMW proved a relatively ineffective lobbying force on behalf of women doctors, especially on the national stage, as it lacked a central body specifically charged with representing female physicians' perspective in medical and national politics. During the First World War, its locally based organisational structure made it practically impossible for the ARMW to assist medical women in their attempts to persuade the War Office to alter its policy of denying female physicians serving with the Army the temporary commissions equal to those afforded their male colleagues doing identical work. Medical women working under these conditions viewed the absence of rank as an issue of paramount importance because while

> Withholding ... a small act of respect due to a doctor [by male physicians and ordinary soldiers] ... because she possesses no official rank may seem a trivial matter ... occurring as these discourtesies did ... day after day, for years, and affecting large numbers of medical women, they amounted *in toto* to a definite slight to the profession as a whole.[21]

The strain of their unfortunate position weighed heavily on female physicians' minds, often making it difficult for them to perform their jobs effectively: as one medical woman complained, 'no one can do first-rate medical or surgical work when subjected to heart-burnings and "pin pricks" all day long'.[22] Frustrated with their inability as individuals to get the government to recognise and reward their status as skilled medical professionals, female physicians working in army hospitals and casualty clearing stations began arguing vigorously for the creation of a new female medical society to take up their cause. Their efforts proved convincing, and in 1917, the 'various associations of medical women in England ... decided to amalgamate into one body'.[23]

Like its predecessor, the MWF was intended to act as a bridge 'between the values of scientific professionalism and those of social feminism',[24] projecting an image of the 'woman professional' as 'equal but not identical' to male physicians and therefore having 'responsibilities and interests [that] are not exactly the same as men's'.[25] However, this new organisation possessed a substantially different mandate from the ARMW in that its founders intended its central function to be that of a dedicated advocate for medical women's professional interests in the formal public sphere of politics, one that would be 'looked upon as a responsible, professional body, able to voice the opinion of medical women on matters of public policy',[26] as well as to work to 'procure changes' in the 'administration of the law ... affecting medicine or medical practice' more generally.[27] Initial membership numbered only 190,[28] a mere fraction of the nearly 1,200 women then listed on the General Medical Council's Register as qualified to practise medicine, but its supporters included several of Britain's most highly regarded female physicians, such as Dr Florence Willey (Lady Barrett) and the eminent surgeon Dr Louisa Aldrich-Blake. Subsequent years saw the Federation's enrolment increase steadily, reaching 385 in 1918; by 1930, its ranks had swelled to include 1,317 members, or approximately 40 per cent of Britain's actively practising medical women,[29] as well as many female medical students.

Throughout the inter-war years, the Federation campaigned incessantly for permanent improvements to what its members regarded as the unprofessional working conditions facing medical women. Following its failure in its immediate task of persuading the War Office to grant medical women rank and commissions, it devoted its energy to a variety of other endeavours, like the removal of marriage bars, raising the retirement age for female physicians to that required for male doctors, and ensuring that medical women received adequate pensions. Nevertheless, its most enduring and successful efforts in this vein came in its work to rectify salary disparities between male and female practitioners working for public health authorities. Whenever the MWF's leaders became aware of a public or private post that proposed to pay medical women less than their male counterparts doing a similar job, they utilised every method at their disposal to get the prospective employer to either pay women equally to their male colleagues or to withdraw the advertisement. In most cases, the pressure tactics employed by the Federation were relatively mild, typically involving letters sent to the offending body articulating its position, but they generally produced the desired result. With more obstreperous employers, the MWF adopted more overtly confrontational techniques, such as personal deputations made by Federation officers to the administrators advertising the posts or, regarding government positions, having Members of Parliament it knew to be supportive of medical women's professional interests ask pointed questions of ministers during Parliamentary sessions. By 1922, the Federation could boast that it had 'made itself felt as a force and a power recognised by government – a force that could get questions asked in the House of Commons and demand justice' for all British medical women.[30]

The Federation pursued this agenda so tenaciously because these pay discrepancies harmed women on a material, and, more importantly, a professional level. The BMA had adopted the idea of 'equal pay for equal work' as official policy in 1907, and both the ARMW and, later, the MWF wholeheartedly pledged to support this principle. As the MWF's President, Frances Ivens, stressed to members in 1925, if female physicians quietly accepted whatever meagre salary employers deigned to offer them, they effectively assisted in 'lower[ing] the prestige of medical women in the eyes of their colleagues and of the public'.[31] These concerns are reflected in the enormous amount of pressure placed on practitioners who did accept these underpaid posts to abandon them.[32] Moreover, the Federation's leadership was also well aware of the fact that in addition to being unjust towards medical women, the enduring problem of unequal salaries could have repercussions on the broader profession. As noted in a 1930 memorandum the MWF received from the BMA:

> this matter [is] not so much … one of injustice to medical women but … one which deeply affects the whole medical profession … If this principle were allowed to extend, it would have a demoralizing effect upon the status and remuneration which the BMA has, during the course of many years, established for medical practitioners. Such an effect would be bad for the profession as a whole and eventually for the public it serves.[33]

Collaborating with the BMA on this issue enabled the fledgling Federation to add additional force and prestige to its arguments, and the unified front the two medical organisations presented during the 1920s clearly proved intimidating: by 1930, a memorandum produced by the BMA and approved by the MWF's Medico-Political Committee reported that the 'campaign has been almost entirely successful',[34] as the advertisements for unequally-paid posts had been drastically reduced and the vast majority of positions within the Civil Service offered equal pay to men and women doctors.

The MWF's efforts to achieve pay equity produced other legacies as well, ones less tangible but arguably more valuable in the long term. Participation in these kinds of activities helped medical women build up the cultural capital essential to furthering their integration within the profession, as their enthusiastic support of these actions did much to convince male physicians that female doctors genuinely cared about issues affecting the entire profession and they could be counted upon to act in solidarity with their male colleagues to achieve mutual goals. But the Federation's success also helped to reinforce the image of 'female professionalism' that it projected to its members, as it showed women that if they banded together and refused to be treated as anything less than men's professional equals, they really could create substantial changes in their status.

As befitted an all-female medical organisation in which scores of its members had long-standing ties to the feminist movement,[35] the Medical Women's Federation also intervened in contemporary debates regarding the changing nature of women's work. For example, the MWF worked to assist medical women claim a larger role for themselves in the public health field, publishing position papers and delivering addresses that argued female physicians possessed special insights in these areas and alleging that it was of 'national importance'[36] that they be able to perform this type of work. In a 1917 speech, Lady Barrett even went so far as to assert that medical women's 'expert opinion[s] need to be available to statesmen when framing Bills affecting women and children throughout the country'.[37] At an MWF gathering five years later, Dr Mary Sturge echoed these sentiments, contending that 'medical women have their share to play in helping the State to make wise decisions concerning such matters as Infant Welfare, Venereal Disease, Child Education, and ... Birth Control'.[38] The Federation also offered its opinion on issues affecting women beyond those impinging directly on its members' professional interests, making public statements on topics ranging from women's fitness to qualify as commercial airline pilots to the current state of research on menopause.

It is important to realise, however, that the Federation's actions on behalf of female physicians during this period did not go uncontested. Throughout the 1920s, female physicians repeatedly challenged the ways in which the Federation's leadership publicly represented the broad coalition of medical women on topics relating to their collective professional welfare, suggesting that its positions did not entirely reflect their individual feelings on certain issues. In essence, these medical women grew increasingly worried that the Federation privileged the interests of certain segments of the community over others in articulating its positions. For instance, the MWF's staunch opposition to marriage bars in employment proved surprisingly provocative within the medical women's community, generating serious friction between the Federation and its members. This conflict first emerged in September 1921, following the St Pancras Borough Council's decision to terminate the employment of Dr Gladys Miall-Smith, its Assistant Medical Officer for Maternity and Child Welfare, who had recently married. Understandably, medical women regarded this development as threatening, both professionally and personally, and the MWF was immediately galvanised to act. The Federation moved quickly to reassure worried members, informing them that the Executive Council 'resolves to take every possible means to prevent at the outset such dangerous infringement of women's liberties as is involved in the exclusion of married medical women from public posts',[39] including forming a Standing Committee specifically 'empowered ... to deal with any cases of interference with the employment of married medical women which may arise'.[40]

While it would seem logical that the entire medical women's community would have instantly rallied in support of Miall-Smith, interestingly, this did not transpire. Instead, married medical women found themselves pitted against their single, often younger, peers, many of whom felt that their married colleagues, who 'had [their] living assured by [their] husband[s'] earnings', had 'no right to take posts which might otherwise fall to the lot of younger women who have to earn their own living'.[41] Unmarried medical women were particularly piqued by what they perceived as a discriminatory Federation policy of 'strongly supporting' the cause of married female physicians 'while their claims to earning a living [we]re ignored',[42] and they relayed their frustrations to the MWF in no uncertain terms. By the autumn of 1921, this swelling undercurrent of dissent within its ranks deeply worried the MWF's leadership: in internal correspondence, the Standing Committee members noted ominously that 'a great deal of support for the dismissal of married women is coming from the unmarried medical wom[e]n who [are] finding it hard to get jobs. They want these jobs for themselves'.[43]

Presenting at least the fiction of a united front remained of paramount importance to the Federation's leaders, as they feared that their efforts to convince municipal and national authorities to rescind these policies might not be taken seriously should the public, male doctors or the employers involved suspect that not all medical women were completely committed to that aim. 'It is [essential] for all of us who see clearly the general principle to influence the thought of these young, unmarried medical women',[44] the MWF executives maintained. To that end, they published a series of articles explicitly directed at medical women who held those opinions. In these pieces, the Federation's directors explained that while they certainly sympathised with 'the stress of economic pressure that exists today', single medical women needed to understand that 'a great principle was involved: the interference with the liberties of and rights of women'.[45] The authors further urged them to remember that though 'it is quite true that the less efficient and less experienced may often be in greater need of … pecuniary help … but if appointments were made in respect of financial need' rather than on the basis of demonstrated professional skill, 'there would be no progress in medical or scientific work'.[46]

Issues relating to co-education also fostered significant discord between medical women and the Federation during this period. Since 1916, London's St Mary's Medical School, had accepted female students for clinical rotations in its affiliated hospital; after 1919, it permitted them to matriculate for the entire course. But in 1924, its Board of Management suddenly announced the termination of this policy following the graduation of the cadre of women then enrolled. In response, the MWF had its president, Lady Barrett, write a letter protesting vociferously against this action to the St Mary's authorities early in the decision-making process. But beyond registering these concerns, the

Federation did surprisingly little on female physicians' behalf in the public domain, a stark contrast to its typical response to attempts to restrict medical women's professional opportunities. Despite pleas by female medical students at St Mary's for it to immediately insert itself into the national controversy surrounding the decision, the officers of the MWF consciously avoiding taking this step as long as possible. When they finally came, the Federation's actions consisted only of writing two short letters to the editors of the national dailies: the first asserted that it 'desired all possible opportunities for experience in the profession',[47] and the second remarked that 'it is strongly felt by a large section of the community that co-education offers the best means of fostering the spirit of cooperation and mutual trust which is essential in any profession in which men and women engage on an equal footing'.[48] As the officers of the MWF explained to a member who expressed dismay at the Federation's uncharacteristically lacklustre response, they 'came to the conclusion that to call further attention to the desire of St Mary's Hospital to exclude women would not be in the interests of medical students themselves',[49] for they feared it might lead to an escalating backlash against the principle of co-education.

Understandably, many medical women were confused and disturbed by the Federation's apparent reluctance to act publicly in what they regarded as their collective best interest, and they did not hesitate to criticise the MWF's approach. In early October 1924, before the letters appeared, a Dr Kettle wrote to the Federation's officers to decry its inactivity at such a crucial moment for medical women, arguing that

> If the only organised body of medical women remains ... silent while other organisations are trying to point out in the press that the decision ... will do harm to existing medical women trained at St Mary's, it can only seem that they don't agree with this ... If the Federation really wants to help, complete inaction after a preliminary private letter does not seem to me the right way.[50]

Dr Mabel Ramsay was even more pointed in her criticism, asserting that the continuing disjunction between the Federation's behaviour and its members' opinions might have potentially serious consequences for the organisation's ability to claim that it spoke for medical women. According to her, this latest incident had led younger medical women to begin speculating about its ability to truly represent *their* collective professional identity:

> The Federation was formed to serve the interests of all its members and a long view has to be taken of such questions. Medical co-education outside London

is usual and even in London is slowly growing, even with the setback of St Mary's ... We have to realise ... that women's practise is not the same as 50 years ago ... One has to realise that in the National Insurance Act the contract made between Dr & the State makes no differentiation between the sexes ... The MWF has to foresee that [in] the present generation of medical [women] is a possible majority ... very much interested in co-education and in obtaining the same start in life as their male comperes.[51]

'I may say', Ramsay continued ominously, 'that I have received a good many protests that the MWF is very backward and are inclined [sic] to support one interest rather than the whole. ... [I]n [the] St Mary's controversy, I think we have not done our best'[52] to convince medical women that that is not the case.

Perhaps the most interesting aspect of the Federation's history during its first decade is that as early as the mid-1920s, signs of fractures had already emerged within medical women's ranks between a faction that argued for the necessity of its continued existence and those who viewed an all-female association as anachronistic in an increasingly gender-integrated profession. Female physicians advocating a separate association tried hard to convince the small, but growing, number of sceptics within their community that the MWF 'was [still] of any use'[53] whatsoever to their professional interests and identities. In November 1929, Dr Ethel Bentham, a MWF member since its inception and Britain's first female physician to be elected to Parliament, addressed this issue directly in the Federation's newsletter:

> One of the practical questions with which we are faced is whether there is still useful work for separate organizations – political or professional – of men and women ... [Is there] still sufficient difference in the point of view of men and women to make it necessary or advisable that they should be organised for public work in separate, even though allied, bodies.[54]

'Yet', she continued, 'even if we agree that ... the ideal to which we are working is a state in which men and women shall think of themselves as co-workers ... and leave sex out of account, that time is not yet. ... For some time to come, it would seem that women can best help by maintaining their separate channels of expression, though side by side and even *more* closely in cooperation with those of men'.[55] 'The help of the medical profession is needed to solve some of the most important and fundamental problems of the day', Bentham concluded. 'Medical women have a double responsibility as part of this research body on one hand and on the other as those who hold the largest possibility of bringing women's special knowledge and experience to its highest use'.[56]

The stress Bentham laid in her closing remarks on the duality inherent in medical women's professional identities reflects the gendered image of professionalism to which the MWF clung, despite increasingly obvious signs that some female physicians no longer shared it. Indeed, younger medical women, particularly those qualifying since 1918, had started raising serious questions regarding the central assumptions in a feminine articulation of professionalism. Having seen how eminently capably medical women performed in 'masculine' roles during the war and noted the substantial growth in cooperation and collegiality between male and female doctors in the years since, these individuals began wondering whether gender should continue to play a role in how they conceptualised 'professionalism'. Dr Octavia Wilberforce, who qualified in 1920, voiced the sentiments of many young women doctors on this point when she noted that in her experience, both she and her male counterparts 'forget half the time that there's any difference between the men and women, ... and that's what you need in medicine. Equality and absence of sex'.[57] If one's identity as a physician could, and perhaps should, be separated from one's gender, these female physicians began asking themselves, then what material benefits could a separate organisation really offer medical women that the BMA could not?

The tensions underscoring the growing debate in the female physician community over the professional image all-female medical societies projected to their members and the role that they might play in medical and national politics were not resolved by Bentham's speech, nor were they even well into the 1930s. Nor were they entirely unique among their female professional contemporaries: as Dina Copelman and, especially, Alison Oram have shown, women teachers became embroiled in strikingly similar discussions over the relative weight to be placed on the core ideas underscoring their professional identities – feminine difference and feminist goals of equality – by the organisations purporting to represent them.[58] More significantly, like medical women, female teachers found themselves questioning the continued relevance of these types of associations in the changed social climate of the inter-war years. The fact remains, however, that in the late nineteenth and early twentieth centuries Britain's medical women did benefit in a broad sense from the establishment of this new kind of women's organisation. Union did provide them strength, as well as some tangible material and professional gains. Divided into tiny, local associations, medical women's professional and social influence was negligible. By collapsing these groups into the ARMW and the MWF, and then working in conjunction, rather than competition, with their male colleagues, female physicians transformed themselves into an increasingly powerful social force, one able to generate positive changes in the conditions of life – and hence the health – of other women and children.

Notes

1   Wellcome Institute for the History of Medicine, Contemporary Medical Archives Centre (CMAC) SA/MWF/Box 24/C.81: Association of Registered Medical Women, 'Speech for Tuesday, 11 January 1916'.

2   Elizabeth Garrett, later Garrett Anderson, qualified in 1865 as Britain's first female physician with the License of the Society of Apothecaries (LSA), a low-status qualification but one which enabled her to place her name on the General Medical Council's Medical Register, thereby permitting her to practise medicine legally. She acquired her MD in Paris in 1870.

3   Royal Free Hospital Archives Centre Press Clippings Collection, Volume 4 (1904–15): *Sheffield Independent*, 23 February 1915.

4   Royal Free Hospital Archives Centre Press Clippings Collection, Volume 5 (1915–20): *The Times*, 9 November 1915.

5   CMAC/SA/MWF/Box 24/C.81: Association of Registered Medical Women, 'Speech for Tuesday, 11 January 1916'.

6   In this chapter, I use the term 'Federation' to refer to the organisation generally. I indicate where I am specifically discussing the opinions or actions of its leaders or those of its members.

7   CMAC/SA/MWF/Box 24/C.81: Association of Registered Medical Women. 'Speech for Tuesday, 11 January 1916'.

8   A. Oram, *Women Teachers and Feminist Politics, 1900–1919* (Manchester, 1996).

9   Dr Frances Ivens, 'Some of the Essential Attributes of an Ideal Practitioner', *Magazine of the London (Royal Free Hospital) School of Medicine for Women*, 9, 60 (November 1914), p. 153.

10 J. Scott, *Gender and the Politics of History* (New York, 1999), p. 168. See also J. Scott, 'Deconstructing Equality Versus Difference: Or, the Uses of Poststructuralist Theory for Feminism', *Feminist Studies*, 14, 1 (1988) and J. Rendell, *Equal or Different: Women's Politics, 1800–1914* (Oxford, 1987).

11 Statistics derived from Table 3.5, 'Active Medical Practitioners, 1881–1891: Analysis by Sex', in M. Elston, 'Women Doctors in the British Health Services: A Sociological Study of Their Careers and Opportunities', PhD dissertation (Leeds, 1986), p. 63.

12 H. Sommerlad and P. Sanderson, *Gender, Choice and Commitment: Women Solicitors in England and Wales and the Struggle for Equal Status* (Aldershot, 1998), p. 119; P. Bourdieu, *The Logic of Practice* (Cambridge, 1990); P. Bourdieu, *Language and Symbolic Power* (Cambridge, 1991).

13 Ibid.

14 Garrett Anderson had been elected to the BMA in 1873. In September 1878, at the annual meeting in Bath, the BMA's membership passed by an overwhelming majority a resolution to insert a clause into the Association's charter preventing women from being declared eligible for admission. The issue of women's membership did not resurface until 1892, when they were permitted membership. See also T. Lamont, 'The Amazons Within:

Women in the BMA 100 Years Ago', *British Medical Journal*, 19 December 1992, for more information on the debate over the inclusion of women.

15 The nine founding members of the ARMW were Elizabeth Blackwell (British-born, but the first woman to acquire a medical degree in the United States and a long-time supporter of the cause of medical women in Britain), Elizabeth Garrett Anderson, Sophia Jex-Blake, Louisa Atkins, Mary Marshall, Eliza Walker Dunbar and Drs Barker, Clarke and McDonogh. These members were present at the Association's first annual dinner, held at the Trafalgar Pub, Greenwich, on 4 May 1880. See CMAC/SA/MWF/Box 26/C.89.

16 E. Friedman, 'Separatism as Strategy: Female Institution Building and American Feminism', *Feminist Studies*, 53 (1979).

17 E. More, 'The Blackwell Medical Society and the Professionalization of Women Physicians', *Bulletin of the History of Medicine*, 61 (1987), p. 603.

18 CMAC/SA/MWF/Box 26/C.89: 'Internal History of the Medical Women's Federation'.

19 Ibid., p. 604.

20 Oram, *Women Teachers*, p. 116.

21 Dr Mary D. Sturge, 'The Medical Women's Federation – Its Work and Aims', *Magazine of the London (Royal Free Hospital) School of Medicine for Women*, 17, 81 (March 1922), p. 38.

22 Ibid.

23 CMAC/SA/MWF/Box 24/C.81: 'Preliminary Leaflet – Medical Women's Association'.

24 More, 'The Blackwell Medical Society', p. 604.

25 CMAC/SA/MWF/Box 24/C.81: 'Preliminary Leaflet – Medical Women's Association'.

26 Ibid.

27 CMAC/SA/MWF/Box 26/C.87: 'Memorandum of Association of the MWF, 1917'.

28 L. Hall, '80 Years of the Medical Women's Federation', *Medical Women: Bulletin of the Medical Women's Federation*, 16, 2 (Summer 1997), p. 6.

29 Figure derived by combining information from the official Census statistics for 1931 regarding 'actively practising' medical women compiled by Elston and the MWF's own membership total for 1930.

30 Sturge, 'The Medical Women's Federation', p. 38.

31 CMAC/SA/MWF/B.2/2: Dr Frances Ivens, 'An Address to Junior Members', *Medical Women's Federation Newsletter*, March 1925, 17.

32 In 1925, one of the members of the MWF's Executive Council suggested that members who transgressed the Federation's principle of not accepting positions unless they paid women equally to men should have their names published in the *Newsletter*. That step appears never to have been taken, and the Federation continued to address this issue in private communications with the offending members. See CMAC/SA/MWF/Box 1/A.1/3/Vol. 2: Minutes of the Meetings of the Council of the MWF, 8 May 1925,

33 CMAC/SA/BMA/Box 55/C.103: Minutes of the Medico-Political Committee, 12 March 1930.

34 Ibid.

35 Medical women's involvement with the feminist movement was a relationship best characterised by its depth and duration. Leading feminists, such as Barbara Bodichon and Emily Davies, had played crucial roles in the movement to open the medical profession to women during the 1860s and 1870s, and some female physicians, like Dr Helen Wilson, became intimately involved in widely publicised 'feminist' causes, such as the campaign to educate British women about venereal disease. The politics and rhetoric of the recent suffrage campaign also resonated strongly with Edwardian medical women, as

they viewed the acquisition of the vote as representing a long-overdue, public validation of their identities as both citizens and, more crucially, professionals. Overwhelmingly, medical women tended to support the acquisition of the vote by non-violent means, with approximately four times as many affiliating themselves with the NUWSS than with the WSPU. Besides serving as members of the executive committees of their local branches of these organisations, medical women also participated in processions, wrote articles in the suffrage press, and placed copies of *Common Cause*, the NUWSS' official organ, in their surgeries' waiting rooms. At least 13 medical women – many of whom were ARMW and, later, MWF members – were imprisoned for militant activities, and at least one, Dr Frances Ede, was forcibly fed. Those imprisoned included Drs Frances Ede, Alice Ker, Mabel Hardie, Marie Pethick, Helen Bourchie, Ethel Cox, Dorothea Chalmers Smith, Elizabeth Knight, Helen H.B. Hanson, Louisa Garrett Anderson, and Flora Murray. The latter two also operated a Notting Hill nursing home to which many of their friends and colleagues were taken after being forcibly fed. See *The Suffrage Annual and Women's Who's Who* (London, 1913), *Common Cause, Votes for Women* and *The Vote* for 1909–14, and *Roll of Honour: Suffragette Prisoners, 1905–1914*.

36   Lady Barrett (Dr Florence Willey), 'Address by Lady Barrett', *Magazine of the London (Royal Free Hospital) School of Medicine for Women*, 68, 12 (November 1917), p. 84.

37   Ibid.

38   Sturge, 'Medical Women's Federation', p. 41.

39   CMAC/SA/MWF/Box 12/B.2/1: Lady Barrett (Dr Florence Willey), 'Married Medical Women', *Medical Women's Federation Newsletter* (December 1921), p. 9.

40   Ibid., p. 8.

41   Ibid., p. 10.

42   CMAC/SA/MWF/Box 41/D.4/1: MWF Secretary to Dr Louise McIlroy, 17 November 1921.

43   CMAC/SA/MWF/Box 41/D.4/1: Minutes of the Standing Committee on Married Medical Women, 17 November 1921.

44   CMAC/SA/MWF/Box 41/D.4/1: MWF Secretary to Dr Louise McIlroy, 17 November 1921.

45   CMAC/SA/MWF/Box 41/D.4/1: Minutes of the Standing Committee on Married Medical Women, 17 November 1921.

46   Barrett, 'Address', p. 11.

47   CMAC/SA/MWF/Box13/B.2/7: Excerpt from a letter written by Frances Ivens, the new MWF president, 11 October 1924, 'St Mary's Hospital', *Medical Women's Federation Newsletter* (November 1924), p. 23.

48   Dr Frances Ivens, 'Letter to the Editor', *The Times*, 27 October 1924.

49   CMAC/SA/MWF/Box 20/C.15: Dr Violet Kelnyack, MWF Secretary, to Dr Kettle, 6 October 1924.

50   CMAC/SA/MWF/Box 20/C.15: Dr Kettle to Dr Violet Kelnyack, 8 October 1924.

51   CMAC/SA/MWF/Box 20/C.15: Dr Mabel Ramsay to Miss Rew, 27 October 1924.

52   Ibid.

53   CMAC/SA/MWF/Box 42/D.9/3: Dr Catherine Chisholm to Dr Violet Kelnyack, 3 July 1928.

54   CMAC/SA/MWF/B.2/2: Dr Ethel Bentham 'The New Position of Women', *Medical Women's Federation Newsletter*, November 1929, p. 20.

55   Ibid.

56   Ibid.

57   O. Wilberforce, *Octavia Wilberforce: The Autobiography of a Pioneer Woman Doctor*,
     ed. P. Jalland (London, 1989), p. 101.
58   See D. Copelman, *London's Women Teachers: Gender, Class, and Feminism, 1870–1930*
     (New York, 1996) and Oram, *Women Teachers*, especially Chapter 5: 'Equal or Different?
     Feminist Strategies, 1920–1939'.

Chapter 9

The Laboratory: A Suitable Place for a Woman? Gender and Laboratory Culture around 1900

Claire Jones

In his inaugural lecture in 1871, James Clerk Maxwell, recently appointed Professor to the soon-to-be opened Cavendish Laboratory at Cambridge University, stressed that his new facility's prime focus would be experimentation for illustration and for research. One of his first projects was to repeat the experiments of the 'great man' to whom the new laboratory was dedicated. In Henry Cavendish's day (d. 1810) there was, as yet, no instrumentation with which to measure an electric current, so Cavendish passed the current through his own body and estimated its magnitude by the intensity of the resulting shock. In keeping with the experimental bravery of his facility's namesake, Maxwell set up similar apparatus at the new Cavendish Laboratory

> ... and all visitors were required to submit themselves to the ordeal of impersonating a galvanometer. On one occasion a young American astronomer expressed his severe disappointment that after travelling to Cambridge on purpose to meet Maxwell and consult him on some astronomical topic he was almost compelled to take off his coat, plunge his hands into basins of water and submit himself to a series of electrical shocks![1]

Not surprisingly, given Maxwell's encouragement of a culture of physical courage and stoicism, women at Cambridge were not welcomed at the Cavendish Laboratory during his tenure. It was only in 1882, during the professorship of his successor Lord Rayleigh, that women were admitted on the same terms as men. An analysis of obituaries, memoirs and biographies of male scientists active in the decades surrounding 1900 presents a striking illustration of the way in which the laboratory was presented as a masculine space where heroic qualities could be tested, developed and displayed. A reminiscence of James Dewar, who experimented on the liquefaction of gases in the early 1900s, highlights the 'personal courage' and 'iron nerve' that his work required. When 'an alarming explosion rent the air of the laboratory' Dewar 'did not move a muscle, or even turn to look'. This memoir continues: 'Dewar never admitted that anything was dangerous. The most he would say was that it was a little tricky. Considering that Lennox and Heath, his two assistants, each lost an eye in the course of the work, this was certainly not an overstatement'.[2] Such daring in the laboratory and the forbearance of uncomfortable physical conditions are common in the recollections of men of science. Even if some of these memoirs are apocryphal, that the laboratory was represented as a site of manly display and the development of moral and physical courage, as well as of the production of knowledge, is significant when considering the experiences of women in science and the representation (or lack of it) of women in the laboratory.

Until recently, women's absence in the laboratory has been explained largely by the growing institutionalisation of science at the end of the nineteenth century, which acted as a barrier to women's participation. As the tradition of home laboratories gave way to new, specialised, experimental facilities, so women were marooned in the domestic sphere from which science had fled.[3] More recent scholarship has revealed a more complex picture by uncovering previously 'invisible' women and following them into the laboratory.[4]

Responding to this new visibility of women, this study suggests that the new professional scientist's need for moral and material status necessitated the representation of a heroic laboratory culture which was antithetical to femininity and, by necessity, ignored female experimenters. This discourse worked alongside the forces of professionalisation and institutionalisation – forces that require unpackaging to reveal the complex mechanisms of inclusion and exclusion. The term 'laboratory culture' is used here in a broad sense to encompass both the shared experiences of workers in the laboratory and the way in which these experiences were represented to a wider public. Anecdotes of laboratory life developed into a mythology which was picked up by journalism and fiction (which in turn reflected it back to the laboratory) and which was shared by both scientific and non-scientific audiences alike. To illustrate this, it is necessary to adopt an inclusive approach that goes beyond the testimony of scientists and scientific writing to include literary, fictional and photographic sources too. In this way, the processes that worked to affect the experiences, expectations and representation of women in the laboratory will be examined, with particular reference to physicist and experimentalist Hertha Ayrton (1854–1923) (Figure 9.1).[5]

Figure 9.1   Mrs Ayrton in her Laboratory

Source: Royal Society Archive © The Royal Society.

Born Sarah Phoebe Marks to modest, Jewish-émigré parentage, Hertha was able to study higher-level mathematics thanks to the support of Barbara Bodichon and her feminist friends who created a loan fund which enabled her to attend Girton College, Cambridge.[6] Hertha's first love was experimental science and, after achieving only average marks in the 1880 Mathematics Tripos, she enrolled on an evening course in electrical and applied physics at the new City and Guilds Technical College in Finsbury, a pioneering educational initiative which marked the beginnings of advanced, laboratory-based technical education in England. The Professor of Technical Physics here was William Edward Ayrton FRS, a well-known telegraphic engineer, electrical physicist and educator. After a 'laboratory romance', Hertha and Ayrton were married in May 1885. Hertha is remembered chiefly for her work on the electric arc and her research into the formation of sand ripples. Arc lights were used extensively for street lighting but their performance was unreliable and they were prone to hissing and spitting. Hertha undertook painstaking experiments on carbons and electrical currents to discover the causes of this instability, producing a 1902 book that quickly became a definitive text on the subject. Although arc lamps were soon superseded by filament lamps, Hertha took out several patents on her technical innovation and advised the Admiralty on applications to searchlights. She spoke before the Institution of Electrical Engineers and became their first female member in 1899.[7] Hertha's next investigation was into the formation of sand ripples in moving water, a popular problem that had attracted the interest of others including Nobel Prize winner Lord Raleigh and Cambridge professor George Darwin (son of Charles). Hertha's findings were read before the Royal Society and there was a move to elect her a Fellow. However this august body was not yet ready to accept a woman in their midst; it would be 1945 when the first female FRS was elected.[8] Nevertheless, the Society awarded Hertha their Hughes Medal for original research in 1906. At the beginning of the First World War, Hertha applied her experimental data on water vortices to air vortices and designed an anti-gas fan to be used in the trenches. Eventually these were supplied to the Front, although their efficacy was a subject of much contemporary debate. In addition to her scientific work, Hertha was an active campaigner for women's suffrage and joined the militant Women's Social and Political Union in 1906.

The closing decades of the nineteenth century have come to be described by historians of science as the years of the 'laboratory revolution'.[9] Between 1880 and 1914 there was an enormous growth in institutional laboratories as the older 'devotee' tradition of research undertaken by gentlemen at home gave way to a new professionalism, and as the universities embraced the newer natural sciences that required experimental facilities. By the end of the century laboratories were used for teaching, research and commercial purposes, plus they could function as workshops and places of production as well as of discovery. The growth of technical teaching laboratories was encouraged by the recommendations of a Royal Commission that reported in 1884 amid fears that Britain was trailing behind Germany in technical innovation. Well-equipped laboratories and workshops became symbolic of national well-being and a key instrument in the race for international competitiveness. In the universities, possession of experimental facilities was becoming increasingly important. By 1900 new laboratories were a prestige-winning formula and reports of opening ceremonies/descriptions of new facilities became a frequent occurrence on the pages of *Nature*. Women's colleges were not left out of the expansion. At Cambridge, chemical laboratories were built at Newnham and Girton Colleges in 1879, and the Balfour Laboratory for Life Sciences for women at Cambridge was opened in 1884. At the end of the century Bedford College, London, possessed six new laboratories, erected at a cost of more than £6,000, and Royal Holloway College, established in 1887, boasted well-equipped chemical and biological laboratories. The former prompted *Nature* to remark that it was 'surely a hopeful sign that a college for the education of women should now be regarded as incomplete unless it contains physical and chemical laboratories specially designed and fitted for the delivery of lectures and performance of experiments'.[10] However, that scientific women in universities were largely catered for with parallel facilities limited their impact on the culture that grew up around laboratory experimentation.

In the limited instances where laboratory facilities were shared, women were a small minority. Only seven women have been identified as 'researchers' at the Cavendish Laboratory in the nineteenth century and Hertha was one of only three women amongst 118 men when she embarked on an evening course in electrical and applied physics at Finsbury Technical College in 1884.[11] At the Central College in South Kensington where, as 'wife-of-the-professor', Hertha carried out her major research on the electric arc, no names recognisable as women's can be found on existing electrical engineering student registers to 1899.[12] Even when the emphasis was on training science teachers rather than on technology and industry, women's participation was negligible. In 1896–97 seasonal courses offered by the Royal College of Science at South Kensington (the Central's partner institution) were attended by 300 men but only six women. The previous year's short summer courses, with an emphasis on practical laboratory work, had attracted 202 male and ten female students. The compiler of these figures, writing in 1897, placed the blame for this under-representation on women themselves for failing to take advantage of the academic opportunities placed within their reach.[13] This is a criticism not unfamiliar to modern ears and one which suggests a more subtle causation of women's absence. Historians of women and science have demonstrated the ways in which the growing institutionalisation of science worked to keep women out. However the cultural meaning of the laboratory and its effects on women have been largely overlooked. The laboratory's moral currency as a venue in which to develop and exhibit manly character, plus the increasing significance to national pride and virility of success in this experimental, knowledge-and-technology producing space, were all elements which interacted to keep women to the periphery. Even the tradition of home-based laboratories, which did not disappear entirely but co-existed with institutional laboratories, did little to render women more visible in science, as Hertha's career illustrates.

The tendency to represent the laboratory as a site of manly display, heroic endeavour and moral bravery, as illustrated in the introduction, created an inevitable ambivalence towards femininity. Writers of scientific memoirs used experimental work as a vehicle for constructing personas that recall the adventurer-heroes of Edwardian fiction such as Conrad's Marlow (*Heart of Darkness*) or H. Rider Haggard's Allan Quatermain (*King Solomon's Mines*). Speaking of the Cavendish Laboratory, one researcher remembered being a near-victim to wires so arranged overhead that they threatened passers by with decapitation, and recalled battery cells containing nitric and sulphuric acids which 'what with the fumes which assailed one's throat and the acid which destroyed one's clothes' were 'a most disagreeable business'.[14] Photographs of Rayleigh's laboratory at the Royal Institution, where he performed work leading to the discovery of argon, emphasised the sense of risk by focusing on a sign hanging from the ceiling that warns simply 'DANGER'. In some accounts, the harsh physical environment of the laboratory is heightened by competitiveness, mainly for scarce equipment, redolent of the public school playing field. The 'danger' of Rayleigh's laboratory was augmented by its laboratory store being 'regarded as a plundering ground by the Scottish marauders from downstairs' (the chemists in the basement).[15] The decades of the laboratory revolution were also when the new genre of 'scientific romances' became popular (examples include H.G. Wells's *The Time Machine* and Robert Louis Stevenson's *Dr Jekyll and Mr Hyde*). Much of the fast-growing output of magazine fiction also used science or scientific ideas as a favourite theme with stories written following the tradition of Faust, Frankenstein and the gothic novel. Here we can see laboratory culture and popular culture spilling over and informing each other. It has been noted that in these texts it is often the laboratory that has 'diabolical connotations' and is the site of danger and evil.[16] It is possible that these representations had associations with the growth of a descriptive language that emphasised courage and manliness in the experimental space. The laboratory signified a place of unease in some parts of popular literary culture and, as these stories often stood alongside 'factual' accounts of science and scientists, it can be assumed that science and science fiction had a reciprocal effect upon each other.[17]

The stereotype of the laboratory as a dangerous place calling for physical and psychological bravery and endurance by necessity omits any feminisation or representation of women. It is difficult to find evidence of the experience of women who worked in this environment; no wonder there is little scholarship in this area. Marsha Richmond has written on the history of the Balfour Biological Laboratory for Women at Cambridge University and notes an undercurrent of prejudice against the few female research workers (as opposed to undergraduate students from Newnham and Girton who attended lectures and demonstrations there) which 'could sometimes turn into hostility and make working there problematic'. She quotes a male researcher talking about Cambridge in the 1890s: 'At that time women were rare in scientific laboratories and their presence was by no means generally acceptable – indeed that is too mild a phrase. Those whose memories go back so far will recollect how unacceptability not infrequently flamed into hostility'.[18] Although laboratories were built at some women's colleges in the first decade of the twentieth century, as previously outlined, these were mostly teaching, not research, institutions. At Cambridge, their function was to offer routine instruction to female undergraduates who were segregated in their own facilities and did not (as a rule) have opportunity to undertake novel experimental work. As a result, these scientific women did not pose a threat to the reproduction of manly values within university-wide facilities that owed their reputation to research. Women were in a precarious position when infiltrating these facilities, their presence often tolerated rather than welcomed and subject to the whim of male dons. In 1887 Adam Sedgwick threatened to turn women out of his morphology laboratory if they did not stop agitating for degrees. The environment at the Cavendish Laboratory could be similarly antagonistic, exacerbated by overcrowding. J.J. Thomson, an assistant and then Professor of Experimental Physics there, recalled an episode in the 1890s that 'appealed to his sense of humour'. A 'lady student' from Newnham or Girton had fainted and a laboratory boy, 'anxious to rise to the occasion, thought it right to turn the fire hose on her!'[19] It was not until 1909 that Cambridge women were finally admitted to the University Chemistry Laboratory and to physiological practicals. If laboratories held significance for masculinity, women's presence could be transgressive – indeed the presence of anything connected with femininity required explanation. When the Central Institute's magazine described the College's research on a vacuum cleaner in 1904, the author felt it necessary to excuse this feminine-related subject 'occupying valuable space' by emphasising that 'the profession of an engineer is the art of directing the sources of power in Nature for the use and convenience of men'.[20] When they do not ignore women altogether, contemporary accounts tend to portray them as objects of amusement. That women were able to undertake an evening course in electro-technics at Finsbury Technical College in the early 1880s was reported with indulgence by the *Electrician* magazine which remarked that 'Women may study electrical science without risk of alarming anybody or of doing any harm to themselves'.[21]

Hertha's prize-winning work on the electric arc had been carried out at the Central Institute where her husband, William Ayrton, headed the electrical engineering department. Despite her researches there from 1893 to around 1904, it is difficult to follow her into the laboratory as her presence is rarely noted in any existing archive of the institution. The College journal refers to her collaboration with her husband in its obituary of William Ayrton; later the journal also carried a review of a biography of Hertha which was written by her friend, the journalist and suffrage campaigner Evelyn Sharp, and published in 1926, three years after Hertha's death.[22] This relative 'invisibility' in college history is significant when it is remembered that Hertha's work here was aided by Central students and led to the award of a prestigious Royal Society Medal – surely an important event for a college striving to win credibility as a professional institution on a par with the universities. Indeed, promoting the original work of its students was an important propaganda tool for the Central in its bid to win credibility and prestige.[23] Yet, most important for the Central, was to prove itself capable of producing 'trained men' and 'professional engineers' who were able to maintain 'the whole status of the profession'.[24] This required promoting an image of itself as producing graduates who were dedicated to giving service to mankind – men whose practical laboratory training and manly integrity equipped them to build dams, construct electric light schemes or create new locomotive systems throughout the world. A woman in the laboratory, no matter how successful her work, would not aid the promotion of this image. A nervousness of showing women in the laboratory was not confined to the Central Institute. For example, an article on Girton College in a contemporary periodical was not untypical in showing well-equipped, tidy but empty laboratories.[25] The new women's colleges were wary of provoking criticism from opponents who argued that women jeopardised their well-being by following a programme of education similar to men's. Darwinian fears that exposing women to hard intellectual work could lead to a loss of health, fertility and beauty, were exacerbated by imagery that presented the laboratory as a harsh and competitive environment that threatened accepted norms of femininity. A woman in the laboratory was inappropriate – and dangerous.

Yet a glimpse of Hertha's experiences in the laboratory can be gleaned from the 1902 book *The Electric Arc*, which resulted from her researches.[26] Far from being a figure of amusement, it is clear that she established warm relationships with the staff and students who assisted her in experimental trials of carbons while following their diploma course. C.E. Greenfield, a student at the Central 1899–1903, later worked with Hertha in her home laboratory after her husband's death. Another co-worker at the Central, her husband's Chief Assistant Thomas Mather (who had worked with Ayrton on arc lights) later rushed to Hertha's defence in a letter to *Nature* in response to an unsympathetic obituary which had accused her of a lack of originality.[27] In the preface to *The Electric Arc* Hertha thanked Mather for his valuable advice and assistance with experiments. Mather had superintended the first set of experiments and made suggestions that simplified their execution. In order to adequately monitor the carbons, a mirror was now used to reflect the phenomenon onto a large screen of white cartridge paper. This improved visibility was vital to Hertha's research, which depended on observing the carbon and spotting minute changes over long periods of time. It was painstaking work, which required keeping an arc under a steady current controlled by hand for periods of an hour or more while monitoring the results (Hertha likened this process to the driving of an obstinate animal after learning its caprices). Effective teamwork and experimental facilities able to host lengthy, controlled experiments were indispensable. The relationships that Hertha achieved with co-workers at the Central were therefore vital to her work. Similar productive relationships have been discovered between male and female co-researchers at the Cavendish Laboratory.[28]

Given recent research revealing women in the laboratory, it is important to ask why their presence has for so long been obscured, not least by 'manly' representations of laboratory life of the kind described above. Despite the growth in number and prestige of laboratories – and the increasing recognition of their key role in achieving trade dominance – any hint of commercialism could still taint a researcher's work: he was no longer in pursuit of disinterested truth. In 1903 astronomer William Huggins, in his presidential address to the Royal Society, made implicit criticism of Fellows who worked not out of ideals of service but for profit when he stated that the Society had achieved its unique position '… by its unwearied pursuit of truth for truth's sake without fee or reward'.[29] Men receiving money as a result of their scientific researches could jeopardise their position; for women to do so would be to transgress middle-class conventions of femininity and jeopardise social standing as well. Emphasising the heroic qualities involved in research – perseverance, bravery, and 'iron nerve' – helped win prestige and moral currency at a time when science was still emerging as a profession. For similar reasons, applied scientists constructed arguments for their own worth based on their profession as a service to mankind. The scientific researcher or engineer was an heroic tamer of Nature – 'directing the sources of power in Nature for the use and convenience of men'.[30] This characterisation contains the gendered, Baconian connotations of Man as investigator of a female Nature, which have been often rehearsed by scholars.[31] Such arguments tended to imbue laboratory methodology – observation, experimentation, reason – with moral worth, a view neatly presented in a Royal Society obituary which remarked that 'Scientific investigation is eminently truthful. The investigator may be wrong, but it does not follow (that) he is other than truth-loving'.[32] Here it is the method of science that bestows moral righteousness, not the correctness of any results that the experimenter may produce. Furthermore, experimental work was valuable for the moral training it conferred. At Oxbridge and public schools, success in the laboratory or site of scientific experimentation was becoming as important as the playing field for the development of moral character.[33] If the laboratory was where manliness was developed and displayed, women's presence was problematic. It is no coincidence that Conan Doyle's Sherlock Holmes, who first appeared in the *Strand Magazine* in 1901, became popular as an icon of rational masculinity, his character aligned with scientific procedure, observation and unemotional logic. For Holmes, women are 'never to be trusted – not the best of them'.[34] This remark reflected views still articulated by some followers of the new Darwinian sciences which, rather than questioning traditional sex divisions, put these divisions on a new, scientific footing. They theorised that women's intellect was not on a par with men's. Women were lower down the evolutionary scale closer to animals and, as chemist Henry Armstrong FRS, Professor at the Central Technical College, opined 'Education can do little to modify her nature'.[35] Women operated on emotion and instinct; men, especially men of science, relied on reason.

A connecting factor that helped to keep women at the periphery of laboratories was the applied sciences' competition with mathematics for status. The Natural Science Tripos at Cambridge had been established in 1851 and, until the mid-1870s, it had been viewed largely as the poor relation to mathematics. Later, pure mathematics, which had been the signifier of genteel manliness, had become distrusted in some scientific quarters as a feminised pursuit unsuited to the active masculinity now exhibited by the applied mathematicians, experimental scientists and engineers who had been in the vanguard of so much technical progress. Although the Cambridge Mathematics Tripos was still an important route of entry into experimental science, the infiltration of a new, abstract and highly logical style of mathematics from the Continent had reinforced the perception of the subject as removed from, and unimportant to, the real world. This led applied mathematician and physicist Lord Rayleigh to remark in a Royal Society Presidential Address that in some branches of Pure Mathematics it is said that 'readers are scarcer than writers'[36]. What's more, by the 1890s students at the new women's colleges had successfully challenged the idea that mathematics was the preserve of men by winning high places in the lists, prompting one Cambridge mathematician to use this as evidence of how the Tripos had become devalued.[37] The applied experimentalists constructed an active, virile identity in the laboratory in part to highlight their difference from the pure mathematicians and so enhance their status relationship.

Whatever the cordial relationships that individual women may have established with individual co-workers in the laboratory, their presence did not rest easily within the culture and image that male workers liked to present. Hertha was only welcome at the Central's laboratory when she was pursuing work that had been initiated by her husband (she had taken over his research on the electric arc) and, after Ayrton's death in 1908, she carried out no further research there. Instead, she transferred her attic laboratory into the drawing room of her London home and it was here that all her experimental work was undertaken until her death in 1923, 15 years later. Historians have written extensively about a late nineteenth-century ideology that divided space according to gender and function. Separate spheres placed the (middle-class) woman in the home and men in the great world beyond; scholars of space have emphasised how women, as signifiers of moral virtue and social status, could not cross social and physical boundaries as men were able to do.[38] Although the explanatory power of separate spheres has been increasingly challenged as providing too rigid a division, especially when applied to the turn of the century, it is clear that men and women shared few spaces on equal terms; women were defined by the home in a way that men were not. Although many male scientists had home laboratories after the 'aristocratic house' tradition, by the late nineteenth century they were rarely the only venue for experimental work to which they had access. That gentlemen's 'country-house' laboratories continued at the turn of the century has been interpreted as a means to reconcile the idealism and spiritual value represented by the older scientific 'devotee' tradition with modern laboratories producing commercial applications alongside new knowledge.[39] This strategy, alongside that of representing the laboratory as a place of manliness and heroism, worked to assuage the new professional scientist's need for moral worth. Lord Rayleigh had developed large laboratories at Terling and a smaller one at his previous home in Cambridge, yet he also researched and held professorships at the Cavendish Laboratory and the Royal Institution, and was later associated with the new National Physical Laboratory. William Crookes experimented at home as well as undertaking joint work at the Royal Institution. George Gabriel Stokes carried out most of his research at a modest home laboratory but simultaneously held a Cambridge Professorship. But these home laboratories were not all modest. Upon inheriting Terling Place in 1873, Lord Rayleigh installed a private gas works to feed bunsen burners and blowtorches, and developed the existing laboratory into a complex of experimental facilities. These consisted of a 'book-room', a workshop, a chemical room and a photographic darkroom. Above these on the main floor was the main laboratory, partitioned into a number of areas, including the 'black room' which was equipped with a helioscope and a spectroscope and used for optical experiments.[40] Crookes's private laboratories consisted of a suite of rooms including a physical laboratory, chemical laboratory, workshop and library.[41] Experimental activities at these home laboratories were endorsed by the Royal Society of London of which all these men were Fellows (and Presidents in the case of Rayleigh and Crookes), a validation and honour denied to women. Working only from home, without position, implied amateur status by the closing years of the nineteenth century. After all, anybody could perform simple experiments in their home, as was encouraged by a series of articles entitled 'Science for the Unscientific' appearing in a popular periodical from 1894. Through experiments to be executed at home the series explored subjects such as electricity, air pressure and optical illusions.[42] Hertha's home laboratory contributed to her remoteness from the networks and standards of the scientific community and had similar effects to her exclusion from the Royal Society.

It seems likely that Hertha's laboratory lacked credibility as a viable experimental site at a time when increasing emphasis was being placed on precise measurement and the use of manufactured instrumentation.[43] Whether experimental findings were to be admitted as knowledge was now dependent on the credibility of their site of production, as well as to the trustworthiness of the men of science who had produced them. Laboratories were becoming privileged epistemological spaces. When Karl Pearson took over Francis Galton's Eugenics Record Office at University College London in 1906, one of his first acts was to rename it 'The Galton Eugenics Laboratory', although much of its work centred on statistical computation, measurement and the compilation of tables. New institutional laboratories vied with each other for prestige based on their laboratory equipment. The Cavendish Laboratory had a 'magnetic room' for experiments in which there would be no magnetic disturbances from iron fittings or pipes. A 100-ton testing machine was pride of place at the new National Physical Laboratory, while the Central College's new electrical laboratories boasted a 5kw Ferranti transformer and a travelling overhead crane to assist in experimentation. The efficacy of Hertha's experimental apparatus was questioned by the Royal Society on several occasions, leading to the rejection of a paper on sand ripples.[44] One referee characterised her research methods as 'crude'.[45] Even sympathetic contemporaries wrote of how hard it was to appreciate her ideas due to the 'toy-like models' used in her laboratory.[46] Another memoir describes Hertha's use of 'a morsel of feather on a single thread of silk, anchored to a hat-pin' with which to test the speed that coal gas is driven through tubes.[47] Yet, there is a gender difference here. Male scientists were applauded for their achievements gained with primitive apparatus, especially when these heightened the danger to the experimenter. Gabriel Stokes was celebrated for experimental work 'executed with the most modest appliances' and Rayleigh's Terling laboratory was famously said by Kelvin to be 'held together with sealing wax and string'.[48] Such characterisation referred back to the romance of the earliest experimenters, such as those who founded the Royal Society in the 1640s, and linked the contemporary 'great men' of science with their forebears. Hertha was limited in the type of work that she could undertake in her laboratory which was simply not equipped to perform, say, electrical experiments requiring precise measurement. She found it increasingly difficult to persuade contemporaries to visit her home to witness her experiments, especially during the first months of the First World War. One commentator, a President of the Institution of Electrical Engineers, refers with ambivalence to Hertha's laboratory as a 'laboratory-drawing room'.[49] A photograph of 'Hertha Ayrton in her laboratory' which, although undated, probably originates from 1906, the year that she received a Royal Society Medal, endorses this perception [Figure 9.1]. Hertha is positioned in front of a bookcase, a potted plant and vase are above each shoulder and paintings hang on the wall above her head. She stands in front of a table upon which is a barely visible glass tank. The edge of another glass tank can just be seen, resting on top of a table covered in a velvet cloth. Hertha herself is dressed as to receive visitors, wearing jewellery, avoiding our eyes by gazing out towards the right of the photograph. The effect is ambiguous. Is this a scientist in the laboratory? Or a hostess/woman in her drawing room? The tidy, domestic values so connected with notions of femininity can also be read from this image. When compared to the messy, busy, active photographs of her contemporaries' laboratories, the visual subtext revealed by Hertha's portrait is that a woman's space is the home, not the laboratory.[50]

When Hertha Ayrton's achievements were reported in the press, the emphasis was on her femininity as a source of wonder and amusement. In 1899, the *Daily News* reported that what had astonished the lady visitors to Hertha's experimental demonstration 'was to find one of their own sex in charge of the most dangerous-looking of all the exhibits, a fierce arc light enclosed in glass. Mrs Ayrton was not a bit afraid of it'.[51] *The Times*, reporting on the award of the Hughes Medal to Mrs Ayrton, noted that her experimental methods were to be appreciated 'with interest and entertainment'.[52] Even a sympathetic novel, *The Call*, written by Edith Ayrton Zangwill and inspired by the life of her stepmother, uses the spectacle of a woman in the laboratory as a curiosity with which to generate humour:

> From the room within came a curious fizzling sound and a faint but still more curious odour. Some demented domestic appeared to be frying a late and unsavoury lunch in her bedroom. No servant would have condescended to a shapeless, blue-cotton overall and, still less, to hideous, dark goggles, made disfiguring by side-flaps ... all was dominated for the moment by a hissing jet of flame that darted out between the small, dark objects held in metal clamps which stood on a table in front of the girl ...[53]

The ambivalence of a woman in the laboratory is a theme of the novel, represented by the heroine's mother who names her daughter's laboratory the 'infernal regions' of the house and feels uncomfortable visiting there. The heroine's suitor also finds accompanying Ursula/Hertha into the laboratory personally uneasy. He remarks that he prefers to meet her in the park because she is 'less scientific, more human, more personal' – by implication, more 'womanly' out of the laboratory than within it.[54] *The Call* was published in 1924, the year following Hertha's death. The scientific experiences of Ursula in the novel follow closely those of Hertha (although the former's family situation is very different to conform to the requirements of a romantic novel). Passages of Evelyn Sharp's biography of Hertha echo word for word episodes in *The Call* and Sharp and Zangwill were in correspondence with each other. Sharp's memoir of her friend also betrays some ambivalence to Hertha's laboratory, this time from her natural daughter, Edie, who is quoted as complaining 'I do wish mother had a boudoir all filled with yellow satin furniture, instead of a laboratory ... like the mothers of other girls'.[55] Interestingly, in the novel Ursula is a Christian (nominally at least, as the fictional family celebrate Christmas) so Hertha's Jewishness is ignored, despite the fact that the author was married to leading Jewish writer Israel Zangwill (who was, therefore, Hertha's son-in-law). Does this imply that Hertha's Jewish status was not a matter that affected her scientific career? Certainly Hertha did not embrace a Jewish identity, lapsing from her religion on her marriage to a gentile and declaring herself an agnostic as far as religious belief was concerned as science was unable to prove the matter either way. Jewish writer Amy Levy, who studied at Newnham College, Cambridge, while Hertha was at Girton, suggested in an 1886 article for the *Jewish Chronicle* that Hertha was one of a number of notable Jewish women who had had to break ties of religion and race in order to pursue interests beyond the family and home.[56] Despite this, Hertha left no record indicating that she believed her Jewishness had affected her career adversely, while for the popular press her gender was novelty enough to warrant their attention. However Hertha's Jewish origins may have enhanced her attraction for the press, at least in the early years of her career, as it added to her exoticness as a woman scientist. When she read a paper before an audience of men at the Institute of Electrical Engineers Hertha was described as a 'little dark-haired, dark-eyed lady' who 'created a sensation'.[57]

As historians of science and gender have illustrated, the accelerating professionalisation of science at the end of the nineteenth century did pose an effective barrier to women's participation. However, this operated in a more complex way than just the closing of institutional doors to women. Justification and naturalisation of women's varying exclusion from the laboratory required the propagation of a masculine laboratory culture – both actual and mythic – which emphasised the physicality of the experimental space and the dangers that could lurk there. The creation of an heroic identity for scientific experimenters also served a useful function in elevating their moral and material worth at a time when the authority and status of their profession was being established. It is interesting to note that the applied mathematical and physical sciences were, at this time, removed from nature to the laboratory while, in contrast, sciences such as botany and geology sought phenomena as they occurred in nature. Women have been associated with the natural biological sciences while becoming virtually invisible in the physical ones. That the laboratory was configured as an unsuitable place for a woman may have contributed to this gender divide.

Notes

1   Alexander Wood, *The Cavendish Laboratory* (Cambridge, 1946), p. 4.
2   Robert John Strutt (Lord Rayleigh), 'Some Reminiscences of Scientific Workers of the Past Generation and their Surroundings', *Proceedings of the Physical Society*, 48, 2/265 (1936), p. 230.
3   For example see 'Introduction' to P.G. Abir-am and D. Outram (eds), *Uneasy Careers and Intimate Lives: Women in Science 1789–1979* (New Brunswick, 1987).
4   See Paula Gould, 'Women and the Culture of University Physics in Late-nineteenth-century Cambridge', *British Journal for the History of Science*, 30 (1997); Marsha L. Richmond, '"A Lab of One's Own": The Balfour Biological Laboratory for Women at Cambridge University, 1884–1914', in Sally Gregory Kohlstedt (ed.), *History of Women in the Sciences, Readings from ISIS* (Chicago, 1999).
5   Hertha Ayrton will be referred to as 'Hertha' in order to distinguish her from her husband, also an electrical engineer, and to reflect her desire to forge a separate identity from him. She adopted the name Hertha at the beginning of her career and was generally referred to as Mrs Hertha Ayrton by contemporaries (not Mrs William Ayrton) and often dropped the 'Mrs' when able to influence the publication format of her papers.
6   Barbara Leigh Smith Bodichon, 1827–91, was a member of the Langham Place Group and co-founder, with Emily Davies, of Girton College, Cambridge.
7   The second woman to become connected in any formal way with the IEE was engineer Gertrude Entwhistle who was elected a graduate member in 1919.
8   In 1945 x-ray crystallographer Kathleen Lonsdale and microbiologist/biochemist Marjory Stephenson were elected Fellows. For an account of Hertha Ayrton's nomination to the Royal Society see Joan Mason, 'Hertha Ayrton (1854–1923) and the Admission of Women to The Royal Society of London', *Notes. Rec. Royal Society of London*, 45, 2 (1991).
9   See F.A.J.L. James (ed.), *The Development of the Laboratory, Essays on the Place of Experiment in Industrial Civilization* (London, 1989).
10 *Nature*, 23 January 1890, p. 279.
11 Gould, 'Women and the Culture of University Physics'; London Guildhall Library, Finsbury Park Student Records, no. 29, 973.
12 London Guildhall Library, Central Institution Student Records, no. 21, 907–8.
13 C.S. Bremner, *The Education of Girls and Women in Great Britain* (London, 1987), p. 181.
14 Robert John Strutt (Lord Rayleigh), *The Life of Sir of J.J. Thomson* (Cambridge, 1942), pp. 51 and 26.
15 Rayleigh, 'Reminiscences of Scientific Workers', p. 226.
16 Peter Broks, *Media Science Before the War* (London, 1996), pp. 41–51.

17　Ibid.

18　Richmond, '"A Lab of One's Own"', p. 256.

19　Rayleigh, *Life of J.J. Thomson*, p. 46.

20　*Central Gazette*, 1, 4 (November 1904).

21　Quoted in Archives of Girton College, Cambridge: Joan Mason, 'Matilda Chaplin Ayrton (1846–1883), William Edward Ayrton (1847–1908) and Hertha Ayrton (1854–1923)' (unpublished manuscript, 1994), p. 6.

22　Ayrton's obituary was published in a special memorial issue of the college journal: *Central Gazette*, VII, 21 (1910), pp. 70–80; M. Soloman, 'Review of Evelyn Sharp's *Hertha Ayrton, 1854–1923, A Memoir*' (London, 1926), *Central Gazette*, XXIII, 59 (1926) pp. 70–72.

23　Graeme Gooday, 'The Premisses of Premises: Spatial Issues in the Historical Construction of Laboratory Credibility', in C. Smith and J. Agar (eds), *Making Space for Science. Territorial Themes in the Shaping of Knowledge* (London, 1998), p. 238.

24　*Central Gazette*, 1, 1 (February 1899).

25　Jean Barbara Garriock, 'Late Victorian and Edwardian Images of Women and their Education in the Popular Periodical Press with Particular Reference to the Work of L.T.Meade' (University of Liverpool, unpublished PhD thesis, 1997).

26　Hertha Ayrton, *The Electric Arc* (London 1902).

27　*Nature*, 29 December 1923, p. 939.

28　Gould, 'Women and Culture of University Physics'.

29　Sir William Huggins, *The Royal Society, or, Science in the State and in the Schools* (London, 1906), p. 40.

30　This summation of the profession of an engineer appeared in 'The Vacuum Cleaner', *The Central*, 1, 4 (1904) p. 148.

31　The classic statement of this is Carolyn Merchant, 'Isis' Consciousness Raised', *ISIS*, 73, 268 (1982). See also Evelyn Fox Keller, *Reflections on Gender and Science* (Yale, 1985) and Ludmilla Jordanova, *Sexual Visions* (London, 1989).

32　*Proceedings of the Royal Society* (LXXV) Obituaries of Deceased Fellows, 1898–1904, George Gabriel Stokes.

33　On the USA see Larry Owens, 'Pure and Sound Government, Laboratories, Playing Fields and Gymnasia in the Nineteenth-Century Search for Order', *ISIS*, 76 (1985).

34　See J.A. Kesiner, *Sherlock's Men: Masculinity, Conan Doyle and Cultural History* (Aldershot, 1997).

35　J. Vargas Eyre, *Henry Edward Armstrong, 1848–1937* (London, 1958), p. 130.

36　Lord Rayleigh, 'Presidential Address', *Proceedings of the Royal Society,* Series A, LXXX (1907–8), p. 243.

37　I. Grattan-Guinness, 'University Mathematics at the Turn of the Century; Unpublished Recollections of W.H. Young', *Annals of Science*, 28, 4 (1972). Famously, it caused a furore when Philippa Fawcett (daughter of Millicent) was placed above the 'senior wrangler' (first-placed male candidate) in the Cambridge Mathematics Tripos of 1890.

38　See Shirley Ardener (ed.), *Women and Space, Ground Rules and Social Maps* (Oxford, 1993).

39　Simon Schaffer, 'Physics Laboratories and the Victorian Country House', in C. Smith and J. Agar (eds), *Making Space for Science: Territorial Themes in the Shaping of Knowledge* (London, 1998).

40　A.T. Humphreys, 'Lord Rayleigh – the Last of the Great Victorian Polymaths', *GEC Review*, 7, 3 (1992).

41　Rayleigh, 'Some Reminiscences of Scientific Workers'.

42 Broks, *Media Science*, p. 37.
43 For discussion of the expansion in scale, cost and time of experiments from this period see Nicholas Jardine, *The Scenes of Inquiry* (Oxford, 1991).
44 Concern was raised that the pressure indicators attached to the tanks of water that she had used could have leaked and distorted the readings. Hertha redesigned the apparatus and her paper was finally accepted.
45 Archives of the Royal Society of London, Horace Lamb, Referee Report 142/1904.
46 Institution of Electrical and Electronic Engineers Archive, A.P. Trotter, unpublished memoirs, p. 587.
47 Evelyn Sharp, *Hertha Ayrton, A Memoir* (London, 1926), p. 282.
48 *Proceedings of the Royal Society*, Obituaries, LXXV, Stokes, p. 211; Humphreys, 'Lord Rayleigh', p. 8.
49 Trotter, Memoirs, p. 587.
50 See photographs in Strutt, 'Some Reminiscences'.
51 Sharp, *Hertha Ayrton*, p. 144.
52 Archives of Royal Holloway College, University of London: *The Times*, 1906, quoted in 'Mrs Ayrton and the Hughes Medal', *Bedford College Magazine* (December 1906).
53 Edith Ayrton Zangwill, *The Call* (London, 1924), p. 9.
54 Ibid., p. 131.
55 Sharp, *Hertha Ayrton*, p. 154.
56 Linda Hunt Beckman, 'Leaving "The Tribal Duckpond": Amy Levy, Jewish Self-Hatred and Jewish Identity', *Victorian Literature and Culture*, 27, 1 (1999).
57 Sharp, *Hertha Ayrton*, p. 136.

PART V

WOMEN AND WAR

Chapter 10

All Quiet on the Woolwich Front? Literary and Cultural Constructions of Women Munitions Workers in the First World War

Angela K. Smith

> Six shell cases to the hour … eight cases to the hour … ten cases to the hour … she sent wishes of death with every shell. 'Do the same, my beauty, do the same to the enemy who killed *him*!'[1]

Pamela Butler, the 'munitionette' protagonist of Irene Rathbone's novel *We That Were Young*, takes up factory work instead of nursing after the death of her fiancé in France. Her motive is very clear: anger. Unable to avenge his death in the conventional way, by serving as a soldier, she determines to make the shells that will kill his enemies. Rathbone uses Butler firstly to highlight the impotent rage of the bereaved, but perhaps more interestingly, to draw connections between the women in this industry and their male counterparts on the Western Front. Working extended shifts, Butler identifies with soldiers at the front, with the physical and mental hardships that they face. She witnesses horrific industrial accidents, women maimed by the alternative machinery of war, and her health is finally ruined leaving her with the lasting legacy of her own battles.

As a cultural construct, Pamela Butler operates to argue for an equality of suffering. The war is as bad for women as it is for men. The factory becomes the front line with comparable physical and emotional implications. This chapter explores this and similar such constructs. Through examination of a variety of literary texts, memoirs and private diaries, it seeks to explore the way in which women workers chose to represent themselves and the way in which they were represented by others. What is the lasting impression of the woman munitions worker? And does it correspond with the military experience of the First World War?

The very notion of experience is complex. Joan Scott has argued that the word itself is problematic. Endowed with multiple meanings and alternative modes of reading, it is often used to 'essentialize identity and reify the subject' in a way that can be misleading.[2] The many representations of experience explored here are diverse and open to a range of interpretations and meanings, which may result in contradictory patterns emerging. As with any form of life writing, and many of the testimonies included here fall easily into that category, it is impossible to separate truth from memory and indeed, memory from fiction. The literary readings of these experiences help to locate them as a part of a wider cultural process.

Scott argues, 'What counts as experience is neither self-evident nor straightforward; it is always contested, and always therefore political'.[3] Rathbone wrote *We That Were* Young in 1932. Her book is a considered fictional commentary, taken from 'real' accounts, of a variety of women's wartime experiences. Part of the project, a distinctly political one, appears to be to reclaim participation in the war as a female as well as male arena. Her female combatants also serve as nurses and do other types of work, completing a picture of a suffering generation.[4] But this impression of the munitions worker as a female soldier was not new. Even during the war, many publications explored the role and the image of the 'munitionette' in an attempt to find an appropriate public space. Theirs was a complex identity. They were women engaged in men's work, work as far removed from conventional 'feminine' roles as it was possible to find. But they were doing it for 'King and Country' and as such it was important to present a positive propagandist image despite the supposed 'unnatural' character of the work.

During the war a range of propagandist texts appeared. These included *The Woman's Part: A Record of Munitions Work* by L.K. Yates, which appeared in 1918 and which sought to present an optimistic and patriotic image of women. It was an exploration of 'the Heroism of the workshop': '… events have proved that the women of Great Britain are as ready as their men folk to sacrifice comfort and personal convenience to the demands of a great cause'.[5] Yates informed the reader that: 'The work has, in fact, called for personal qualities usually thought to be abnormal in women … The heroism of the battlefields has frequently been equalled by the ordinary citizen in the factory; whether man or woman'.[6] Yates used the rhetoric of the heroic tradition to bring this type of women's work into line with that of men, oblivious to the notion that the First World War may have, by 1918, rendered this rhetoric obsolete.

In *Munition Lasses (Six Months as a Principal Overlooker in Danger Buildings)*, A.K. Foxwell's writing used an insider's advantage to illustrate this heroism for the general public. Foxwell intended, 'To give the general public an insight into the life of the munition worker – a life which, while sympathetically spoken of by the nation at large, and at last included in the nation's prayers, is practically unknown to all but the initiated'.[7] Foxwell lacked the missionary zeal of Yates, but instead used experience to argue for authentic representation. But even 'true' stories have a tendency towards the quaint in these early texts as the title of another such publication indicates: *TNT Tales and a Few Food Fancies*, collected from the mouths of munition girls by T.A. Lamb.[8] Here the peculiar juxtaposition of the violence of industry and the domestic in the Barnbow shell-filling factory attempts to soften the impression of the workers, who retain some of the innate femininity so threatened by work previously positioned as masculine. I will return to the complex ideas held within this juxtaposition later. It is clear that these early works had a political agenda of their own and the writers used claims about the authenticity of the experiences they described to promote their own message.

The cultural stereotype created by 'the heroism of the workshop' appeared as early as 1916. *Lloyd George's Munition Girls* by Monica Cosens appears to be a personal memoir by a woman who wanted nothing more than to be 'Miss Tommy Atkins'.[9] Cosens's account created caricature figures, 'Khaki girls' referred to generically throughout, who do their bit just like their soldier brothers. The tone is gentle and humorous, perhaps slightly mocking. While being applauded, the 'khaki girls' are not quite taken seriously. As strange labels such as 'khaki girls' and 'Miss Tommy Atkins' suggest, Cosens attempted to equate the experience of the work with life in the trenches. When fumes from a charcoal brazier make the girls ill, the foreman refers to it as being 'gassed'. The minor injuries received by the girls are their 'wounds', 'She [Miss Tommy Atkins] is proud of her wounds. After all, they have come about in the service of her country'.[10] As she loses her looks through the hard work and exposure to dangerous substances, this is compared to the loss of a limb, (although it is admittedly not quite as bad). Of course the khaki girls of this publication never receive life-threatening or disabling wounds, and it would be inappropriate to make a comparison that close to men's experience in a text of this type.

The munitions workers in Monica Cosens's book are, for the most part, well-respected and respectable, admired by the public for the important work that they do and even acknowledged by the real combatants. After receiving some flowers picked by wounded soldiers Cosens wrote: 'Here was real proof that Mr Tommy Atkins thought about us. It made us feel we were sharing the war with him. It drew us together, and we felt for the first time we were working *with* our soldiers and not *for them*'.[11] But they never claim equality and these flowers emblematically endorse their feminine status.

Angela Woollacott has argued that the uniform representations of women in such narratives is inaccurate:

> The danger of phrases like 'Tommy's sister' is that it implies a homogeneity among women munitions workers that simply did not exist. The women who made up this cohort were a mixture of ages, classes, sexualities, races, ethnicities and regional and national origins and represented enormously varied standards of living, cultures, and political views.[12]

Indeed, during the war Annie Purbrook noted:

> Very soon there was a great demand for workers in munitions factories. All sorts and conditions of people left their ordinary occupations and went, as they said, to 'do their bit' … It is astonishing how eagerly the girls take on the rough, dirty and tiring work, cheerfully, uncomplaining … all sorts and conditions, gentle well-bred girls side by side with those used to factory work. Truly this war is a great leveller.[13]

But other contemporary records often ignore these differences in order to create the impression of the propagandist 'khaki girl'. Gabrielle West, who served firstly in munitions factory kitchens and then as a woman police officer in various factories, tended to generalise when discussing the women workers. She describes the workers at Woolwich thus: 'The girls are very rough, regular cockneys, but mostly amiable if not rubbed the wrong way. If they are it is Billingsgate gone mad'.[14] This application of stereotype in a private document is interesting and suggests a level of uniformity amongst the women that denied the individuality of the worker. Middle-class Peggy Hamilton, a Woolwich worker, was clearly unusual. However, in her published memoir, *Three Years or the Duration*, she acknowledged her own class difference, but at the same time emphasised how much she enjoyed the uniformity: 'I felt a curious satisfaction and happiness in being just an ordinary worker pushing my way in through the gates with hundreds of others'.[15] Perhaps the sense of belonging, of 'doing your bit', seemed more important than individual backgrounds at the time. Alternatively, Sharon Ouditt has suggested that the notion of classlessness cultivated in women's industry was designed to negate ideas of a new power that grew out of the widening employment opportunities. Many such representations were intended to 'naturalise women's involvement in war work and play down its radical implications'.[16] Ouditt goes on to argue against the anonymity of these constructions of women workers: 'Stereotyping the jolly working classes from this bemused, bourgeois perspective renders them interchangeable; disempowers them while claiming to celebrate their power'.[17] There is perhaps an element of social control in some of these early representations of women munition workers, indicating a vague, underlying fear of the potential that they embody.

Rathbone's novel acknowledges social and cultural difference, placing the middle-class Butler alongside working-class co-workers, but all are 'khaki girls' when it comes to patriotic duty. Faced with working gruelling triple shifts in order to deliver a particularly tough order, all the workers volunteer and all pull together despite exhaustion. In order to get herself through it Pamela compares herself with the soldiers at the front:

> The second night ground on. It was no use pretending any more that you were at a dance. A far stronger stimulus than that was required. The Front. The dark glutinous desolate Front. Think of *that*. The soldiers. Your eyes were red-hot coals, your spine a red-hot poker, your arms a mass of leaping tortured nerves. But what did it matter? You were warm and safe, which the soldiers were not. You were regularly fed, which they were not. Noise crashed around you, but it was only the noise of machinery – not of shells. Stick it! Stick it![18]

The direct address of the narrative invites the reader to share the experience. While Pamela assures herself that she is better off than the soldiers, Rathbone offers a different subtext. She has done everything possible here to recreate the sensations of trench life. The lack of sleep is paramount, the eternal noise, the monotony. Indeed, the monotony for the women actually involved repetitive, continual hard work, as opposed to the waiting around that made up a large part of trench life. Their food breaks are short and limited. And of course, as Rathbone shows us, through two horrific and detailed industrial accidents, the work is not as safe as Pamela intimates. Is this then, the female front?

Contemporary diarists tend to avoid the issue of serious injury.[19] Ethel Wilby recorded, 'On some of the lathes I got the raw sockets cutting off the brass, and the bits used to fly up. If I got a cut finger I'd have a bit of brass in it, or a bit in the eye'.[20] Similarly Edith Airey recalled, 'Small bits of brass seemed to be a target for my eyes and I was for ever at the first aid post having bits extracted'.[21] These actual testimonies do not seem very glamorous and do not really bear comparison with the trench experience. In contrast, Gabrielle West acknowledged the possibility of serious injury, but used its avoidance to accentuate the heroism of the girls:

May [1918]

Quite a big explosion. Recently a new machine has been put in for water-proofing the dry gun cotton. In the middle of the night it blew up. Two girls were working it. The shed was wrecked & the machine blown to chips & the girls shot out on to the bank opposite. One found that her shoes were alight so calmly kicked them off & both trotted up to the canteen. Meanwhile agitated firemen were hunting for their dismembered remains.[22]

This insouciant attitude towards danger gives the impression of bravery which seems to comply with at least one representation of the munitions worker at the time – the 'plucky survivor'. West developed it:

The girls are very plucky during a raid & really very good tempered too considering the cold & discomfort of a raid. There are now shelters of a kind. They are called 'dugouts' but there is no digging about them. They are very little huts made of packing cases with a few sand bags & brush wood on the roof.[23]

These shelters do not sound as though they would inspire confidence, but did not, apparently, dent the courage of the women whom they shielded. Similar language recurs in other accounts to confirm this image. Writing to her sister during the Second World War, Geraldine Kaye recalled, 'At Woolwich I had 400 women and girls in my three workshops (I was principal overlooker on my shift) and I used to feel very proud of their wonderful pluck when all the lights were put out when the Zeppelins used to come over'.[24] This is a 'pluck' that unites Mr and Miss Tommy Atkins in the eyes of the public.[25]

But Irene Rathbone wants more for her women and she makes a bigger claim. It is not enough to share a similar heroic mythology. To prove that equality of suffering she has to go further.[26] Liz Fanshawe foolishly removes her 'jelly-bag' hat to allow her head to breathe for a moment. It is enough: her hair is caught in the wheel of a drilling machine ripping off the front part of her scalp. Later, Elsie Thompson, 'a stodgy girl, with a thick white face',[27] loses a finger to a capstan machine. Both women are in shock, but they are rapidly moved to the casualty clearing station, that is, the dispensary. Rathbone also focuses on the reactions of the witnesses, the psychological trauma of war. Pamela's neighbour, Nellie Crewe, is sick at the sight of Liz's scalping. Pamela herself 'punched on in a frenzy, fighting her nausea. One did not faint. If one had any stamina, any pride, one – did – not – faint'.[28] There is surely a danger here, of shellshock setting in. But later, as she watches the bits of flesh being cleaned out of Elsie's machine, she has a more conventional, patriotic reaction:

This other was more like a soldier's wound, of which she had seen many. She wondered that she felt no greater pity for Elsie, but the only thought that went through her mind was: 'Wounded for her country. Almost wish it had been me. Wish I could lose a finger – an arm – my whole life.'[29]

Pamela's identification with the soldiers reinforces Rathbone's point. By laying themselves open to wounding and death as a result of the technology of war, while in the process of war production, these women are soldiers too, with their own dangers to face. This is not quite the front line, but close enough.

But this construction of munitions workers as soldiers and as heroes was by no means universal. On the contrary, the image of the masculinised woman munitions worker caused great offence to many. Soldier George Wilby, serving in Africa, wrote to his fiancée, '… don't take on a man's job or go into a factory. I think it disgusting the way women are going on at home. When us chaps come home we shan't know the women from the men'.[30] Wilby went on, 'I'm so afraid if you go into a factory or any other rough work it will take all the womanly qualities out of you, Dear, and leave you coarse and unlovable like most other girls'.[31] It is interesting to contrast this with the 'Tommy's' voice quoted by Monica Cosens, 'it's fine what you're doing kiddie, and all of us out here think you great'.[32] The text aimed at promoting the role of the munitions worker cannot afford to enter into this debate and acknowledge that such work may compromise a woman's 'womanly' status.

George Wilby voiced a double common concern that women would lose their femininity: firstly through doing hard, physical, men's work, and secondly through the independence granted by higher wages. Munitions work, for many, meant a temporary end to economic dependence. Women who don't need men pose a serious threat to conventional power structures and to notions of femininity. The cultural construction of the munitions worker as a 'good time girl', perhaps an inevitable response to this threat, was well established by 1918 and is demonstrated by Madeline Ida Bedford's parodic poem, 'Munition Wages':

> Earning high wages? Yus,
> Five quid a week.
> A woman, too, mind you,
> I calls it dim sweet.
>
> Ye're asking some questions –
> But bless yer, here goes:

I spends the whole racket
On good times and clothes.

Me saving? Elijah!
Yer do think I'm mad.
I'm acting the lady,
But – I ain't living bad …

…We're all here today, mate,
Tomorrow – perhaps dead,
If Fate tumbles on us
And blows up our shed.[33]

The poem, first published in 1917, creates a caricature picture of the munitions worker, exaggerating both the language and the lifestyle. The speaker of the poem is identified linguistically as working class. The use of slang places her in a distinct category, a woman used to less, making the most of more. Despite acknowledging the possibility of danger in the factories, the main emphasis is on high living; indeed, the danger is cited as a justification for this fabled lifestyle. Like the soldiers at the front she needs to make the most of life while she can in case 'fate tumbles on us / and blows up our shed'. The poem is both exaggeration and parody. Other commentators, such as Peggy Hamilton, suggest that the 'five quid a week' of Bedford's munitionette may be optimistic. Equally her preoccupation with 'good times and clothes' creates a rather limited image and one that may be apt to give the women a bad reputation despite her claims that she 'ain't living bad'. While the poem does not, perhaps, present a very convincing impression to the modern reader, this and other such representations made an impact during the war.

Ethel Wilby was quick to disassociate herself with both this way of living, and the money that allegedly financed it. Wilby entered the factory towards the end of the war: 'It was at the time when they were slowing down on making them, coming to the end of the war, and you weren't making the money like they did in the first place, when they were supposed to have bought fur coats and goodness knows what with the money they earned'.[34] Wilby was clearly aware of the mythology surrounding the munitions workers, although she did not appear to have experienced it herself.

Peggy Hamilton further undermined the myth in her published memoir, recalling an argument that took place in her boarding house. Responding to a woman's accusation – 'I think it's disgraceful all these munition makers and their fur coats; they're getting too much money' – Hamilton returned, 'I told her I was a munition worker, that no one I knew owned a fur coat, that we worked 7 to 7, six days a week, for £1 a week and what sort of fur coat did she think she could buy after paying her living out of that?'[35] The truth is probably somewhere in between. For single women moving from more traditional, lower paid work (such as domestic service), the wages probably did provide the opportunity for a more extravagant life style – new clothes instead of 'tatters' – but doubtless the poem exaggerates the level of luxury available to them. For married women, now often breadwinners, the better wages could have meant the difference between keeping a family and poverty, not a ticket to the high living that Bedford suggests.

However, the high wages paid to munition workers gave them some scope at least to reinvent themselves, although accounts of decadent living may have been little more than further constructs. But their 'femininity', their dependent status, indeed, the gender balance within society, might be threatened by this new economic power. And for people such as George Wilby the notion of women working in munitions was also dangerous on a more ideological level. Here women are involved not only in hard physical labour (as they may be in a range of other jobs), but also in the processes of death. For many people, both women and men, this was a crime against nature. Women were intended to create life, not destroy it. Another poem written during the war – Mary Gabrielle Collins' 'Women At Munitions Making' – articulates this view:

> Their hands should minister unto the flame of life,
>   Their fingers guide
> The rosy teat, swelling with milk,
> To the eager mouth of the suckling babe …
>   But now,
> Their hands, their fingers
> Are coarsened in munition factories …
> They must take part in defacing and destroying the natural body
> Which, certainly during this dispensation
> Is the shrine of the spirit.
>   O God! …[36]

This poem, melodramatic as it is, presents a view shared by many at the time, that there was something *essentially* wrong with women becoming involved with war, on any level, but particularly one that involved them in the processes of killing.[37] Women create life, so must not destroy it. Intimate images of motherhood exaggerate this role and are repeated throughout the poem. The Madonna-like picture of the mother and child is juxtaposed with the rawness of the battlefield through the image of the hands, once soft, now 'coarsened' by the unnatural work. It is fundamentally against nature; the natural body, the property of woman, is destroyed. It is also against God. Women, like their belligerent men-folk, blaspheme when they destroy the 'shrine of the spirit'. Like Bedford's poem, 'Women At Munitions Making' presents an extreme view, and one that does not sit comfortably with the patriotic agenda of the country at war which was prepared to turn a blind eye to such 'unnatural' processes. However, for many the potential masculinisation of women presented a serious threat, not just to the balance of patriarchal society, but to the future of society itself.

Ethel Wilby did not listen to her fiancé's advice. Perhaps she did not even receive it in time, but she entered a munitions factory in June 1918. George received the news in October and was very unhappy:

> Fancy – my little girl helping to make shells to blot out human lives – you know Darling, you weren't made for such a thing – you were really made to bring lives into the world wasn't you … after the war we will see about the 'bringing in' process to make up for the damage *you* have done.[38]

Wilby got over his immediate anger, justifying her actions to himself through the understanding that it is the enemy that she will be killing. But note the phrasing. After the war they will have children to make up for the damage that *she* has done: the ultimate re-feminising process to reclaim her for womanhood, although she may remain tainted by having deviated. Ethel's own retrospective account of her war experience, recorded in 1984, seems to suggest that she was quite happy in munitions (despite concern that her angry fiancé would not like her wearing trousers!). But even writing years later she was troubled by the paradoxical representation of women workers, 'People didn't think much of munitions girls, but they had to do it. I thought I was doing the right thing, but evidently I shouldn't have …'.[39] In 1984, she still believed that she had done the wrong thing. The ethical problems wrapped up in making munitions leave a legacy of guilt that does not appear to fade with the years.

These various constructions of munitions workers circulated during the war years, both via the media and within private writings. But certainly, from a propagandist point of view, much less emphasis was placed on the 'reality' of the experience. Creating the right public image was the most important thing. Just as Monica Cosens made light of the workers' 'wounds', so she paid little attention to the conditions of factory life, many of which left something to be desired. Gabrielle West, however, made sure to record these details in her diary account, ranging from the technicalities of the work itself, to the state of the medical and hygiene facilities available to the women workers.

> July 22nd 1916.
> Today I went over the factory as a real favour. First I saw the cordite made in charges ... then I saw the lyddite works. This is a brilliant yellow powder & comes in tubs. It is then sifted. The house, windows, floors, walls in which this is done is stained bright yellow. As soon as you go in the lyddite in the air gets into your nose and mouth and makes you sneeze and splutter as if you had a violent hayfever. It gives you a horrid bitter taste at the back of your throat ...[40]

Reading this, it is easy to visualise the yellow skinned women workers – the 'canaries'.

> 10th March 1917.
> The ether in the cordite affects some of the girls. It gives them headaches, hysteria & sometimes makes them unconscious. If a worker has the least tendency to epilepsy, even if it has never shown itself before, the ether will bring it on ... when the girls get taken ill we are generally called in to render what assistance we can & to take them up to the surgery on stretchers. In this way we have begun to win the confidence of the girls & some, who were most aggressive in attitude towards the women police are beginning to get quite friendly.[41]

These practical dangers seem to have been exacerbated by the lack of appropriate facilities.

> April 10th 1917.
> This factory is very badly equipped as regards the welfare of the girls. The changing rooms are fearfully crowded, long troughs are provided instead of wash basins & there is always a scarcity of soap and towels ...
> Although the fumes often mean 16 or 18 casualties a night there are only 4 beds in the surgery for men & women & they are all in the same room ... There are no drains owing to the ground being below sea level ... there were until recently no lights in the lavatories, & as these same lavatories are generally full of rats & often very dirty the girls are afraid to go in.[42]

West's private commentary on the poor conditions in the factories echoes the more public writings of women such as Sylvia Pankhurst, who used her socialist paper, the *Dreadnought* to argue for reform,[43] but this image of the 'munitionette' as oppressed worker is not one that took hold in the public imagination. West's role as a woman police officer seems to have fired her interest in the welfare of the women, but this was problematised when the women themselves took action to better their position. While working at factories in Hereford and South Wales, West recorded frequent strike activity. The above diary entries suggest that some of this was justified, but West was not always sympathetic. In Hereford, 'strikes are more sport than just filling shells', and the women 'always get their own way & they know it'.[44] While this industrial action was obviously commonplace in factories such as those that West described, the image of the munition worker as a political militant is not one that was given much publicity during the war. Such behaviour, like the occasional protests of soldiers, was considered to be unpatriotic and bad for the morale of the country. Women may well have found their political feet during the First World War, with so many more of them in industry and a level of trade-union recognition previously unmatched.[45] This gives another very different impression of munitions workers, one which, while retrospectively fascinating, was perhaps, quite deliberately, not allowed to form a part of the contemporary mythology of the First World War. As Sharon Ouditt has argued, propaganda controlled public perceptions of women workers, often hiding reality.[46]

During the war these contrary cultural constructions of women working in munitions competed, arguably putting pressure on the workers themselves. Perhaps as a consequence, there were public, and open propagandist attempts to draw these various representations together, to create an overriding, positive stereotype. At its most extreme this is blatant propaganda. Mrs Humphrey Ward illustrated women working round the clock, with no sign of fatigue, but rather, feminine and efficient with the habit of singing 'Keep the Home Fires Burning' as they worked. Another, perhaps more subtle, example of this kind of literary representation can be found in Rebecca West's article written for the *Daily Chronicle*, 1916, 'Hands that War: The Cordite Makers'.[47]

West's future as a novelist can be seen clearly in this piece. She uses language with effective, often poetic, precision to blend the constructions of the munitions workers into an heroic whole. The cordite factory is located in a rustic idyll, a world of colour and sensation 'polished to brightness by an east wind'.[48] The women workers, who are 'pretty young girls' throughout are 'clad in a Red-Riding-Hood fancy dress of khaki and scarlet'.[49] The connotations here are many. The fairy tale association makes them at once innocent, a blatant denial of the 'bad' character of some impressions. Red Riding Hood also suggests a vulnerability, hinting at the dangerous nature of their work. They are both 'khaki girls' and 'scarlet' women, combining duty and knowledge with that innocence in a rather unsettling way. The khaki and scarlet are emphasised throughout, making the piece extremely visual. The women stand out in this grey factory environment, valorised against the monotony. The women are likened to children which has the effect of reinforcing the notion of innocence, yet is not infantilising. Instead, they are empowered as this impression is juxtaposed with the hard physical work and long hours of factory life. There is a delicate blend of the danger with the domestic, constructed in order to prevent the loss of that valued femininity, '… the next hut, where girls stand round great vats in which steel hands mix the gun-cotton with mineral jelly, might be part of a steam-bakery. The brown cordite paste itself looks as if it might turn into very pleasant honey-cakes …'.[50] There is something particularly comforting about this metaphor. The reality of the work is softened to the point of acceptability by the mist of the 'bake-house' steam. There are echoes here of that strange juxtaposition, *TNT Tales and a Few Food Fancies*. The domestic imagery helps retain femininity against all the odds.

The scarlet hoods, however, are more than they seem. They have been dipped in a solution to make them fireproof, a kind of enchanted protection against the dangers of explosion that are an every-day possibility in the cordite factory. This danger takes us back, once again, to the troops on the front line. 'Surely,' West wrote, 'never before in modern history can women have lived a life so completely parallel to that of the regular army.'[51] For this hard work, courage in the face of danger and the introduction of an added grace and beauty to barrack life, West, the feminist journalist, asked only that the women be accorded military rank, a formal acknowledgement of the equality of 'Miss Tommy Atkins'.

So, the First World War munitions worker was both despised and revered, a masculine bringer of death and a feminine preserver of life, a good time girl, a patriot, and a soldier. The social and cultural constructions are many and diverse, testimony perhaps to the individuality of the thousands who signed up 'for the duration'. Many women enjoyed the work. Mrs P.L Stephens found great freedom, working around the country riding her Triumph motor-cycle.[52] Others, like Ethel Wilby were less sure. Later literary constructions, such as Pamela Butler, open up the possibility of giving voice to West's pretty young girls in khaki and scarlet, and equally important, to whom they might become after the war. In *The Woman's Part: A Record of Munitions Work*, L.K. Yates argued, 'Indeed, many of the girls passing through this strange war-time adventure have assuredly gained by their pilgrimage precisely in those qualities most needed by the wives and mothers of the rising generation'.[53] Presumably these were spiritual qualities rather than the knowledge of how to fill a shell case. It is interesting to note the need, as the end of the war approached, to reaffirm those vital feminine qualities. That little brush with masculinity, in propagandist terms, served to make women better wives and mothers rather than taint them for their future roles.

The reality was mass unemployment among women following demobilisation.[54] For Pamela Butler, the dreams of becoming an actress, treasured before the war, are destroyed by a weak heart, the lasting legacy of her war work. With two dead fiancés behind her and ruined health ahead, she settles for rural spinsterhood looking after her parents. This is a very Victorian plight that seems to deny the possibility that the war did much for women's emancipation, suggesting that they were simply sent back home until they were needed again. The multiple images of the 'munitionette' linger on, in a range of different texts, private, public, non-fictional and fictional, but the post-war reality suggests a limited social or cultural legacy. As Ethel Wilby puts it:

> People were hoping they were going to get better things out of winning the war, so as to be better than they were beforehand. The same with the second war; they thought it was going to be a war to end wars. Strikes me as being the other way round. I should have thought with all the wars we've had it would be understood that wars don't benefit anyone. Everybody's worse off really – except those who make the munitions.[55]

Notes

1   Irene Rathbone, *We That Were Young* (London, 1988), p. 268 (first published 1932).
2   Joan W. Scott, 'The Evidence of Experience', *Critical Enquiry*, 17 (1991), p. 797.
3   Ibid.
4   Rathbone herself served as a nurse during the First World War. She also worked in a YMCA rest camp in northern France at the beginning and again at the end of the war. She left details diaries of her experiences in this last camp, which are now held at the Imperial War Museum (henceforth IWM), Department of Documents. Pamela Butler's experiences are based on those of one of Rathbone's close friends.
5   L.K. Yates, *The Woman's Part: A Record of Munitions Work* (London, 1918), p. 9.
6   Ibid., p.12.
7   A.K. Foxwell, *Munition Lasses (Six Months as a Principal Overlooker in Danger Buildings)* (London, 1917), 'Statement of Intention'.
8   T.A. Lamb, *TNT Tales and a Few Food Fancies* (London, 1919).
9   Monica Cosens, *Lloyd George's Munition Girls* (London, 1916).
10   Ibid., p. 71.

11   Ibid., p. 67.

12   Angela Woollacott, *On Her Their Lives Depend* (Berkeley, 1994), p. 37.

13   IWM, Department of Documents, Annie Purbrook, 'Notes 1914–18'.

14   IWM, Department of Documents, Miss G.M .West, unpublished diary, 22 May 1916.

15   Peggy Hamilton, *Three Years or the Duration* (London, 1978), p. 37.

16   Sharon Ouditt, 'Tommy's Sisters: the Representation of Working Women's Experience', in Hugh Cecil and Peter H. Liddle (eds), *Facing Armageddon: The First World War Experienced* (London, 1996), p. 739.

17   Ibid., p. 742.

18   Rathbone, *We That Were Young*, pp. 274–5.

19   It is important to note that contemporary accounts by munition workers are in very short supply, due to the fact that most were working class in origin and lacked the time, education or indeed motivation to keep a written record. See Ouditt, 'Tommy's Sisters', pp. 745–6.

20   IWM, Department of Documents, Ethel Wilby, unpublished memoir, typescript 1984.

21   IWM, Department of Documents, Edith Airey, unpublished memoir.

22   West, Diary, May 1918.

23   West, Diary, undated entry, probably early 1918.

24   IWM, Department of Documents, Mrs Geraldine Kaye, letter to her sister, Eileen Hutchinson, 24 January 1940.

25   Peggy Hamilton, *Three Years*, p. 34, gives this a different slant. She talks about how the women were too tired to move during air-raids, suggesting that they would as soon be hit there as anywhere else.

26   For more detailed information about the facts and figures of industrial accidents see Woollacott, *On Her Their Lives Depend*, pp. 79–80 and 84–8.

27   Rathbone, *We That Were Young*, p. 269.

28   Ibid., p. 267.

29   Ibid., p. 270.

30   IWM, Department of Documents, George Wilby, letter, 20 September 1917.

31   Ibid.

32   Cosens, *Lloyd George's Munition Girls*, p. 158.

33   Madeline Ida Bedford, 'Munition Wages', in Catherine Reilly (ed.), *Scars Upon My Heart* (London, 1992), p. 7. The poem was first published in Madeline Ida Bedford, *The Young Captain* (London, 1917).

34   Ethel Wilby, Memoir.

35   Quoted in Woollacott, *On Her Their Lives Depend*, p. 129.

36   Mary Gabrielle Collins, 'Women At Munition Making', in Reilly (ed.), *Scars Upon My Heart*, p. 24.

37   See for example, Margaret Kemester and Jo Vellacott (eds), *Militarism Versus Feminism* (London, 1987).

38   George Wilby, letter, 3 October 1918 (my emphasis).

39   Ethel Wilby, Memoir.

40   West, Diary, 22 July 1916.

41   Ibid., 10 March 1917.

42   Ibid., 10 April 1917.

43   See for example, Sylvia Pankhurst, 'Lloyd George in Wonderland', *The Women's Dreadnought*, 19 February 1916.

44   West, Diary, 10 June 1917.

45 Many men's trade unions were reluctant to accept women workers in the first instance, but later realised that they needed to protect the position of women in order to protect the position of men. If women were paid lower wages for equal work then there may be reluctance on the part of factory owners to re-employ men at the traditional higher rates after the war.

46 Ouditt, 'Tommy's Sisters', p. 739.

47 Rebecca West, 'Hands that War', in Margaret R. Higonnet (ed.), *Lines of Fire: Women Writers of the First World War* (New York, 1999).

48 Ibid., p. 123.

49 Ibid., p. 123.

50 Ibid., pp. 123–4.

51 Ibid., p. 125.

52 IWM, Department of Documents, Mrs P.L. Stephens, Recollections, 1976.

53 Yates, *Woman's Part*, p. 64.

54 See Woollacott, *On Her Their Lives Depend*, pp. 105–12.

55 Wilby, Memoir.

Chapter 11

Eve in Khaki: Women Working with the British Military, 1915–18

Lucy Noakes

The movement of women into most spheres of public life, and into all the professions, has been a defining feature of twentieth-century British society. During the twentieth century, the labour participation rate for women grew from 30 per cent in 1900 to 65 per cent in the 1990s.[1] The gendered wage gap narrowed over the same period from a position in which women earned approximately 50 per cent of the male wage at the beginning of the century to 28 per cent of the male wage by 1994.[2] However, the movement of women into occupations and professions traditionally perceived as male has long been resisted by the men working in those occupations and by their trades unions, who feared that the 'feminisation' of their occupations would denude them of status. When women have moved into the military, this fear can be seen even more clearly. The female soldier threatens to destabilise established discourses of both masculinity and femininity because she encroaches closely upon an occupation which has been so closely linked with masculinity as to sometimes appear as a natural, fundamental function of it. Early psychological studies of warfare, which attempted to account for cases of shell shock during the First World War, found that male combatants suffered breakdowns during the war because of the passivity and anonymity of trench warfare, not because of the acts of violence demanded of them.[3] The figure of the warrior hero has long been central to Western discourses of masculinity. A British recruitment poster of 1914 categorised men according to their willingness to take up arms: 'There are three types of men. Those who hear the call and obey. Those who delay. And the Others. To which do *you* belong?'[4] The woman in military uniform threatens this naturalised linkage between masculinity and militarism; she is both 'woman out of place', undermining traditional discourses of femininity, and also a figure which challenges the close connection between the military and the masculine.

The movement of women into the military threatens not only cultural constructions of gender, but also the established relationship between the military and civil society. As Dandeker and Woodward and Winter have both commented, there is a tension between the need for the military to be both separate and distinct from the rest of society, and a socio-cultural need for it to reflect the mores and values of the civil society which it represents.[5] This tension could be viewed as gendered, as the categories of military and civilian are often perceived as, respectively, masculine and feminine. British men in the First World War were informed that their labour was needed 'to defend your mothers, wives and sisters from the horrors of war' whilst British women were told that 'perhaps the most important thing that women can do in the way of helping in the war is to keep themselves and their families in the best possible state of health'.[6] Women in wartime symbolise the domesticity to which the male combatant will return, and the home which he is defending. However in times of total war, and in times of high employment, when the armed forces may experience difficulties in recruiting and retaining sufficient numbers of recruits, the military has had to draw upon a non-traditional pool of labour, recruiting both women and men who would not normally qualify for military service because of age or physical fitness. A tension thus exists between the need to draw women into the military in order to ensure the continued successful organisation of the armed forces, and the symbolic need for women to remain within the home, representing the values of the civil society which the military is defending. This tension can be understood as a conflict between the organisational and economic needs of a society at war for women's labour, and the cultural necessity of maintaining existing gender roles. The movement of women into the armed services destabilises not only cultural constructs of gender, but also the civil-military nexus.

Military organisations are, by their very nature, hierarchical in structure, socially conservative organisations which mirror patterns of social stratification within wider society. Historically, the British Army was relatively late in its adoption of a professional organisational culture, and until at least the mid-twentieth century was dominated by a gentleman-officer culture which celebrated amateurism and social background over technical or managerial expertise.[7] However, despite the class based chain of command found in the British Army, the military still functions to efface some of the divisions of civilian life as the collective nature of military life functions to reconstruct male civilians as male soldiers. Within this structure, the highest status is awarded to those men whose work within the army can be most clearly defined as masculine: the combatants whose role is to fight in the front line of battle. Lower status men in the army are those whose work can be most closely aligned with tasks traditionally undertaken by women in civil society; working in the support roles of nursing, cleaning and sustaining the combat troops. The military thus functions to reinforce cultural and social divisions of both class and gender within its organisational structure and workplace culture.

However, women were quick to don khaki during the First World War. A number of voluntary organisations grew up during the early years of the war and in 1917 the War Office began to recruit women into the Women's Army Auxiliary Corps (WAAC). The eagerness of many women to participate in the war effort can be accounted for by a number of factors, including a 'patriotic' urge to work for one's country in wartime and to demonstrate women's citizenship in relation to the suffrage campaign. Furthermore, women's struggle for an expanded public role in the years preceding the war had seen middle-class women work to professionalise traditionally female nurturing activities in occupations such as nursing, health visiting and social work. Millicent Garrett Fawcett of the National Union of Women's Suffrage Societies, the umbrella organisation of pre-war suffragists, called in the *Contemporary Review* for women to ensure that men returning from the war 'find that women at home have been doing work no less vital for the health of the nation'.[8] Although both the NUWSS and the militant Women's Social and Political Union (WSPU) swiftly called a halt to the suffrage campaign, the existing organisations built on their networks of communications and active members to create numerous women's voluntary organisations in the first months of the war. In August 1914 *The Times* listed 12 London-based organisations in its 'Work for Women' list, including the Women's Emergency Corps, the British Women's Patriotic League, Harvest Work for Women and the Women's Suffrage National Aid Corps.[9] The Women's Emergency Corps (WEC), organised by the NUWSS to act as a clearing house for voluntary and unpaid labour identified the cause of women with the cause of the nation in its recruiting poster 'The Call of the Country', arguing: 'Women! Your country needs you. Today the country needs every woman no less than it needs every man … Give of your best in the same spirit in which your brothers have answered the nation's call'.[10] The WEC used a militarised language to place women's work in wartime alongside the male work of combat, and although the suffrage organisations explicitly argued that they were not undertaking war work in exchange for political enfranchisement, a suspicion of women's labour in wartime remained.

Women serving in military organisations during the First World War threatened the status quo in at least three ways. They threatened to disturb existing gender roles by wearing khaki and undertaking a militarised role, disrupting the naturalised discourse of the male as soldier and warrior. As a wider aspect of this gendered disruption they challenged the civil-military nexus, when, symbolising civil society and the home which the armed forces existed to defend, they appeared and acted in a militarised manner. Finally, the existence of the pre-war suffrage movement, and the transformation of many of its leaders and members into pro-war activists led to a widespread perception of women in military organisations as 'playing at soldiers'.[11] They were thus seen as undermining the role and reputation of the male combatants whilst at the same time attempting to take advantage of wartime conditions in order to achieve their pre-war aim of female suffrage, an aim which was seen by many conservative critics as challenging and subverting the natural order in which 'war and the government of this Empire are the business of men'.[12] Women in khaki, although often vital to the success of the British war effort, were widely perceived as disruptive and transgressive since they were difficult to contain within existing dominant discourses of femininity. Women's quasi-military voluntary organisations were singled out as especially problematic.

The Women's Volunteer Reserve (WVR) was launched in December 1914 as an adjunct to the WEC. The WVR was the largest and most visible of the uniformed women's voluntary organisations which appeared in the first year of the war. Other uniformed organisations included the Home Service Corps and the Women's Reserve Ambulance Corps, and although all were treated with some suspicion by a public unused to seeing women in military uniform, it was the WVR which was the most highly criticised. The WVR dedicated itself to organising women to defend the nation in the case of invasion and to serve in any other way possible. The declared aims of the organisation were twofold. Firstly, it desired to 'free more men for the firing line' by providing support services for the military, and secondly to 'organise more succour for the helpless ones in the community'.[13] Thus it combined a patriotic appeal with the traditionally female role of helping and supporting those in need, and with the appearance and some of the activities of a male, militarised organisation.

By January 1916 the WVR had approximately 6000 members and 40 branches in the United Kingdom.[14] Although it was founded and led by women of the upper and middle classes, the WVR claimed for itself a classlessness, declaring that all members would join as privates, regardless of their social standing. How well this worked in practice, however, was questionable, with contemporary reports suggesting that the WVR mirrored the organisational structures of the male military. The *London Opinion* reported occasions where 'mistresses have had to transfer to another company because they found themselves forming fours with their own servants, which did not seem quite the thing'.[15] Despite the claim of the London battalion that 'the rank and file

consists chiefly of business girls, typists, shop girls and servants' the perception
of the WVR as 'upper-class amazons' was widespread, particularly as well-
paid employment opportunities for working women gradually expanded as a
result of the war.[16] Nevertheless, the WVR remained a popular organisation
for women with enough time to dedicate to it who wished to appear as if they
were taking an active part in the war. The military appearance and quasi-
military activities of the WVR allowed women to visibly identify themselves
with the sacrifice and service of the male soldiers.

Newspaper coverage of the launch of the WVR emphasised the
organisation's patriotism and devotion to duty, commenting that 'the women
are not one whit behind the men in patriotism', but also drew attention
to the military appearance of the corps, whose members were known as
privates and officers, wore khaki uniforms, practised military drill, called
their local groups battalions, and were offered the opportunity of training
to bear arms.[17] Criticism of the organisation began almost as soon as it was
formed. Perceived as a feminine encroachment upon a masculine sphere
of activity, the WVR embodied for some the worst aspects of the suffrage
movement's espousal of the war effort, providing an opportunity for women
to dress as soldiers, undertake military activities and generally 'assume
military attitudes'.[18] Parallels were drawn in the press between the peacetime
demonstrations of the suffragettes and the wartime drills and marches of the
WVR, leading E.D. Smethitt, the organising secretary of the WVR to write
to the *Bournemouth Echo* in April 1915 to refute 'the idea that the WVR is
a suffrage organisation', arguing that 'we have no politics whatsoever'.[19]
However, the appearance of women in military uniform, learning to drill and
undertaking route marches through city streets, continued to be viewed with
distrust within a society in which the men were frequently told that their duty
was to fight to protect women and children.

The khaki uniform and the drill and arms training provided by the WVR
all drew particular criticism, as the three aspects of the organisation which
threatened most clearly the linkage between masculinity and militarism. The
spectacle of 'khaki clad women in colourful imitations of military clothing
swaggering about with short canes and even giving military salutes to soldiers'
challenged the gender divisions of wartime in which men were expected to go
and fight whilst women's role was to 'send them cheerfully on their way'.[20]
Whilst women claimed that their militarised appearance simply denoted that
'they are as patriotic as their brothers in the trenches' suspicion remained that
'men wear (uniforms) because they must; women because they love them'.[21]
Indeed, this claim to a patriotic impulse was itself attacked as damaging,

commentators claiming that 'khaki is sacred to those for whom it forms a shroud … it is the garb of fighting man who goes out to war risking life and limb for England, home and his woman-kind; and it should not be lightly donned'.[22] Female appropriation of this uniform, it was claimed, destabilised not only gender roles, but degraded the sacrosanct nature of male military service and sacrifice.

The response of the WVR and their supporters to such criticism was threefold. Firstly, the practical necessity of both a uniform and of drill and route marches for members was emphasised. Smethitt wrote that the uniform was adopted for purely practical reasons as 'a serviceable dress of some kind which shall be the same for all is absolutely necessary in a large body of people', adding somewhat disingenuously that the colour khaki had been chosen simply as the colour 'least likely to show dirt'.[23] Drill and route marches had a similarly practical basis, as they were 'intended to keep the girls physically fit and teach them discipline and co-operation', activities which, it was implied, were beneficial not only to the health of the individual woman, but also to the future health of the nation as the WVR members were not only fulfilling a useful role in the present, but were also potential future mothers.[24] The sense of duty and patriotism felt by women in the Reserve was also emphasised. A poem in the *Women's Volunteer Reserve Magazine* claimed less prosaic reasons for the organisation's use of khaki than Smethitt, using explicitly religious imagery to link the sacrifices made by female volunteers with those of the combatant man:

> When we are gone
> You will remember then
> We wore the khaki soberly
> As did the men …
> For outward sign
> The colour shall suffice
> The inward spirit of the sacrament
> A sacrifice.[25]

Finally, the feminine nature of the work of the Reserve was stressed. An article in the *Ladies Pictorial* in February 1915 stated that 'there is nothing unfeminine about the Women's Volunteer Reserve. On the contrary, it is distinctly a womanly movement' as the work of rendering 'first aid and guidance to the aged, infirm, panic stricken and helpless who can do nothing for themselves' in case of air raid or invasion was simply an extension of woman's established peacetime role as carer and nurturer.[26]

In 1915 the Women's Legion was formed as an offshoot of the WVR to provide 'the many kinds of war work that could not be managed on the quasi-military lines of the Reserve'.[27] Lady Londonderry, the Colonel-in-Chief of both the WVR and of the Women's Legion was privately convinced that elements within the WVR *were* too militaristic, commenting in her autobiography that 'we had to contend with a section of she-men who wished to be armed to the teeth'.[28] Comprised of both paid and voluntary members the Women's Legion did not practise drill and although they wore uniform the bulk of their work, such as cooking and serving in military canteens, remained clearly within an established female sphere. Perhaps because of this the Women's Legion proved to be a far more acceptable organisation than the WVR and by 1915 the WEC, which oversaw both organisations, was claiming in its Annual Report that the WVR was simply one aspect of the Women's Legion.[29] The Women's Legion was recognised by the Army Council in February 1916 and the Military Cookery Section and the Motor Transport Section began to work directly with the army within the British Isles. These women worked directly with men, taking into the military sphere the already established idea of dilution, by which women in industry replaced men as they moved into combat positions. The work of these women, although signifying the first recognition by the British army of the need for female labour, also helped to reinforce established gendered patterns of employment, as their prime function was to 'take the place of men in the firing line' by performing work better suited to women.[30] Although the activities of the uniformed, quasi-military WVR, and its less contentious sister the Women's Legion represented a movement of women towards the male, military sphere of employment, they can also be seen as a product of the wartime division of gender roles. It was against this background of a grudging recognition of the necessity for women's militarised labour, combined with a desire to maintain the military as a masculine organisation, that the WAAC was founded in 1917.

Male conscription, enforced by the Military Service Act in March 1916, led to a reconsideration of women's contribution to the war effort. To a large extent this debate was concerned with the possibility of conscripting women in order to 'free a man for the front'. Female conscription was considered both as a means of tackling 'slackers in petticoats' and as a way for women to demonstrate their own willingness to serve.[31] An article in *The Times* in June 1916 was archetypal in its criticism of 'women who will not work', calling for 'women recruiting sergeants ... with the authority to ask any young woman seen restaurant haunting or shopgazing to ask what she is doing for her country'.[32] However, female war service was rarely considered in the same terms as male military service. Women's role in wartime was still predominantly seen as that of helping and supporting the vital male work of combat, whether this help be achieved through working in the munitions industry, nursing or working directly to provide support services for the military. Women's work in this military sphere, although firmly feminine in character, was still subject to criticism, Violet Markham remarking on the 'facetious analogies circulating at the moment of an "army of women" mobilised alongside an army of men'.[33] Debates about women's war service were rarely framed within the same parameters as those concerning male service. Although it was becoming increasingly apparent that a formalised system of female service was going to be necessary, early debates concerning this service reflected the concurrent concerns that, if women were to be mobilised, actual and symbolic gender divisions would need to be defended.

Despite the influx of conscripted men into the forces in 1916 the need for more manpower remained urgent, and following the catastrophic casualty rates of the Battle of the Somme, Lieutenant-General H.M. Lawson was commissioned to carry out a study assessing which occupations within the army could be carried out by older men or by women, thus relieving men for the front. The Women's Legion Cookery and Motoring Divisions were already working for the Army in Britain; Lawson suggested expanding their numbers and the work being carried out as well as, crucially, extending their work to France. Although women had a long history of servicing the Army as camp followers in the eighteenth and nineteenth centuries, Lawson's Report marks the first official recognition by the army of the necessity for those services in a designated war zone.

However, the suggestion that women's labour should be utilised by the army on a large scale was resisted in many quarters. Field Marshall Douglas Haig, Commander-in-Chief of the British Armies in France, whilst broadly acknowledging the necessity of some female labour, remained sceptical about the type and amount of work that women would be able to undertake. Whilst Lawson had suggested that women should be substituted for men, Haig argued that they should be employed as dilutees, suggesting a ratio of 200 women to replace 134 men as clerks and in domestic service.[34] Haig also insisted that there were many areas of support work in which women could not be successfully employed. Fearing the disruptive influence of women upon army life, he argued that the employment of women at Base Depots was not to be recommended as there would be 'more likelihood of sex difficulty occurring in these depots than elsewhere'.[35] Haig also felt that the specific conditions of service with the army were often unsuitable for women. Whilst accepting that trained women could 'at once be usefully employed as motor-car drivers, motor-ambulance drivers … cleaners, telegraphists and telephonists' he was adamant that other areas of work should remain the preserve of men.[36] Nursing, already an established occupation for women, was only grudgingly accepted by Haig, who commented that 'it is quite certain women could not have stood the enormous and incessant strain' experienced by army medical personnel during the battle of the Somme.[37] Work carried out by non-combatant men behind the lines was seen by Haig as essentially masculine work which could only be taken on by women in the direst necessity. One way of ensuring that women's work remained separate from that of men can be seen in Lawson's suggestion that women utilised by the army should not be integrated but 'must form part of definitive units provided with their own women officers and NCOs'.[38] The introduction of women into the army was to be managed in such a way as not to destabilise the existing naturalised linkage between masculinity and soldiering.

Discussion about women's work with the army continued at weekly War Office conferences throughout January 1917. Debate focused around the terms under which women would be employed, with Florence Ellis of the Women's Legion insisting that 'women would like to feel they were taken on by the Army, and that they were more or less soldiers'.[39] The men attending the conferences resisted any suggestion that women be enlisted in the same way as male combatants, arguing that as women were not being employed on active service 'that treatment would not do' and proposing instead that a woman's service could be ensured by emphasising 'the moral obligation'.[40] It was eventually decided to enrol women for service with the army rather than enlist them along the same lines as male soldiers. The new organisation would be based on 'a military scheme of organisation' but its members would have the legal standing of civilians working with the army and not be treated as soldiers, ensuring that women's legal status was that of camp followers.[41] The position of military women was deliberately ambiguous: working with the Army, they were recruited through the Women's Legion and the Ministry of Labour, subjected to military discipline as civilian employees. Thus defined, they remained separate from the male army; subject to discipline and punishment if their behaviour was found to be wanting yet denied the status associated with male military service.

The desire to maintain a distinction between men and women in military uniform permeated much of the discussion of the minutiae of organising a female corps for service with the army. One area which was the subject of detailed discussion was the levels of pay applicable to women so employed. The use of dilution, as suggested by Haig and by Sir Auckland Geddes, Director of Recruiting at the War Office, who had argued that 'in civil life it takes 10% to 20% more women to do the work of male clerks', eventually provided the War Office with a means of paying women less than the male soldiers that they served alongside.[42] The question of uniforms for women was also discussed at length, one War Office memo commenting that:

> Three thousand women now at work at home have done without it. Why should we incur the expense of uniforming them now? The supply of khaki for the men of the Army is becoming increasingly difficult and there is no cloth to spare for women who can work just as well in garments of other hue and texture provided, as hitherto, at their own expense.[43]

It was eventually agreed that women enrolled for service would wear uniform, as Lawson's original Report had suggested, although the motivation behind this decision appears to have been motivated less by a desire to build an *esprit de corps* than by the belief that the provision of uniforms or badges 'would prevent unauthorised females entering camp areas'.[44] Female motivation for working with the army overseas was seen as inherently questionable. Any patriotic stimulus was virtually dismissed in these discussions, debate instead focusing on the best means of controlling women whom the men of the War Office and the Army Council believed to be motivated primarily by a desire for excitement, higher rates of pay, and the opportunity to mix with the male soldiers.[45]

The WAAC was created by Army Council Instruction 573 in March 1917, and the first draft of women, all prior members of the Women's Legion, left Dover for France on 31 March. There were five broad areas of employment for the WAAC: domestic, cookery, mechanical, clerical and tending war graves. Army Council Order 1069, which permitted the WAAC to serve at home as well as overseas, clearly set out the gendered nature of the new service, and also highlighted the difficulties inherent in attempting to manage an influx of women into the military without disturbing gender relations. The principle of dilution was written into the formation of the corps, the order stating that 'four women clerks will be considered an equivalent to three soldier clerks ... four technical women ... will be considered an equivalent to three technical soldiers'.[46] The feminine nature of the service was also underlined, as areas suitable for female work were defined as including 'Officers' messes, clerks, Sergeants' messes, tailors, cooks, librarians, company storemen, shoemakers'.[47] The novelist F. Tennyson Jesse argued in her book about the WAAC, *Sword of Deborah*, that the women so employed 'send a fighting man to his job by taking on the jobs that are really women's after all. For is it not a woman's earliest job to look after man?'[48] The work of tending war graves in particular was seen as a proper and correct extension of this nurturing role, and the women who undertook this work were described as carrying out 'an act of reverence towards the heroic dead'.[49] Women were to be employed primarily as carers and nurturers for the male combatants. Although the nature of their employment was in some ways revolutionary, as they wore official uniforms and worked alongside the army, in other ways it served to reinforce the gendered division of labour which existed in civil society.

The WAAC was organised along army lines and overseen by the War Office, with Mona Chalmers-Watson as Chief Controller of the Corps, based in London, and Helen Gwynne-Vaughan appointed as Controller of the WAAC in France. Both women had supported the suffrage campaign before the war, and both came from upper-class, professional backgrounds. Chalmers-Watson was a medical doctor from Edinburgh, the sister of Sir Auckland Geddes, Director of Recruiting at the War Office and niece of Elizabeth Garrett-Anderson, the first female doctor in Britain. The widowed Gwynne-Vaughan had been a lecturer in Botany at Birkbeck College, a profession she returned to between the wars before becoming Director of the Auxiliary Territorial Service in 1939. Grades within the WAAC, as in the army, were closely linked to social class. The majority of members were working class, but were supervised by women of the upper classes, and although articles in the press made claims similar to those made for the WVR, that the WAAC uniform meant 'there is no sense of class distinction whatsoever', existing structures of social class were embedded within the organisation, and the role of officers was largely that of supervising the welfare of the corps' workers, a position similar to that of the lady welfare officers in the large munitions factories.[50] Despite this creation of an 'officer class', these women were not referred to as officers, but as controllers and administrators, the equivalent grades to NCOs and privates being forewomen and workers. Thus the existing army structure was utilised as an efficient means of organising women without giving them the symbolic male appellations associated with military service.[51]

Although the regulation of women's labour in the WAAC meant that gender divisions were not broken down by the movement of women into military service, they were threatened, particularly when women in uniform appeared to be acting in ways that could be defined as masculine. The military nature of the service was played down by Chalmers-Watson, who chose to emphasise

the 'home like conditions' in the women's barracks, stressing that 'these are
no Amazons but the girls we have known, the wives and mothers and sisters
who were the light of our homes in the old times and who will return to lighten
them again'.[52] However, the appearance of large numbers of women in military
uniform, sanctioned by the state, did act as a visual reminder of the shifting
patterns of gender caused by the war. The uniform of the WAAC was widely
seen as symbolic of this changing role, and, as such, was carefully managed
in an attempt to ensure that the women's femininity was emphasised over and
above their militarism. Although khaki was eventually agreed upon as the
uniform's colour, other signifiers of militarism, such as badges of rank and
saluting, were resisted. Gwynne-Vaughan, working with the corps in France,
pushed for the WAAC to take on as many of these symbols of militarism as
possible, as she believed that they would help to ensure discipline amongst the
women. Her insistence on this resulted in the following plea from Chalmers-
Watson in London: 'I feel sure you ought to take off the badges … I am
awfully sorry but it will have to be done … Also, all saluting will have to
stop, and the military salute amongst the women'.[53] An eventual compromise
was reached whereby women did wear distinguishing badges of rank, but
the crowns, crosses and bars of the army were replaced by a set of flower
insignia, predominantly the rose and the *fleur de lys*. The woman in uniform
walked a tightrope, combining the necessary symbols of military life with the
signifiers of femininity. She had to preserve her femininity without seeming
too feminine, as femininity was seen as inimical to military life. At the same
time she could not take on too many of the trappings of militarism as this was
seen as devaluing the work and the 'sacrifice' of the male combatants.

By early 1918 the positive early press reports of the WAAC had been
largely replaced by a widespread suspicion about the motivations of women
in uniform, the WAAC serving in France in particular being the subject of
rumours about sexual misconduct. France was already widely perceived in
the British imagination as a hotbed of vice and prostitution, with the regulated
system of brothels, the *Maisons Tolerées*, being a particular cause for concern
amongst hygiene campaigners such as the Association for Moral and Social
Hygiene.[54] Women working in France may have suffered by association,
as their lives were largely hidden from the public eye, and rumours about
their conduct quickly spread. In April 1918 a primitive methodist minster in
Congleton was prosecuted for 'spreading false reports about the WAAC'.[55]
A letter from Chalmers-Watson to Gwynne-Vaughan in France set out some
of the statements made to her about the WAAC:

Ninety women from Rouen sent back for misconduct … A maternity home, eight hundred beds, every encouragement to procreate, fifty pound bonus to each woman, state adoption … Another old and aristocratic bird asserts that the War office is sending out professional prostitutes dressed in our uniform.[56]

Concerned about a fall in recruits for the WAAC, the Ministry of Labour convened a Commission of Enquiry to investigate the rumours. The commission, which was made up of six women, published their report on 20 March 1918, finding that 'not only are the rumours untrue, but … the number of undesirable women who have found their way into the Corps has been very small'.[57] The report went on to suggest that the bulk of rumours had their basis in letters sent home by troops who were motivated by 'jealousy and hostility towards the WAAC' when they were 'dislodged from non-combatant tasks in the bases' by the women's arrival.[58] The publication of the report was overshadowed by the sudden and successful German offensive that began the following day and in which nine members of the WAAC were killed during bombing raids at Abbeville; their funeral, with full military honours, appeared to demonstrate that women, like men, had 'confirmed their right to khaki', making them 'one in sympathy and sacrifice with the fighting troops'.[59] The WAAC was renamed Queen Mary's Army Auxiliary Corps (QMAAC) in April 1918, with Queen Mary assuming the title of Commander in Chief.

At the war's end in November 1918, between 80,000 and 90,000 women had served in the auxiliary services, the majority in the WAAC and the remainder in the Women's Royal Naval Service (formed in November 1917) and the Women's Auxiliary Air Force (formed in April 1918).[60] They had worked as clerks, store keepers, cleaners, cooks, waitresses, mechanics, telephonists and drivers. Although British women did not take part in combat they had worked close to the front lines in France and Belgium, and repeatedly came under fire in the German offensive of 1918. Although their work came to be widely regarded as an essential contribution to the war effort, women's war service was never seen in the same way as men's. Women remained auxiliary, their organisation allied to, but separate from, that of the military. They worked to serve and support the fighting men, and although they may at times have been working alongside the men, symbolically they remained subordinate to them. This separate status was reinforced in the Representation of the People Act of January 1918, which extended the male franchise on the basis that no man who had served in the military should be denied a vote, whilst women were awarded voting rights based on their age and marital status, not on their war service. Indeed, politicians arguing against female suffrage emphasised the distinction between the fighting man and the civilian woman, arguing that 'it is upon men that the dangers of battle and the ordeal of service fall … is it right that women should have a controlling vote in these things, and that men should have so indescribably greater a share of the suffering?' [61] Although the very presence of women in uniform and close to combat threatened to undermine the distinction between home front and war front, female and male war experience, the regulation and control of every aspect of female service meant that these boundaries were largely maintained. With the war's end they could be rebuilt.

Notes

1   D. McCloskey, 'Paid Work', in I. Zweiniger-Bargielowska (ed.), *Women in Twentieth-century Britain* (Harlow, 2001), p. 165.
2   Ibid., p.174.
3   J. Bourke, *An Intimate History of Killing* (London, 1999), p. 248.
4   Imperial War Museum (IWM), Department of Art, Catalogues and Posters 1914–1918, PRC103/PST/5041, Parliamentary Recruiting Committee poster 1914.
5   C. Dandeker, 'Don't Ask, Don't Tell and Don't Pursue: Is a Pragmatic Solution the Way Forward for the Armed Services in Today's Society?', *Royal United Services Journal*, 137 (1999), pp. 87–9; R. Woodward and P. Winter, 'Discourses of Gender in the Contemporary British Army', *Armed Forces and Society*, 30, 2 (2004), pp. 279–302 .
6   IWM, Department of Art, PRC49/PST/5102, Parliamentary Recruiting Committee poster 1914; *Daily Mail*, 18 August 1918.
7   E. Kier, *Imagining War: French and British Military Doctrine Between the Wars* (Princeton, 1999), p. 113.
8   M. Garrett Fawcett, 'Women's Work in Wartime', *Contemporary Review*, CVI (December 1914), p. 782.
9   *The Times*, 31 August 1914.
10 IWM, Women's Work Collection (WWC), Volunteer Corps, Women's Emergency Corps, 2/1.
11 This was a term widely used to describe women in militaristic voluntary organisations. See for example, letters to the *Newcastle Chronicle*, 19 March 1915.
12 Lord Finlay (Lord Chancellor), 'Representaton of the People Bill', *Hansard, 5th Series, House of Lords*, 27, col. 472, 10 January 1918.
13 IWM, WWC, Volunteer Corps, 2/27, WVR Recruitment Pamphlet.
14 *Women's Volunteer Reserve Magazine*, 1, 1 (January 1916).
15 *London Opinion*, 20 January 1915.
16 IWM, WWC, Volunteer Corps, 2/25, Report of London Battalion.
17 *Bayswater Chronicle*, 12 December 1914.
18 Letter to the *Morning Post*, 18 August 1915.
19 *Bournemouth Echo*, 22 May 1915.
20 *Ladies Pictorial*, 21 August 1915, *Evening Standard*, 26 August 1914.
21 Letter to the *Morning Post*, 26 July 1915, *Evening News*, 24 January 1918.

22 *Globe*, 19 August 1917.
23 *Evening Standard*, 21 August 1915.
24 *Northern Mail*, 12 March 1915.
25 'Sacrament of the Dust', *Women's Volunteer Reserve Magazine*, 1, 12 (December 1916), p. 240.
26 *Ladies Pictorial*, 20 February 1915.
27 *Daily Express*, 24 August 1915.
28 Marchioness of Londonderry, *Retrospect* (London, 1938), p. 112.
29 IWM, WWC, Volunteer Corps, 2/3, Women's Emergency Corps First Annual Report.
30 J. Cowper, *A Short History of the QMAAC* (Aldershot, 1957), p. 10.
31 *Bystander*, 21 June 1916.
32 *The Times*, 13 June 1916.
33 Public Record Office (PRO), Home Office (HO), Women's Service Committee, Violet Markham, Notes on Organization of Woman Power, 1 December 1916.
34 PRO, War Office (WO) 32/5093, Letter from Haig to Lord Derby, Secretary of State for War, War Office, 25 February 1917.
35 PRO, WO32/5093, 11 March 1917.
36 Ibid.
37 PRO, WO32/5093, 28 January 1917.
38 PRO, WO32/5093, Lieutenant-General H.M. Lawson, *The Number and Physical Catalogue of Men Employed Out of the Fighting Area in France and an Economy of Manpower in the Fighting Areas in France*, January 1917.
39 PRO, WO162/31, Conference on the Organization of Women Employed by the Army (In Connection with Compulsory Service), 15 January 1917.
40 Ibid.
41 PRO, WO32/5253, Women's Army Auxiliary Corps – Status Of, May 1917.
42 PRO, WO32/5251, Women's Service in the Army, 18 December 1916.
43 PRO, WO32/5530, Organization of WAAC, 1917.
44 Ibid.
45 For further discussion of attitudes towards female patriotism in wartime, see K. Robert, 'Gender, Class and Patriotism: Women's Paramilitary Units in First World War Britain', *International History Review*, XIX (1997).
46 National Army Museum (NAM), Women's Royal Army Corps (WRAC) Collection, *Army Council Instruction 1069 of 1917*, 9401–247–433, p. 2.
47 Ibid., p. 3.
48 F. Tennyson Jesse, *Sword of Deborah: First Hand Impressions of the British Women's Army in France* (London, 1919), p. 59.
49 *Daily Telegraph*, 24 November 1917.
50 *Daily Chronicle*, 1 October 1917.
51 This argument was made by Helen Gwynne-Vaughan in her autobiography, *Service with the Army* (London, 1942), p. 16, where she commented on the civilian titles 'which, I suspect, were given to keep us in our place'.
52 *Weekly Dispatch*, 2 September 1917.
53 NAM, WRAC Collection, Gwynne-Vaughan Papers, 9401–253–13.
54 *The Vote*, 8 March 1918.
55 *Western Daily News*, 14 February 1918.
56 NAM, WRAC Collection, Gwynne-Vaughan Papers, 9401–253–20.

57 Ministry of Labour, *Report of Commission of Enquiry into Women's Army Auxiliary Corps in France* (1918), p. 3, para. 3.
58 Ibid., p. 6, para. 11.
59 *The Times*, 1 June 1918.
60 PRO WO 162/6, *History of the Development and Work of the Directorate of Organization August 1914–December 1918*.
61 Earl Loreburn, *Hansard: 5th Series, House of Lords*, 27, col. 416, 9 January 1918.

Chapter 12

'Singing While England is Burning': Women Musicians as Working Music Travellers in Wartime Britain, 1940–43

David Sheridan

On 11 June 1940 Sybil Eaton, professional violinist and Music Traveller, organised and performed in what locals described as the very first art music concert in the small village of Shotley, rural Suffolk, England. Art music, the term used in this chapter for what is more generally classified as 'classical' music, came to this small village at the time of the evacuation of Dunkirk, just before the onset of the Battle of Britain in the summer of 1940. The audience of 50, comprised mostly of farmers, farm hands and their wives, included a 'sympathetic parson, one Mr. Chetwynd, who reported the audience was a bit shy, and feared that they wouldn't "understand" what they were about to hear'.[1] In her report sent back to London, Eaton described further how, in spite of the parson's fears, the audience soon warmed up. In so doing, they became 'lovely listeners', so lovely that 'when we ended with the slow movement of the Mendelssohn followed by the National Anthem, I couldn't see a dry eye in the house and Mr. Chetwynd tried to speak, and broke down and I wondered whether a funny man would not do better'.[2]

This short description conveys many of the challenges, rewards and perceptions shared by working musicians on the British homefront, and in particular, female musicians. These musicians helped spread musical opportunities to a wide variety of Britons, many of whom had little or no prior interaction with art music.[3] This group of women musicians known as the Music Travellers provided entertainment, musical education and, according to their correspondence, believed that they helped foster both community and national identity at a time of great peril. This concert at Shotley is one example that demonstrates a form of female work not usually discussed in traditional stories of women in war – women's professional musical work.

The Music Travellers originated from an idea of the British composer Henry Walford Davies, who served as Master of the King's Musick from 1934 to

1941 and was also a leading member of the Council for the Encouragement of Music and the Arts (CEMA).[4] CEMA was the first publicly-supported arts organisation in Britain. The organisation began its work in late 1939 during the early months of the 'phoney' war period and was supported initially by a £25,000 grant from the Pilgrim Trust. This Trust was set up in 1930 with a £2 million grant given by American millionaire Edward Harkness, whose intent was to foster Anglo-American cultural endeavours. In early 1940, the British Board of Education matched the Pilgrim Trust's investment and state funding of the arts was underway. With little public debate, the wartime government chose to invest in Britain's arts culture at a time of national crisis, suggesting their belief in its importance to homefront morale and its imagined role in the 'Britain' which the nation at large was fighting to protect.

CEMA's original mission was a dual one: to maintain the highest possible standards of the arts while keeping them accessible to the general population during wartime – in other words, continuing 'the things of peace'.[5] Davies, cognizant of the limitations imposed on Britain's rural music life at the war's beginning, envisioned a set of 'pioneer travellers' roaming throughout the length and breadth of Britain. These pioneers, a group of professional musicians, would be based in various geographical regions, offering musical expertise and assistance to existing music-making groups in addition to performing their own concerts to war workers and others. Though musical opportunities continued to be available in London, the Travellers' work brought them into rural areas. Therefore, Davies was able to recruit his Music Travellers with the financial backing of the CEMA-sponsored Rural Music School Council.[6]

With support in place, Davies needed musicians willing and able to act as music educators, administrators and performers in disparate areas of Britain. The wartime reality of military service eventually pulled many male musicians away from their peacetime musical endeavours, creating more musical work opportunities for women. As a consequence, a majority of the Travellers were women.[7] Davies initially approached the distinguished professional violinist, Sybil Eaton, organiser of the Shotley concert described earlier and offered her a leadership position. Eaton, one of the few women established as a prominent musician before the war, accepted Davies's offer to lead the Traveller movement.[8] With her leadership assured, Davies recruited five other Music Travellers to start the programme, including Imogen Holst, daughter of well-known English composer Gustav Holst, herself an accomplished musician and educator.[9] As the programme grew to include more Travellers, these musicians were assigned to the various civil air defence regions in England,

Wales, Scotland and Northern Ireland. By late 1939, the Travellers formed the bulk of CEMA's effort to provide publicly-funded art music entertainment and education to the nation's workers and to the general population outside London.

The set-up of the Travellers dictated the nature of these women's work. Davies and other CEMA elites insisted that the Music Travellers be well-versed and trained in the Western art music tradition. They also needed to organise concerts and use music to educate in places with very diverse existing musical cultures. Some regions had local orchestras or were close enough to London for people to attend music performances there regularly. More remote areas might be limited to local choir festivals, regional theatre or local organ concerts in churches.

As the job was defined, the Travellers encountered situations in which their abilities as musicians were not adequate for all job requirements. Not only did their training and taste reflect a rather 'elite' schooling in the methods and techniques of traditional Western art music, but they were asked to face situations in which these qualities might count as less important or might not be respected at all. These workers were asked to negotiate between identities as musical professionals in larger, more metropolitan areas and as educators who oversaw existing amateur and regional musical opportunities.

This is not to suggest that these women used their musical training as a conscious means to 'distinction' or used their taste in music only to 'affirm their class', while considering only 'legitimate' pieces of music worth performance.[10] Neither did they believe they propagated a national movement to squelch different notions of worthy musical culture. Rather, the musical language from which they drew for performance was a result of their training as musicians schooled in the Western canon (in itself an endeavour contingent upon one's economic and educational background). However, the formally-trained musicians who served as travellers soon realised that the qualities and skills necessary to succeed as art musicians in London differed from those required in provincial areas to make their CEMA work successful. These women (and the few male Travellers) had the immense task of deciphering how to be both professionals and simultaneously to use their particular musical language to communicate Davies's ideals.

The previously mentioned wartime call-up of many male musicians was not limited to the 1940s. As both Paula Gillett and Cyril Ehrlich point out, women musicians also witnessed increased opportunities during the First World War, especially work in professional orchestras.[11] As in other areas of employment, however, these gains were short-lived since, when the war ended in 1918, male musicians largely returned to their previous positions. As a result of this return by men musicians, women musicians, though growing in stature since the late nineteenth century, found fewer professional career opportunities compared to men during the inter-war period.

What was distinctly different regarding musical work opportunities for women during the Second World War was the state-supported effort to bring musical experiences to the British populace. This national funding, along with the programme's unique mission of fostering musical life in a variety of regional settings as both performers and administrators, provided the Travellers with an administrative power which was not available to women musicians during the previous conflict.[12] Offering the best of musical art and stimulating amateur music-making opportunities formed the crux of the Travellers' work and created interactions with local musicians and musical authorities. Many of these experiences called on the Travellers to assess and react quickly, to use their musical expertise to educate and to lead and supervise challenging situations.

Davies's idea was soon realised, but the group he organised and recruited is rarely the focus of historical studies of Britain's wartime homefront. More surprisingly, this organisation of mostly female professional music workers is not discussed in women and work historiography. Their work has remained largely unexplored, though there have been discussions of CEMA and its post-war successor, the Arts Council of Britain.[13] Though an extensive historiography of women and work in Second World War Britain exists, most studies focus on public policy towards women workers in what is considered 'traditional' wartime work in factories, wartime military service, agricultural work and nursing, whilst ignoring other forms of wartime work.[14] One reason for this omission is that musicians are rarely considered to be workers by most music historians or historians interested in artistic and popular culture. Composers' musical output is often analysed, but the process by which their music is produced has not figured significantly as an object of study. Until most recently, musicologists, music historians and other scholars have not rigorously interrogated musical life and culture. Rather, the discipline has remained largely transcendent, as if music just 'happens', existing only as a text to be studied formalistically. What has been left in the dark are the various processes that comprise music's creation, performance and consumption.[15]

In part, the work of wartime women musicians deserves attention for no other reason than that two of the most famous and now iconic women on the wartime homefront, Vera Lynn and Myra Hess, were female musicians. Scholars of the general public have rarely, if ever, considered these two women's wartime activities as 'work'. Vera Lynn's wartime ballads, with images of nightingales and white cliffs, and Myra Hess's piano playing at her famous National Gallery lunchtime concerts series, are now both evoked frequently in nostalgic representations of Second World War Britain as the soundtrack to the war. These two women provided memorable musical experiences to audiences in very different venues. Hess's work took place in one of the sacred cultural institutions in Britain, under the dome in the National Gallery, while Lynn's music making took place in larger venues and was aided by modern technology in its global mass transmission.[16]

Although these women are usually discussed in terms of what they represented, they can be examined also as musical wartime workers. The product of their labour was not material, but cultural. One reason that Hess's and Lynn's efforts have not been considered work is that their product (the music they performed and its effect on Britons) has always been the object of scrutiny – not the labour involved in that product's creation. During the war and certainly since then, Lynn's and Hess's musical performances have been portrayed as 'soothing' the nation at war. With their femininity displayed along with their musical talent, these women have been portrayed less as workers and more as symbols of the Britain that British men fought to protect. With these iconic images of musical women etched in popular memory, it is no wonder that the Music Travellers and other women musicians have not been examined as war workers.[17]

If we dig beneath the myths and nostalgic stories of British wartime experience that continue to be propagated even as recently as the 2000 BBC/HBO co-production of the film *The Last of the Blond Bombshells*, we uncover female musicians who contributed their labour to the war effort as did other British women of different classes and educational backgrounds.[18] Myra Hess and Vera Lynn are only the most prominent musical women war workers. Their cultural work to console, strengthen and entertain the homefront through their use of music during war was duplicated and expanded by CEMA's Music Travellers.

Although the number of women undertaking musical work funded by the state during wartime Britain is small, this work should nevertheless be treated as one segment of Britain's larger wartime work culture. Their work is significant beyond its emotional impact. However, the psychological effect of their labour continues to be emphasised as it is repeatedly linked to memorials of the war in popular visual and recorded representations of the Second World War. This continued focus on music's aesthetic qualities links it with remembrance and nostalgia and obscures the ways in which musical performance expanded women's work opportunities during the war.[19]

The Music Travellers' work duties were varied and demanding. This work entailed travel over long distances – a difficult prospect under wartime conditions, with the constant threat of German aerial bombing. The Travellers worked also with regional arts administrators and planned music opportunities, found and encouraged local musicians in their efforts, organised community singing, performed secretarial duties as needed, composed monthly reports and completed other tasks deemed essential with little or no help. Music Travellers' monthly reports, in which they recorded their experiences providing music and concert opportunities throughout wartime Britain, offer insight into the difficulties and rewards of this form of women's wartime labour.[20] Through these opportunities, women musicians integrated into the administrative side of a male-dominated profession as they organised, programmed and auditioned musicians for concerts and musical opportunities.

Analysing these women's musical work invites scholars to question what exactly constitutes work in a wartime economy, while broadening how we conceive work and the types of labour that contributed to the greater British 'total' war effort. By conceptualising what constitutes 'work' in this broader fashion, scholars are not only limited to labour resulting in material products benefiting the war economy. Cultural products such as musical performance are also valuable in a wartime context. CEMA believed musical performances and educational opportunities in disparate areas of Britain were central to increasing and solidifying morale. Though the programme's success in raising morale on the homefront is not easy to quantify, this form of work was one on which the government decided to spend its valuable wartime funds. Those in government considered this to be important work, a belief shared by the musicians who worked for CEMA. Most significantly, whether or not the product of musical performance is quantifiable, this national programme created a situation in which professional women musicians found musical work opportunities beyond those available in peacetime. This wartime reality suggests that musical work should thus be included in the larger historiography of women and work.

That the Travellers' work was considered crucial to the war effort is evidenced by the fact that they were exempted from National Service requirements in order to perform their duties for CEMA.[21] These women perceived their work to be contributing directly to the war effort as well. The Travellers' representation of their work in monthly reports to CEMA supervisors reflects their belief that they were centrally involved in homefront work. At the same time, these written accounts reveal how gender and perceptions of class and taste shaped their interactions with people they encountered in their assigned regions. The tensions they describe in their monthly correspondence illustrate the complexity of the homefront, countering characterisations of it as homogenous which support the notion of an imagined 'people's war'.[22] The Travellers encountered Britons who did not share their understandings of the importance of this musical labour. Some viewed the Travellers' sex, educational training and artistic taste as threatening or suspect, and these perceptions at times obscured the women's 'mission' to provide entertainment and buttress morale.

CEMA's programmes reflected what its elites believed Britain's arts culture should represent and how it should function. The correspondence of these elites and that of the Travellers in the field further casts doubt on the 'people's war' myth. The Travellers' correspondence reveals that though people shared the common objective of surviving and winning the war, the homefront remained fractured along gender, class and regional lines. These cracks demonstrate the difficulty in forging a national arts education programme in spite of the common goals and national unity at Britain's 'finest' hour.

CEMA officials believed the work of the Music Travellers to be so culturally important that a significant amount of the first public subsidy of art by the British government was earmarked for the Travellers' efforts throughout Britain. The concept of Music Travellers roaming throughout the British countryside fitted perfectly with CEMA's overall goals. These goals were articulated at an early meeting of the council (when it was still called a 'committee'), which stated its mission to include the 'preservation of the highest standards of the arts of music, drama painting and design'. In so doing, CEMA would provide for the 'widespread provision of opportunities for hearing good music and for the enjoyment of the arts generally and the encouragement of music making … by the people themselves'. Through these activities, CEMA would give 'indirect assistance to professional singers and players who may be suffering from a wartime lack of demand for their work'.[23] This early rationale from CEMA indicates much of the artistic aesthetic held by CEMA and those eventually working for the body. Their role was to provide the 'best' in 'good' music, which certainly suggests their desire that art music be implemented in much of the Travellers' work.

At its very beginning, the Traveller project was instituted around a particular taste and stylistic preference for art music. This taste dictated the types of musicians that Travellers chose to perform for CEMA. Some of these issues of taste are revealed in an account of Sybil Eaton's work in Wiltshire. Providing concerts that replicated those found in London was impossible, but Eaton and the other Travellers attempted to maintain performance standards driven by their professional training, which emphasised quality and a specific technique in the music and the performances they organised.

In May 1940, Eaton coordinated a concert, along with her fellow professional Mabel Ritchie, in which the Pewsey and Gare choirs were combined and conducted by Mrs. Wardle, the rector's wife. This concert is illustrative of one situation Travellers encountered. In the provinces, rectors' wives could be music directors in place of trained choral directors and these areas often had very few technical resources. Discovering, upon her late afternoon arrival, an 'impossible piano' in the performing hall, Eaton

> ... found the Wiltshire piano tuner by chance outside the hall, who led me to a Bechstein whose owners were delighted to lend it; then on to the village shop who summoned men to move and who utterly refused payment the next day having so much enjoyed the concert. It was the time of Dunkirk and several people in the audience said they had enjoyed it when they hadn't expected to![24]

Beyond demonstrating conflicts between the Travellers' professional expectations and the realities they encountered in the field, this reveals how these women often needed to be able to improvise on the spur of the moment and rely on the musical resources of locals. This snapshot of Eaton's workday clearly establishes several of the Travellers' responsibilities. It also reveals the constant uncertainty and anxiety involved in organising regional musical performances. Eaton set up the concert, recruited another professional musician to perform along with her, coordinated the site, surveyed the limitations of the piano available and deemed it not playable. As she dealt with this small emergency, she used her skill and tact to acquire what she believed was a superior instrument and located supportive locals who shared her understanding of the type of instrument appropriate for art music. This support from locals did not have to be repaid with CEMA funds, perhaps a testament to Eaton's reputation or ability to deal effectively with local music enthusiasts. The reference to Dunkirk and the audience response to the concert suggests that the war's larger events encroached upon this evening concert, and that the music not only diverted people, but played a psychological function at one of Britain's most uncertain periods.

The concert in Wiltshire suggests, also, the ways in which the Travellers' ethos directed their approach to wartime work. Their commitment to communicating the 'best' in music to the British public is evident in Eaton's securing of the Bechstein piano, which she felt was a superior instrument.

Her report that people had 'enjoyed' themselves when they had not 'expected' to do so attests to the concert's historical setting during an uncertain time of the war. However, this might also be a reference to her concern about the accessibility of the concert and that many in the audience might consider the music 'high-brow'. In fact, much of the Travellers' correspondence suggests that they expected to meet with some audience resistance to their programmes. Eaton describes such an encounter at a concert in Elvington, a mining village near Dover. Like Shotley, this Eaton-organised event was said to be the first of its kind, and she was informed by the warden the villagers 'had been terrified of it being a lot they called "high-brow"'. According to Eaton, these reservations were overcome and the audience 'loved it', asking for another a few months later.[25]

The experience of Music Traveller Mollie Lake illuminates many of the challenges faced by these women as they negotiated their roles as workers, performers and administrators. For the remainder of this chapter, I will focus primarily on her experiences. Lake, a young professional soprano in her mid-twenties, was assigned to the Birmingham region along with another Music Traveller, Tom Harrison, one of the few male Travellers. Her professional training as a musician did not necessarily prepare her for the challenging nature of the tasks she undertook as a Traveller. Often, she dealt with the intricacies of local music scenes and their accompanying political and personal circumstances. She assumed the duties from the previous Traveller, Mary McDougall, in July 1941 and moved to the West Midland region from Somerset to begin her work.[26] Enthused by the opportunity to contribute her skills to the war effort, Lake initially called her work 'thrilling' and hoped that she would 'make something of it'.[27] After being exempted from National Service work with the assistance of CEMA Secretary, Mary Glasgow, Lake created billings, set up concerts and initiated new musical contacts. In her monthly reports, she expressed satisfaction and excitement about the new opportunities she encountered in a region of Britain with which she was unfamiliar.

Just as often, however, she mentioned the difficulties of her work. She discerned quickly that her bicycle was not adequate for the amount of travelling she undertook, and although she did not have a licence and was not financially well-off, she borrowed £10 from CEMA to purchase a 1934 Morris 10 motorcar for £50. Securing reliable transportation was not her only obstacle. Hiring the necessary musicians required for CEMA's concerts was not always easy. Without musical contacts in the region, she was forced to evaluate musicians in ways that at times insulted fellow performers, some of whom seemed uncomfortable taking direction from not only a woman, but also a woman from outside the West Midlands. An example of this occurred only a few months after starting in mid-1941, when she refused to hire a quartet without auditioning them first. The cellist and leader of the quartet

> ... seemed a little ruffled to think that his word was not enough for me. I am constantly having this difficulty with people like him, whose names are quite well known in the Midlands, but who I feel I cannot accept completely on trust. They all look at me as though I was a little whipper-snapper with no experience which may be true, but I still feel that CEMA ought not to engage an entirely new quartet without a hearing first.[28]

Lake made the necessary artistic decisions her CEMA supervisors expected, but her sex and, most likely, her age made these decisions difficult. She was not always perceived to be an administrator, or even a musician. In one monthly report from March 1942, Lake discussed the extent to which her never-ending duties as administrator/performer/concert organiser/secretary were almost impossible to accomplish and often under-appreciated or even uncomprehended by the people with whom she worked in some communities.

One young man from Hereford, whom she called 'slightly mental', failed to understand what her work as a Traveller entailed. He visited her to ask for her help because he 'imagined [she] wasn't finding much to do'. Lake recalled that:

> When I asserted that I was finding *plenty* to do, he looked at [me] with great interest and surprise, and said 'Oh *really*? I *am* glad'. After which unpromising start, he proceeded to explain that he was getting up a performance of the 'Pirates of Penzance' with the evacuee school-children in his village (10 miles from Hereford) and he wondered if I could come to the two performances and *turn over* for him![29]

Lake seemed to delight in recounting this event to her supervisors in London, and ended this month's report saying, 'Ah well, it does all CEMA travellers good to be taken down a peg or two sometimes, but I did think I had a loftier destiny than that!'[30] What she does not comment on is to what extent her sex evoked such a comment from this 'young man', and led him to believe she would be thrilled to turn pages for a community theatre production. The fact that she was a woman, and 'young' herself, must surely have informed this man's opinion of her responsibilities and talents. While suggestive of gender relations in the 1940s West Midlands, this example also indicates just how seriously Lake took her identity as a professional musician and the respect she believed she was owed for her skills. It also reveals that she viewed herself in a superior position in relation to local professional musicians. Her 'loftier destiny' as a musician and administrator indicates her own assumptions about her place as a professional working woman.

While Lake spent much of her monthly reports discussing the many challenges of her work, there are also many examples of rewarding work experiences. She enjoyed her concert tour of Land Army hostels in Worcester in March 1942 which she characterised as having 'excellent results', and was certain this was 'an enormously worthwhile field'. She stated further that '[t]hese Land Girls are placed in isolated villages, often miles from the small town and cinema … they all agreed that it was the loveliest thing that had ever come to the hostel, and begged for a return visit'.[31] Lake was also pleased each time her audiences participated full-heartedly in community singing and whenever they appreciated music she regarded as particularly difficult to perform.

The difficulties of negotiating her dual identities as performer and administrator came to a head after two years of gruelling work for the Travellers. After months and months of organising concerts, dealing with the demands of local musical politics as well as those of CEMA bureaucrats in London's Belgrave Square, and the necessary sacrifices this work meant for her own performance opportunities as a musician, Lake resigned her position. In her resignation letter to Mary Glasgow at CEMA headquarters, she cited the difficulties of keeping up her own musicianship while trying to fulfil so many demanding and ultimately compromising positions as a Traveller. With her work and abilities as a performing musician suffering, she revealed the stress she endured and the personal sacrifices she made while negotiating her duties by remarking that

> I realized … this job was not one which any person would keep on doing indefinitely, if they want to be a performing artist. There must always be a compromise in it between performing and organizing, but I have always considered it a compromise which any artists worth their salt should be willing and glad to make for a time under war time conditions. … I feel I have reached the point where I am both organising and singing badly, and that means it's time to stop. … I do feel that I could be quite a good singer, and that the time has come when I ought to give myself the chance to be.[32]

As a professionally-trained musician, Lake believed her war work compromised the skill and practice time required to maintain her professional musical capabilities. Though CEMA viewed the Travellers primarily as people who implemented excellent musical programmes in support of national morale, they often failed to recognise the immense effort that went into maintaining professional-level musicianship. Additionally, CEMA officials did not appear to conceptualise their Travellers as musicians with post-war careers. This perhaps reveals an unspoken assumption by some CEMA elites that these women would not have music careers after the war or that for them, a musical career in peacetime was not guaranteed. Whatever the case, Lake was obviously determined to maintain a skill level that would allow her to seamlessly return to her peacetime role of professional singer. She continued to consider her identity as professional musician and the occupational value of her skills beyond their possible contribution to the war effort. The added excitement and duties created by their wartime employment with CEMA gave Travellers unprecedented professional power, but also compromised their professional work identities in ways that perhaps they had not anticipated. Nonetheless, these opportunities gave them the power to create and sustain British art musical culture at a time when music was felt to be of the utmost importance.

The important and unique nature of the Travellers' work is displayed in a monthly report postscript that captures succinctly the dual nature of their work. The postscript describes both the powerful effects the Travellers' work had on audiences and offers insight into how they thought their work contributed to the war effort, whilst also acknowledging the frustrations faced by musician workers:

> [T]here have been many moments in the last week when one has been tempted to chuck the work and go to the nearest ARP [Air Raid Precautions] post and enrol. The feeling that one may be singing while England is burning is sometimes difficult to withstand, but one is continually, daily held to the work by the most moving gratitude of those people for whom one does it and with whom one sings. There can be no mistaking the deep sincerity of their thanks – those who say that singing and laughing for an hour has given them new heart and fresh courage and made the black days seem more bearable. In the face of this unanimous testimony one cannot but feel that one is after all making the right contribution.[33]

This Traveller voiced her frustration with work that was quite rewarding, but doubts also crept into her description as she wondered whether her work actually mattered to a nation at war. Although to this woman musician, musical work sometimes seemed a frivolous contribution to the war effort, especially while 'England burned', the Travellers at times also portrayed themselves and their work as 'soothing the nation', providing 'new heart' and 'fresh courage'. These beliefs resonate with the symbolism, both then and since, attributed to the roles of Myra Hess and Vera Lynn during the conflict. This Traveller's depiction of her work does indicate one way she viewed her unique mission, but it does not obscure the reality that the Travellers were government employees who were often overworked, unprepared for the land mines of regional musical work and not given enough practical resources to accomplish their work easily.

Through the struggles of undertaking their work duties, the Travellers reflected their own musical tastes and aesthetic and, undoubtedly, that of CEMA elites as well. The importance of providing music that was 'good' infused much of their effort. CEMA officials certainly hoped their efforts would contribute to the creation of a more musically-literate British public. Whether this actually occurred is the subject of another study. Investigating the everyday work of CEMA's Music Travellers suggests, though, that their work was much more than an effort to establish 'distinction' or create new forms of it in the provinces. The Travellers' work cannot be taken out of its context, and the historical specificity of wartime Britain imbues this work with contextual meanings beyond issues of class, taste and hegemony. Often, concert organisers and performers attempted nothing more hegemonic than merely searching their own musical vocabulary, which consisted largely of pieces from the Western musical canon, for poignant and effective pieces of music they believed spoke to the cultural moment of Britain at war. Evidence suggests that at times these pieces operated as an effective language speaking across boundaries of class, educational background or taste. In these instances, this music communicated messages that helped people cope with the crisis Britain at large was facing, if only for a particular evening, or perhaps during one particular piece of music. As the Shotley concert suggests, what constituted poignant music varied according to time and place. At times it could be Bach, at other times 'I'll Be Seeing You'. As this concert also indicates, affecting music could be the National Anthem – a tune and text charged with extraordinary meaning at this particular historical moment. Whilst not without its own political message during wartime (and in times of peace), what this piece suggests as a concert finale in 1941 would differ dramatically in a different historical and political moment. Additionally, the regional location of the performance and the particular audience make-up would be pivotal.

Music and its performance and consumption not only mark one's social distinction, but can also serve as a language used to communicate and formulate a myriad of identities. As Peter Martin suggests, 'the ability of musical practices to proclaim and affirm group values should not be thought of as restricted to the display and consolidation of social class differences'.[34] During significant historical moments music may be designated as nationally relevant, as it was in Britain during the Second World War. Beyond serving at times as a marker of class, music can become in different contexts anything from a symbol of a generation's identity politics, a signifier of sexuality, gender or ethnic experience, to an expression of national culture or mode of completing employment and creating a professional work identity.

The work of CEMA's Music Travellers offers scholars strong evidence of women's wartime work, and I argue they should emerge from the shadow of Myra Hess and Vera Lynn and join the larger narrative of the historiography of women's wartime work. The Travellers' employment indicates a new type of women's work and adds the musician to the category of labourer – both during war and peace. Their story illustrates how women faced obstacles presented not just by their jobs, but also by gender, taste and regional differences. In disparate areas throughout wartime Britain, these particular women learned to use their skills to persuade others to interact with art music, many of whom would not have appreciated music in ways the Travellers thought appropriate.

The Travellers' work illuminates connections between music, nation and 'total' war. By creating a cultural product through their own labour, CEMA's Music Travellers helped forge connections between the state and music. Their work both changed the nature of Britain's wartime musical culture and had implications beyond the wartime context in which they worked.

Notes

1   Victoria and Albert National Art Library, Blythe House, London, EL 2/46. The description of the Shotley concert is located in a monthly report, sent by Eaton to CEMA headquarters in London's Belgrave Square.
2   Ibid.
3   Though the term 'art music' itself is certainly not a neutral one, I employ its use since most musicologists, music historians and other scholars who examine musical life use it in their work when referring to what the general public classifies as 'classical' music. In using the term, I refer largely to music composed and performed in the Western musical tradition. Most of the music considered appropriate for performance during the wartime period covered by this essay was music from the eighteenth to the early twentieth centuries, including musical styles such as Baroque, Classical, Romantic and late Romantic/Impressionist. This music includes pieces written in various forms, from solo songs for voice, works for piano and other keyboard instruments, music for string instruments (written for a variety of numbers of players) and works for string and full orchestras.

The majority of the music performed during this period included compositions from the Continental European tradition, particularly that from the Austro-Germanic territories including the composers Bach, Handel, Schubert, Mozart, Beethoven, Mendelssohn and Brahms. Though not the focus of this essay, it is fascinating to note the irony that much of the music being performed was Germanic. It would also be remiss, in a collection focusing on women and work and issues of gender, not to mention that these composers were all male Europeans. Though I do not explore them here, issues of canon and gender have come to the forefront in the last 15 years for several musicologists and music historians. See in particular, M.J. Citron, *Gender and the Musical Canon* (Cambridge and New York, 1993).

4   British composer Henry Walford Davies's (1869–1941) historical legacy draws more on his radio broadcasts and educational work for the BBC than for his composing. His two broadcasting series – 'Music and the Ordinary Listener' (1926–29) and 'Everyman's Music' (1940–41) – were popular and indicate his interest in the educational possibilities of art music for the larger British population. This interest no doubt also manifested itself in the Music Traveller scheme discussed here. The literature on CEMA is extensive. It includes J. Minihan, *The Nationalization of Culture: The Development of State Subsidies to the Arts in Great Britain* (New York, 1977); J. Pick (ed.), *The State and the Arts* (Eastbourne, 1980); A. Sinclair, *Arts and Cultures: The History of the Fifty Years of the Arts Council of Great Britain* (London, 1995); R. Witts, *Artist Unknown: An Alternative History of the Arts Council* (London, 1998); E. White, *The Arts Council of Great Britain* (London, 1975). More recent work discussing CEMA features in N. Hayes and J. Hill (eds), '*Millions Like Us'? British Culture in the Second World War* (Liverpool, 1999).

5   EL 1/1.

6   Ibid.

7   In fact, all of the six original travellers were women. In addition to Eaton and Holst, they included Christine Godwin, Mary McDougall, Ursula Nettleship and Anne Wood. Mary 'Mollie' Lake, whose experiences I discuss at more length later in the essay, replaced McDougall.

8   EL 1/21.

9   *CEMA Bulletin*, No. 1, May 1940. These bulletins were monthly newsletters highlighting and discussing all of CEMA's work, compiled and distributed by CEMA bureaucrats in London.

10 P. Bourdieu, *Distinction, A Social Critique of the Judgement of Taste*, translated by R. Nice (Cambridge, 1984), pp. 8 and 16.

11 C. Ehrlich, *The Music Profession in Britain Since the Eighteenth Century: A Social History* (Oxford, 1985), pp. 186–90 and P. Gillett, *Musical Women in England: Encroaching on All Man's Privileges* (New York, 2000), p. 224.

12 One exception to this is the case of Lena Ashwell (1872–1957). Musically educated at the Royal Academy of Music, she gained fame on the London stage at the turn of the century. During the First World War, she organised music concerts throughout France for Allied troops, using professional musicians.

13 See note 4.

14 Again, this literature is extensive, and is led in the case of Second World War Britain by Penny Summerfield's work. Some prominent examples are G. Braybon and P. Summerfield, *Out of the Cage: Women's Experiences in the Two World Wars* (London, 1987); M. Cooke and A. Woollacott (eds), *Gendering War Talk* (Princeton, 1993); P. Summerfield, *Women Workers in the Second World War: Production and Patriarchy in Conflict* (London, 1984)

and P. Summerfield, *Reconstructing Women's Wartime Lives: Discourse and Subjectivity in Oral Histories of the Second World War* (Manchester and New York, 1998).

15   Of course musical scholarship has a tremendous historical legacy, back to the Middle Ages and Antiquity. Within the Western academy, however, the complexity of the lived musical experience (composing, rehearsing, performing, consuming, etc.) has remained largely underexplored, with an emphasis instead on formalist musical analysis. It is only relatively recently that music has even been considered something 'historical'. With the work of historians, sociologists of music and musicologists informing the 'New Musicology' over the last several decades, this silence has been radically challenged. This includes work by such scholars as Peter Martin, Dave Russell, William Weber, Tia DeNora, Susan McClary, Rose Rosengard Subotnik, Lawrence Kramer, Richard Leppert, Phillip Brett and Joseph Kerman.

16   Hess's concert series was also broadcast across the globe through the BBC, though not in the same ways, obviously, as the music of Vera Lynn.

17   In discussing Hess and Lynn, I am well aware of the differences in their musical backgrounds, musical careers and ways their music was consumed and approached by the British populace. For the purposes of this chapter, however, I treat them as musical workers and am most interested in conceiving of them both as such.

18   The British experience in the Second World War remains for historians and the larger lay public as a rich source of fascination. Certainly, the war has figured greatly in how Britons have imagined themselves since, and its subject has created a tremendous variety of texts (books, articles, novels, plays and musical works, both scholarly and otherwise) for the British public to consume. This is especially so in terms of film, as the subject of the Second World War has created a practical industry for both Hollywood and British film production companies. I mention specifically *The Last of the Blond Bombshells* due to its direct relevance in exploring (at least theoretically) women and their experiences as musicians during the war. What is striking are the ways in which the film, in flashbacks to the war, creates nostalgia for the period, especially by its use of wartime popular music. Perhaps most intriguing is that the film, featuring an internationally star-studded cast including Oscar-winning actresses Judi Dench and Olympia Dukakis and French film legend Leslie Caron, spends much more time chronicling the women musicians duelling for the romantic (and sexual) attention of the one male 'bombshell' – the drummer, who appears in drag on stage – rather than their experiences surviving (and working) during the war. Needless to say, although music is presented as a muse for several of the 'bombshells' (becoming a life-time career for three of them), their role as musical 'workers', during the war or after, receives scant attention by the filmmakers.

19   Scholarly discussion as to the war's impact on women's work opportunities is divided and complex. See some of the work cited above in note 14. Here, I contend that in a general sense, the war did create more wage-earning work opportunities for British women during the years 1939–45.

20   These duties are discussed in monthly reports sent by the Travellers to CEMA headquarters in London, found in the EL series at Blythe House.

21   The National Service Act (No. 2), passed in December 1941, allowed the British government to conscript women into munitions factory work and into the women's services. Mary Glasgow, CEMA Secretary-General, often personally intervened and requested the Travellers be deferred from this work. For the case of Mollie Lake, see EL 2/56.

22   The concept of the Second World War as the 'people's war', in which a largely classless democratic Britain united at war against Nazi Germany has a long historical trajectory,

especially in popular British memory. Scholarly debate on this issue has been intense. This literature includes A. Calder, *The People's War* (London, 1969) and A. Calder, *The Myth of the Blitz* (London, 1991); K. Morgan, *Labour in Power 1945–1951* (Oxford, 1984). Paul Addison has touched on this concept in *Now the War is Over* (London, 1995). More recently, Hayes and Hill (eds), *'Millions Like Us?'* offers new interpretations of the usefulness of the phrase.

23 EL 1/11, 'Memorandum to the Application', March 1940.
24 EL 2/46.
25 Ibid.
26 EL 2/55.
27 Ibid.
28 EL 2/55, letter to Mary Glasgow.
29 Ibid.
30 Ibid.
31 Ibid.
32 EL 2/56.
33 *CEMA Bulletin*, No. 3, July 1940.
34 P.J. Martin, *Sounds and Society: Themes in the Sociology of Music* (Manchester and New York, 1995), p. 233.

Index